THE·NAKED·EYE

GREAT PHOTOGRAPHS OF THE NUDE

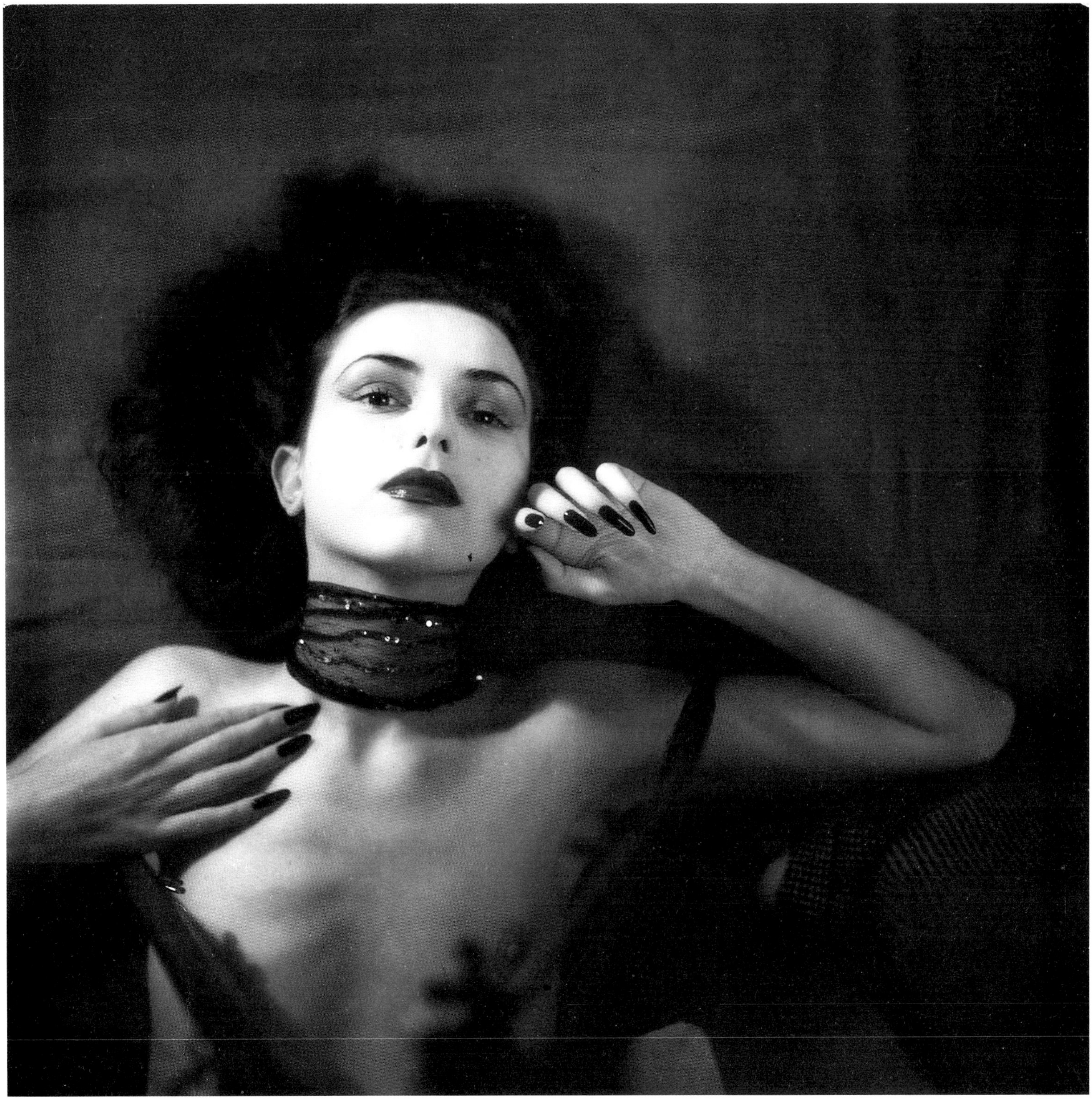

THE·NAKED·EYE
GREAT PHOTOGRAPHS OF THE NUDE

selected and introduced by
DAVID BAILEY

text by Martin Harrison

PLATE I
JACQUES-HENRI LARTIGUE
Florette, Paris 1944
Association des Amis de Jacques-Henri Lartigue, Paris

Lartigue was the ultimate photographic original, influenced by nobody. From the age of seven he took candid pictures, full of life, movement and tenderness. This is one of the first photographs he took of his third wife, Florette, who he described as a "rare human specimen, unspoiled by growing up . . . always natural, beautiful in the morning . . . always natural, beautiful in the evening."

AMPHOTO
an imprint of Watson-Guptill Publications
New York

First published in 1987 in the United States
by Amphoto, an imprint of Watson-Guptill Publications,
a division of Billboard Publications, Inc.,
1515 Broadway, New York, New York 10036.

Library of Congress Cataloging-in-Publication Data
Harrison, Martin, 1945-
The naked eye.

1. Photography of the nude. I. Bailey, David.
1938- . II. Title.
TR675.H368 1987 779'.21 87-19140
ISBN 0-8174-4990-6

Printed and bound in Italy by Motta, Milan

CONTENTS

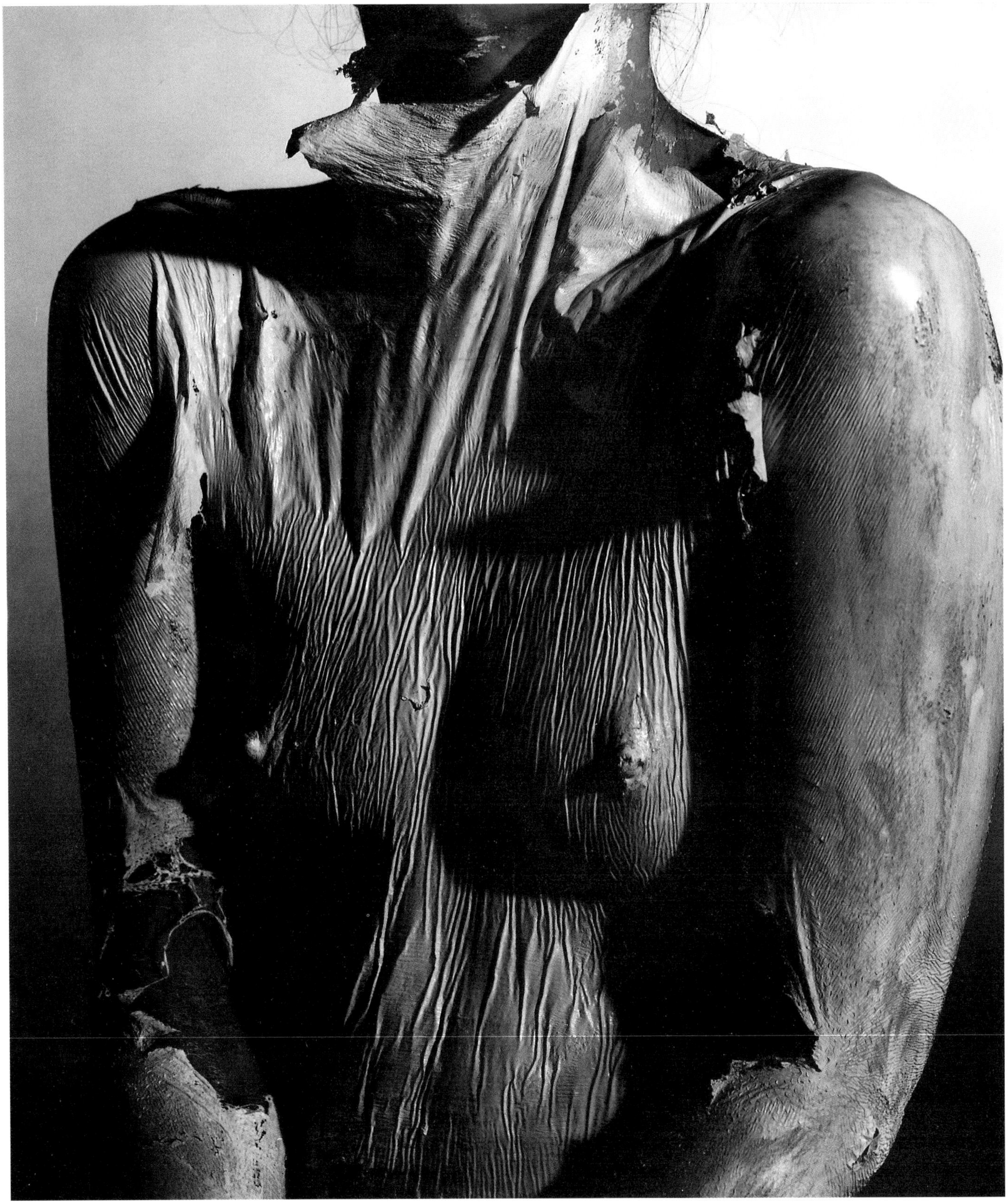

INTRODUCTION

T

PLATE II
DAVID BAILEY
Untitled 1982

increased. In fact, many female photographers take nude pictures of themselves and most male nudes are by men. In the final count, the two most famous nudes, Venus and David, will give both sexes equal billing, with women still at a disadvantage, because Venus has no arms to defend herself. Maybe that is what made her so famous in the male-dominated past.

The choice of pictures in this collection is very personal and in no way a history of the nude. In this respect it is much like the recent Victoria & Albert Museum fashion photography show which I also curated with Martin Harrison, whose presence is very much felt in the present collection and whom I cannot thank enough. Our grateful thanks are due to all the individuals and institutions who have so kindly co-operated in supplying photographs. They are all credited individually elsewhere in this book, but we should especially like to single out Chris Hudson (J. Paul Getty Museum) and Mark Haworth-Booth (Victoria & Albert Museum) for their untiring assistance. Private photographic galleries have helped to provide many key works and our thanks also to Agathe Gaillard (Paris); George H. Dalsheimer (Baltimore); Sidney Janis Gallery (New York); Staley-Wise Gallery (New York); Joseph Vasta (New York); Hamilton's Gallery (London); Robert Miller Gallery (New York); Julian Hartnoll (London) and Zelda Cheatle of the Photographers Gallery (London). Philippe Garner, of Sotheby's, London, was generous with both his time and encouragement, and we should both like to record our indebtedness to Graham Ovenden, for his hospitality as well as for letting us choose from his wonderful collection.

I would like to leave the final say to D.H. Lawrence, with his poem *Innocent England*.

INNOCENT ENGLAND

Oh What a pity, oh don't you agree
That figs aren't found in the land of the free!

Fig trees don't grow in my native land;
there's never a fig-leaf near at hand

when you want one; so I did without
and that is what the row's about.

Virginal pure policemen came
and hid their faces for very shame

while they carried the shameless thing away
to gaol, to be hid from the light of day.

And Mr. Mead, that old, old lily
said: 'Gross! coarse! hideous!' – and I, like a silly

thought he meant the faces of the police-court officials,
and how right he was, and I signed my initials

to confirm what he said, but alas he meant
my pictures, and on the proceedings went.

The upshot was, my pictures must blush
that English artists must finally learn

when they painted nude, to put a *cache sexe* on,
a cache sexe, a cache sexe, or else begone!

A fig leaf; or, if you cannot find it
a wreath of mist, with nothing behind it.

A wreath of mist is the usual thing
in the north, to hide where the turtles sing.

Though they never sing, they never sing,
don't you dare to suggest such a thing

or Mr. Mead will be after you.
–But what a pity I never knew

a wreath of English mist would do
as a cache sexe! I'd have put a whole fog.

But once and forever barks the old dog,
so my pictures are in prison, instead of in the Zoo.

D. H. LAWRENCE

NOTE: Unless stated otherwise, all photographs reproduced in this book are taken from silver gelatin prints.

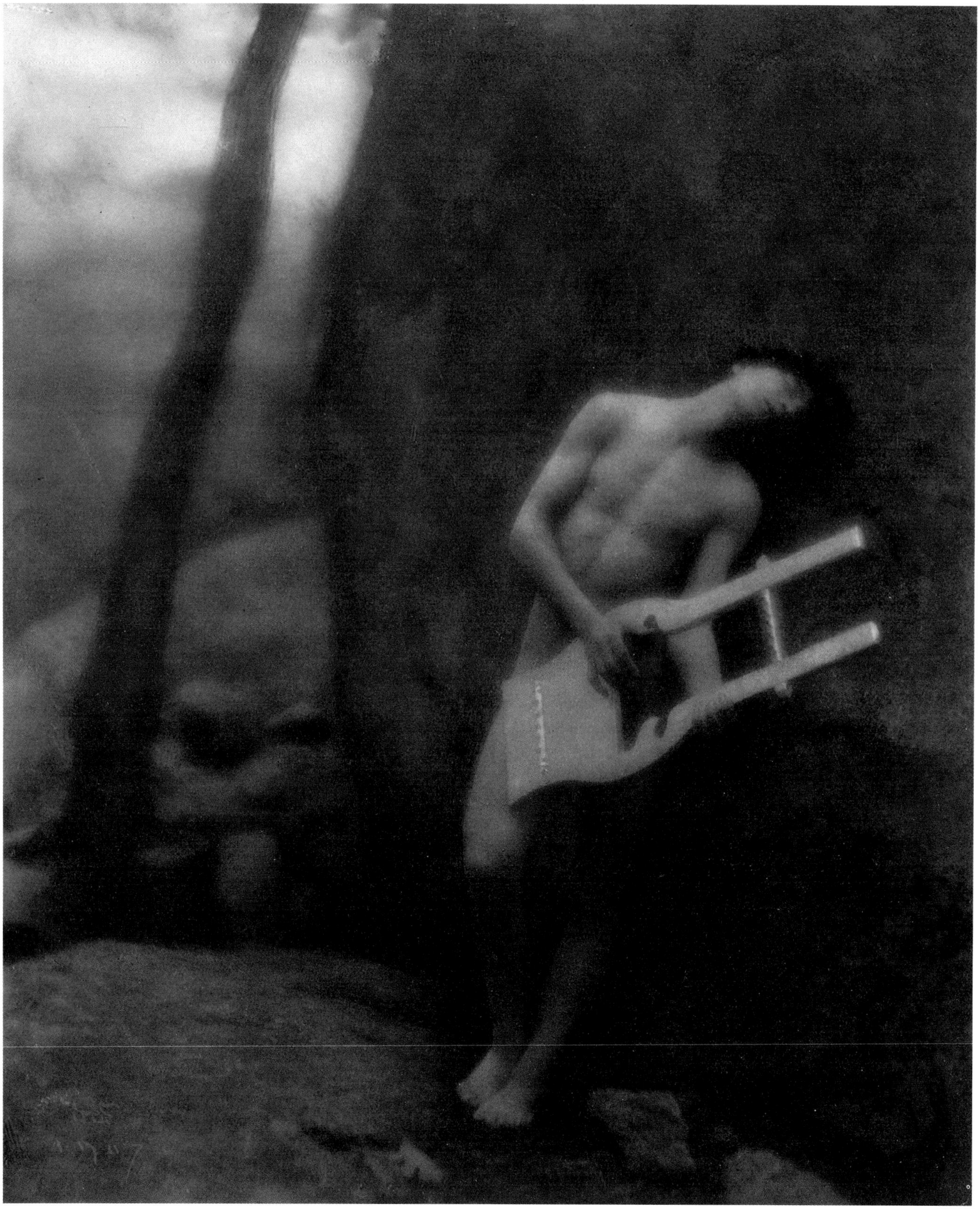

EARLY NUDES

PHOTOGRAPHERS AND ARTISTS

I

PLATE III
FREDERICK HOLLAND DAY
Apollo 1907
PLATINUM PRINT
Robert Miller Gallery, New York

This photograph is part of an extensive series of "Apollo" studies, apparently inspired by Keats. Day had a lifelong obsession with Keats and bequeathed his massive and important collection of Keatsiana to the Keats Museum in Hampstead, London.

In contrast, a French artist of the generation after Delacroix, the Impressionist EDGAR DEGAS, presents an altogether more complex relationship between painting and photography. He was one of many painters whose work benefitted from the stop-action sequence photographs of animals and humans in motion published by Eadweard Muybridge in the 1880s. The list of subscribers to Muybridge's work in England alone included G. F. Watts, Holman Hunt, Millais, Whistler and Sargent. The pastels and sketches of galloping horses which Degas based on Muybridge's studies are well known; much more radical was the influence which "instantaneous" photographs had on the violent cropping of his painting in the 1870s, and the manner in which the exaggerated spatial recession of some photographic lenses caused Degas to flout established rules of perspective in European art. His figures, cut off at the waist or knee, placed asymmetrically, gazed out of the picture frame in a seemingly accidental snapshot manner.

But Degas was a private, almost secretive individual, and we have little direct evidence about the way in which he used photography. What is certain is that towards the end of his career he took up photography himself. His eyesight had begun to fail and, after the 1870s, finding oils too difficult to work with, he turned to pastels and to sculpture. He also became increasingly preoccupied with the nude as his principal subject matter. It is not certain whether he operated the camera himself when he began to make photographs about 1890, but it matters little since he was clearly directing the operations. One of the few nude photographs by Degas to come to light has been described as "one of the greatest nudes in all photography," a view with which Bailey wholeheartedly concurs (PLATE V). This, and perhaps even more particularly its companion (PLATE VI), is especially interesting in the light of Degas' comments in 1891: "The nude has always been represented in poses which presuppose an audience, but these women of mine are honest, simple folk, unconcerned by any other interests than those involved in their physical condition. Here is another; she is washing her feet. It is as if you looked through a keyhole." It should perhaps be added that the "keyhole" reference should be understood as advocating non-intervention as opposed to voyeurism. Degas was in any case no great lover of women in this sense, and could even be described as a misogynist.

Nudes by leading English photographers of the Victorian period are comparatively rare, although the double standard of Victorian morality ensured there was a flourishing "underground" market in such pictures. Bailey's own serious interest in nineteenth-century photographers started when the first photography auctions in the 1970s began to turn up a wealth of early material. His collection now contains important works by Fox Talbot and Julia Margaret Cameron along with many others, but his greatest enthusiasm is reserved for ROGER FENTON. Fenton is probably still best known for his pioneering coverage of the Crimean War in 1855, though his architectural photographs and stunning landscapes have in many ways never been surpassed. He worked as a solicitor before taking up photography in 1851, though he had originally trained as a painter under Paul Delaroche in Paris. It was Delaroche, incidentally, who declared on first seeing a photograph: "From today, painting is dead." Fenton's great achievements in photography were accomplished in a surprisingly short career – he retired in 1862. His oeuvre contains only one known nude (PLATE 10), which Bailey regards as "a masterpiece, touching yet completely assured." Fenton's house overlooked London's Primrose Hill, only one hundred yards from Bailey's own home since 1964 and the location for some of Bailey's famous portraits.

Almost contemporary with Fenton's nude is the charming study by JOHN WATSON, who ran a Bond Street studio, dating from 1850 (PLATE VII). More academic than the Fenton, there is nevertheless a relaxed feeling to the pose of the model that Bailey finds appealing and that saves the photograph from Victorian conventionality. Apart from O. G. Rejlander, none of the other important English photographers of this period showed an interest in the nude and the subject ceased to claim serious attention until the turn of the century. This was doubtless due to a moral climate which was hardly conducive to the open display of such subjects. Alfred Wall, writing in *Photographic News* in 1860, felt it necessary to write defensively about a Rejlander nude of a reclining woman viewed from the rear. "Well, what is the suggestion here?" he asked. "Gross and indelicate? Anything at all like that created by a sight of those partially nude abominations now disgracing so many London shop windows? By jingo, I guess not!"

In spite of Delaroche's alarmed prediction that photography would kill off painting, this did not happen. Much of the debate about photography was concerned with its relationship with painting, just as the question "Is Photography Art?" has continued into the twentieth century. The critic John Ruskin initially welcomed the daguerreotype as a "handmaiden to art"; in the 1840s he made frequent use of them as aids to his drawings of architecture, where they complemented perfectly his dictum of optical veracity or "truth to nature." By 1870 he had concluded, in his usual contradictory way, that photographs were "merely spoiled nature."

EUGENE ATGET did not photograph nudes, but the many hundreds of views he made of the streets and gardens of his beloved Paris are now so highly regarded that Atget is widely accepted as one of the greatest of all photographers. Bailey holds his work in such high esteem that he decided to

stopped to talk to him and, intrigued, invited this unusual character to his studio. Very much in the tradition of Atget, Paul Barkshire photographs the buildings of London. His work is meticulously contact-printed and selenium-toned; he rarely works to a commission, preferring to risk being able to sell the results to libraries or other interested parties. The photograph included here is not typical of Barkshire's work, since it is a close-up study, in high-key, of a sculpture, but its delicate tonality and careful craftsmanship are ever-present virtues in his photographs.

Staying for a moment in the present day, we come to a painter and photographer, GRAHAM OVENDEN, with whom Bailey has only relatively recently struck up a friendship. They have in common a profound interest in reviving old printing techniques. The photograph of sleeping children (PLATE XLI) is from a remarkable series documenting life in London's dockland, made while Ovenden was still in his teens. Inspired by Charles Dickens' accounts of London's East End, he set out to record this area before the docks fell into disuse. The negatives were printed more recently on either platinum-sensitized paper or by the print-out method. The example included in this collection was made on conventional silver bromide paper from an intermediate negative on X-ray film.

ARTIST PHOTOGRAPHERS

"T

The most extreme practitioner of the Photo-Secessionist school was FREDERICK HOLLAND DAY. Eccentricity and decadence were taken so far in his photographs that Bailey says: "You have to admire Day's commitment, if not always the results." In the 1890s, Day exhibited works such as "Ebony and Ivory" and "Beauty is Truth" which, despite homosexual overtones, escaped accusations of indecency. In 1898, he embarked on his most bizarre project, to depict himself as Christ in a series based on the Crucifixion. The series marked the end of Day's experiments with sacred subjects starring himself as Christ, though he returned to a religious theme in 1906 with his photographs depicting St. Sebastian. The model for these pictures was almost certainly the same one who played "Apollo" (PLATE III), the following year, not a Greek God but an Italian youth who repaid Day's affections by skipping English classes to chase girls. Throughout most of his career, Day had made his prints in platinum, which was notable for the subtlety of its tonal rendition. In 1917, the Russian Revolution prevented supplies of platinum metal getting through from the Urals, and the commercial production of platinum printing papers immediately ceased. As a result, Day, along with Robert Demachy and the English photographer Frederick Evans, gave up photography. This was clearly a contributory factor to the depression that took Frederick Holland Day to his bed, where he remained for another sixteen years, until his death in 1933.

Hardly less eccentric than Day was another Photo-Secessionist, and later fashion photographer, Baron ADOLF DE MEYER. Cecil Beaton called him "the Debussy of the camera" and it was the inability to outgrow his hazy romanticism which caused his eventual commercial downfall. His origins are unclear, but he was born and brought up in Paris. By 1895 he had moved to London where, in 1899, he married the beautiful Olga, daughter of the Duke

Cavaceniko. They became intimates of the social circle around the future King Edward VII. Olga was believed to be one of his illegitimate daughters and she and her husband certainly benefited from a grace-and-favour residence on a Royal estate in Dorset. Wishing the couple to attend his coronation in 1901, Edward persuaded his cousin, the Duke of Saxony, to give Adolf the title of Baron. Already a prominent figure in London's artistic society, the added cachet of a title increased de Meyer's social standing; it was a considerable coup for Condé Nast when he signed the Baron as the first contract photographer for *Vogue* and *Vanity Fair* in 1914.

De Meyer's 'Masked Woman' (PLATE XXXIX) is a powerful and mysterious portrait, the purpose of which is unknown. It had been in the collection of Alfred Stieglitz, who had exhibited de Meyer's photographs in his New York gallery in 1907 and 1911. The balletic pose would suggest a stylistic connection with the series de Meyer made in 1912 of Nijinsky dancing *L'Après-Midi d'un Faune* and other Russian Ballet productions by his friend Diaghilev.

A photographic amateur, FREDERICK H. EVANS was even closer to the heart of the [illegible] than either Holland Day or de Meyer. Yet his snapshot-like informality is diametrically opposed to Day's carefully posed outdoor tableaux or de Meyer's elaborate studio theatricality. Evans's photographs, made with available lighting in his own house, possess a seemingly casual directness which is prescient of much later developments in photography. Indeed, Banks [illegible] the group shot (PLATE XXIV) precisely because it seems to anticipate Diane Arbus — an Arbus without the technical sophistication.

The four pictures chosen by Banks (PLATES XXII–XXV) originate from one of Evans's private albums and were all made in 1896. If he was unsophisticated in the technical sense then the two photographs of Amelia Palumbo (PLATES XXII and XXIII) lose nothing by this. Indeed, their stark, grainy quality now appears strikingly modern in many ways and is part of their appeal. Louys' technical naivety was something he had in common with other French artists-turned-cameramen, notably Degas, Vuillard and Bonnard. Ironically, the work of all four shares a spontaneity and graphic strength (the latter due partly to the "risks" they took with using available daylighting) that is rarely evident in the photographs taken by their more self-conscious professional contemporaries.

Pierre Louys is chiefly remembered today as a Parisian dandy, one of the leading poets and writers of the French Symbolist movement. Much of his output was erotic, most significantly the prose poems *Chansons de Bilitis*, published in 1894. Louys claimed they were translations from the Greek of a poetess contemporary with Sappho, which turned out to be a very effective hoax, like Ossian deceiving many eminent scholars. A group of German antiquarians even took an expedition to the Greek East, seeking physical evidence of the fair Bilitis. In the context of his photographs *"La Femme et le Pantin"* (1898) also deserves to be mentioned, since it chronicled the gradual breakdown of a man who became enslaved to a worthless woman.

The Symbolist circle which Louys inhabited included among his intimates Oscar Wilde, Mallarmé, Valéry, André Gide and Debussy. He frequently collaborated with Debussy (Louys has been described as the director of his literary conscience), who set *Chansons de Bilitis* to music in 1897. Debussy used to compose and play for his friends on Louys' melodeon – described by J. E. Blanche as a "wretched instrument" – which dominates the background of the domestic nude (PLATE XXV).

Socially, geographically and intellectually far apart, there is nevertheless

ANONYMOUS NUDES

The approval of painters like Delacroix, Ingres, Courbet and Degas led eventually to a thriving business in the production of nude photographic studies for the use, ostensibly at least, of artists. Published under suitably discreet titles, *Etudes Academiques* or *Academies*, such volumes were significant factors in the widespread dissemination of nude photography. The boom in the photographic postcard in the first decade of the twentieth century was also reflected in an even greater proliferation of nude postcards, mostly originating from Paris. Little serious research has been carried out into this aspect of photographic history and so the authors of most of these images remain, as they intended, anonymous. These anonymous nudes are not difficult to find, which is in itself an indication of the sort of numbers they were produced in, and consequently can often be picked up quite cheaply. Bailey takes a particular interest in two varieties: those which were so contrived as to appear comic, and those which depict an uninhibited sexuality that looks surprisingly modern.

His three choices from *Academies* of 1892 (the copy of which had, incidentally, originally belonged to Pierre Louys) illustrate the criteria. The girl with the apples against a background of kitchen utensils (PLATE IV) suggests a lighthearted symbolism, but still possesses a naive charm; the pose of the model with her arms aloft (PLATE XX) might well have fulfilled a useful function for artists, but Bailey was intrigued because he felt her almost aggressive frontality was most redolent of recent work by Robert Mapplethorpe. The nude lying on the couch (PLATE XXI) transcends kitsch associations in its straightforward elegance and sensuality.

The earliest anonymous image is the French stereo-daguerreotype, dating from c.1855-60 (PLATE XXVIII). Stereo nudes of this period are again not uncommon, Bailey choosing this example because of the offhand self-composure of the model. While clearly not everyone who bought nude photographs was in reality an artist, their use as aids to study was genuine enough. Discussing the paintings in the 1861 Paris Salon, the critic Théophile Gautier noted: "The daguerreotype, which has neither been given credit for nor medals, has nevertheless worked hard at this exhibition. It has yielded much information, spared much posing of the model, furnished many accessories, background and drapery, which have only to be copied and coloured."

To claim that photographs were intended as artists' studies was of course an easy way to side-step laws of obscenity. Despite such laws, there was a flourishing underground market in obscene photographs. In 1874, the police raided the London studio of photographer Henry Hayler and confiscated no fewer than 130,248 photographs they considered indecent. That this was the stock of one studio indicates the scale of the trade and also shows that it was not only French photographs which were undermining British morality. In his book *The Fleshly School of Poetry*, published in 1872, Robert Buchanan, besides continuing his vicious attacks on Swinburne and the Rossettis, also drew attention to the London shop windows filled with photographs of "nude, indecent, hideous harlots in every possible attitude that vice can devise." Buchanan's vituperation was levelled at images which few would find pornographic today. Then as now, that sort of material was inside the shop, under the counter. What offended Buchanan and other upholders of Victorian morality was doubtless the openness with which photographs of naked women whom they believed to be prostitutes were displayed. This went counter to their repressive belief that only males could exhibit sexuality and that wives should remain passive recipients; real sex was a covert activity reserved for mistresses or prostitutes.

French photographers were brought to trial for dealing in obscene images, they were adept at finding ways around the law. One method was to sell their wares as studies for artists, another to circulate photographs by mail order. It is doubtful, on the other hand, whether many Edwardian erotic postcards were in fact ever sent through the post, since to do so was presumably to risk arrest. Bailey found the coyness of the "Ebony and Ivory" postcard (PLATE XLV) amusing, in contrast to the almost blatant sexuality of PLATE IX. The most unusual postcards are the anonymous multi-baby collages (PLATES XXXII-XXXIV) dating from c.1904, partly based on studies by Monteboni of Milan (PLATE XXXV), which Bailey finds strange, disturbing and wonderful, reminding him of Richard Dadd, Bosch and the Surrealists.

The ethnographical book was an alternative means of publishing the nude and avoiding legal problems. PLATE XLVII, the African woman with "conical breasts" (as the original caption described her) was chosen by Bailey from a German book published in 1900 on the grounds of the woman's "stunning, streamlined beauty." A later German publication, *Erotik*, signalled the more open sale of both books and magazines showing nude photographs. Its attractive Art Deco cover art is a clue to its date, 1925, and it ushered in the period in the present century when nudity, within limits, began to be more widely acceptable (PLATE XXIX).

PLATE IV
ANONYMOUS
(from *Academies*) 1892
Graham Ovenden Collection

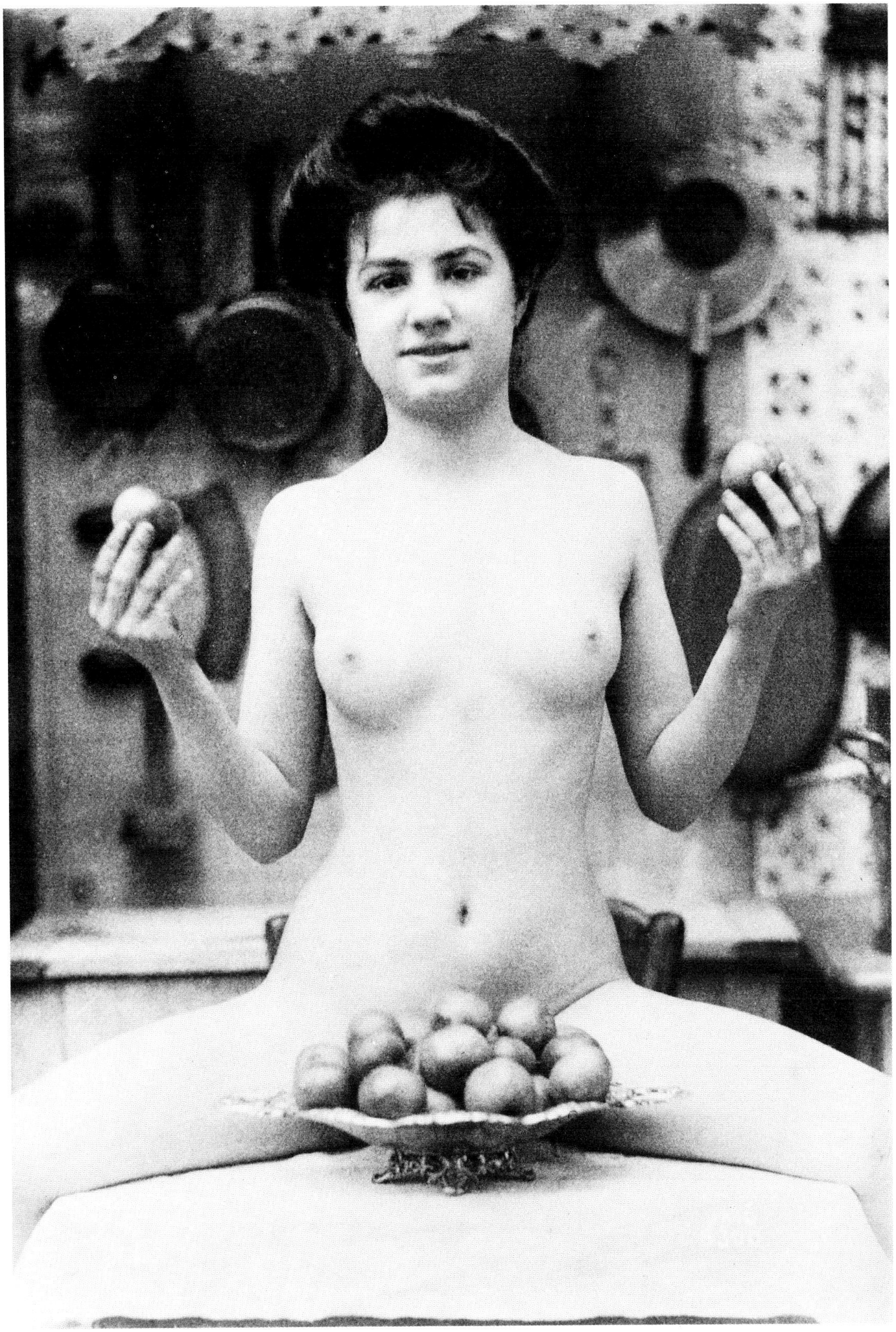

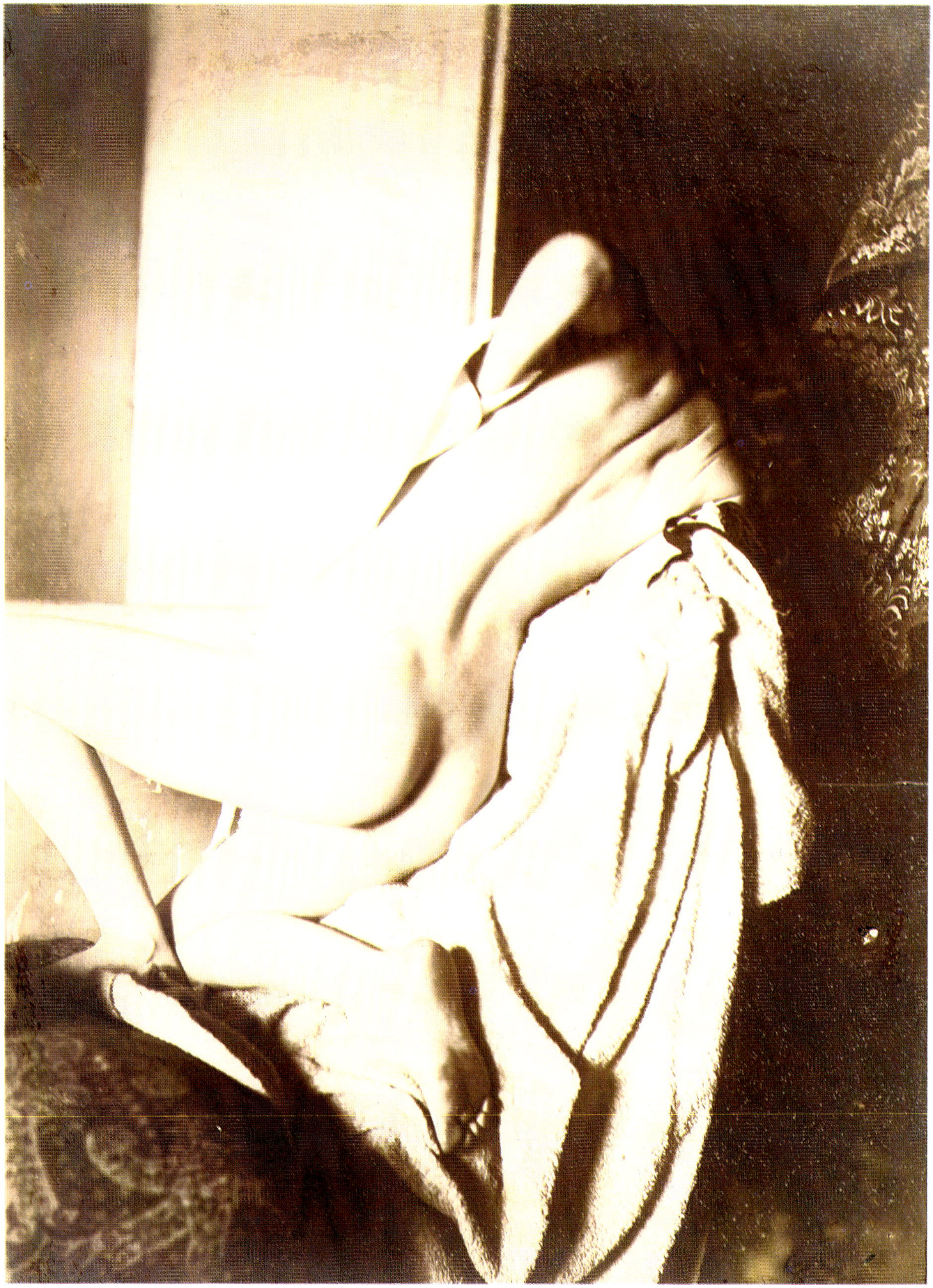

PLATE V
EDGAR DEGAS
Untitled c.1890
17×12 cm (6¾×4¾ in)
J. Paul Getty Museum, Malibu

These exquisite nudes appear to relate most closely to the nudes Degas showed at the final Impressionist exhibition in Paris, in 1886, whose unadorned naturalism was considered shocking at the time. Each is quite different: the seated nude has the air of snapshot realism, while in PLATE V the model strikes a dramatic and unconventional pose that would seem to have been directed.

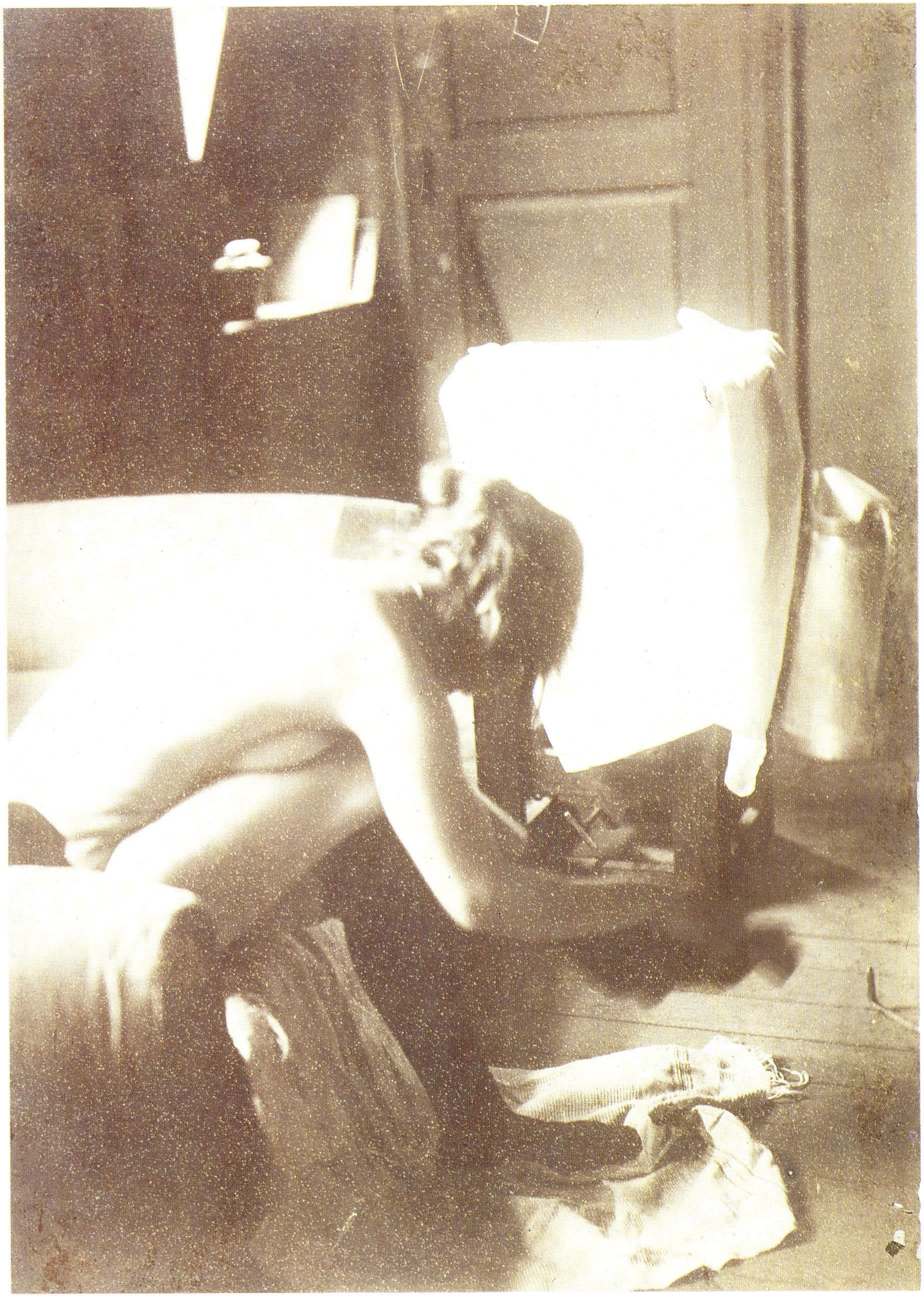

PLATE VI
EDGAR DEGAS
Untitled c.1890
16.5×12 cm (6½×4¾ in)
J. Paul Getty Museum, Malibu

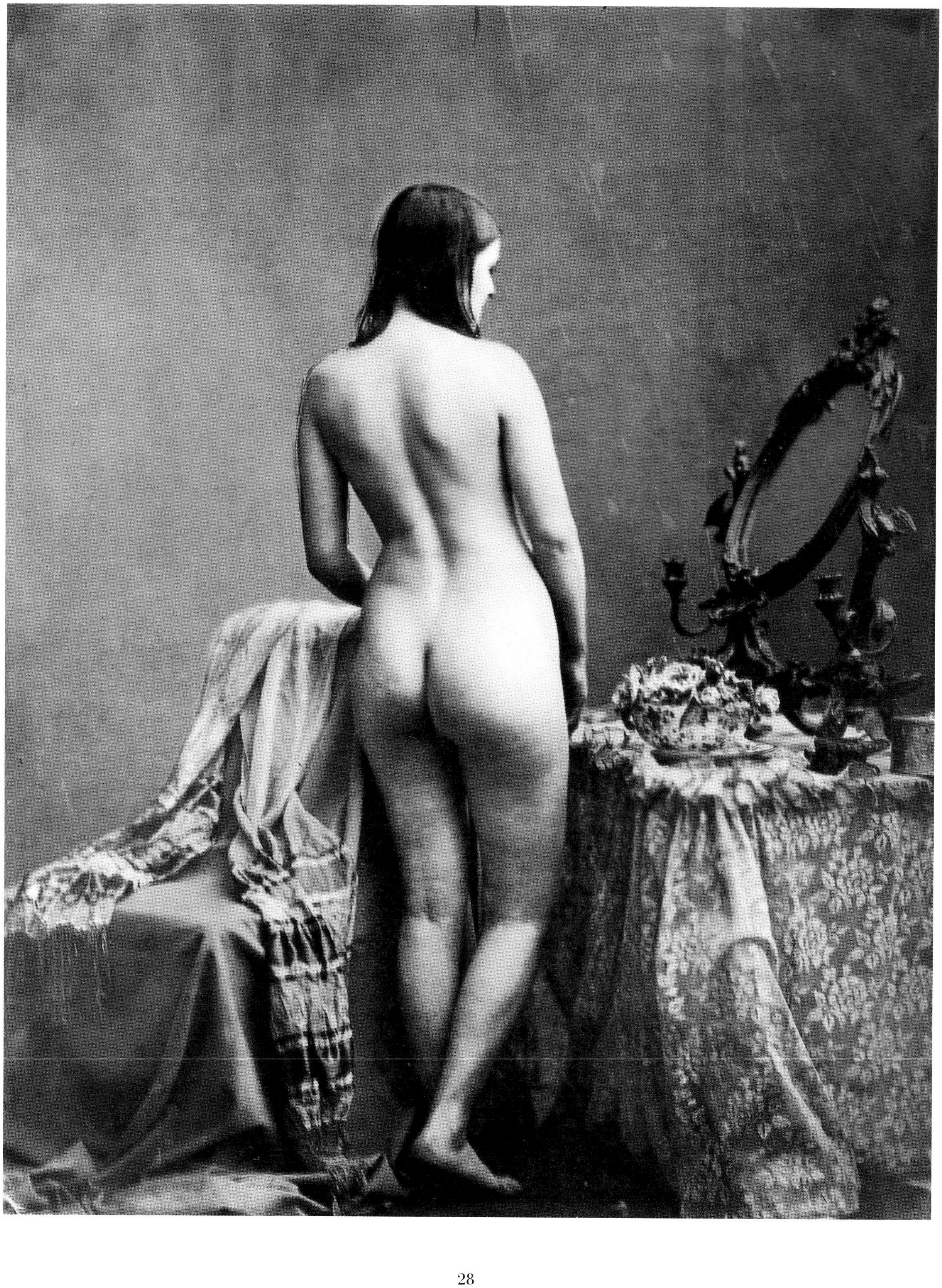

PLATE VII
JOHN WATSON
Nude Study c.1856
ALBUMEN PRINT
Victoria & Albert Museum, London

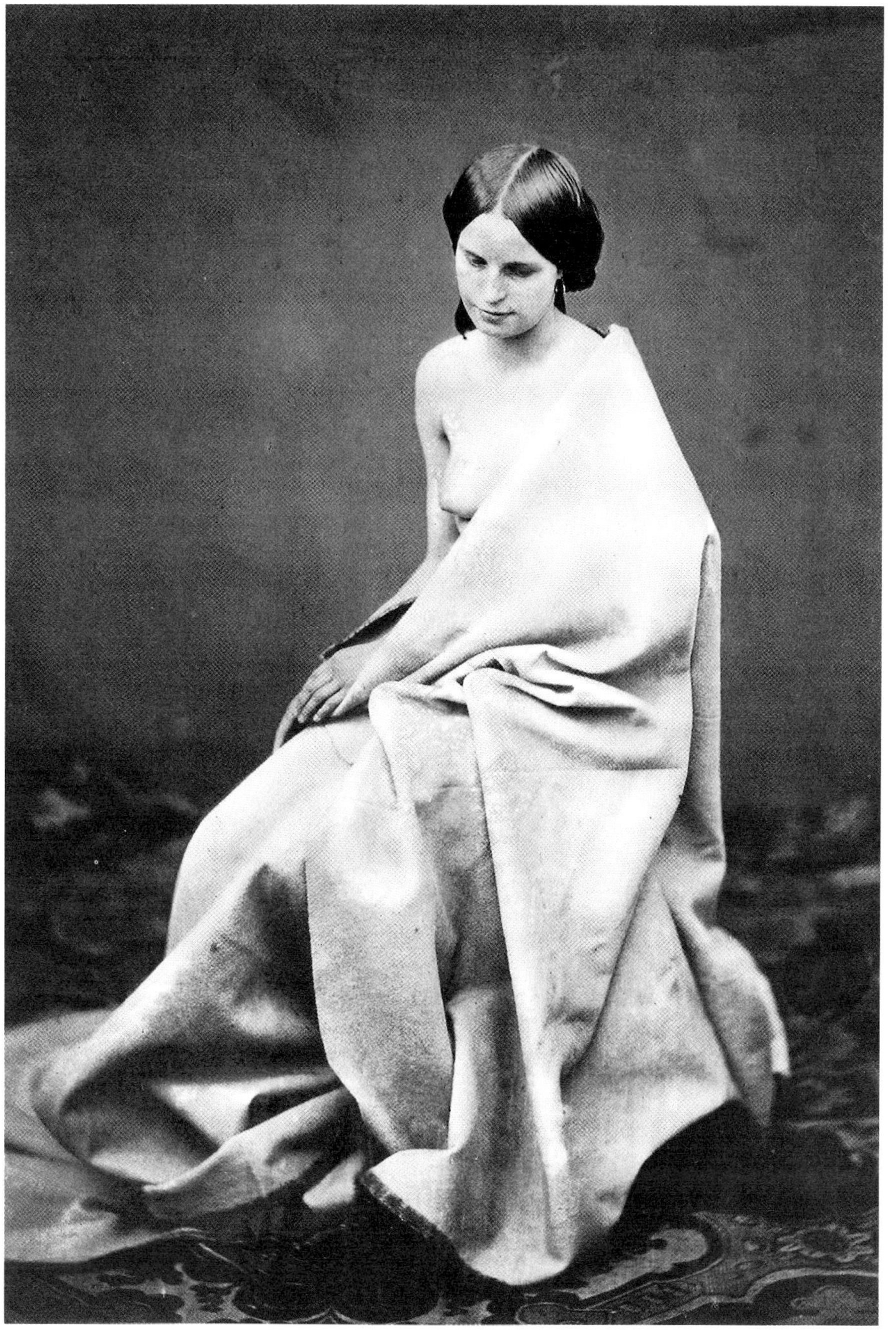

PLATE VIII
ROGER FENTON
Nude Study c.1855
SALTED PAPER PRINT
Victoria & Albert Museum, London

Fenton photographed Queen Victoria on the same rug and against a similar plain backdrop. Like his royal portraits, this unique nude has remarkable directness and informality, rather than the pomp and artifice of the period.

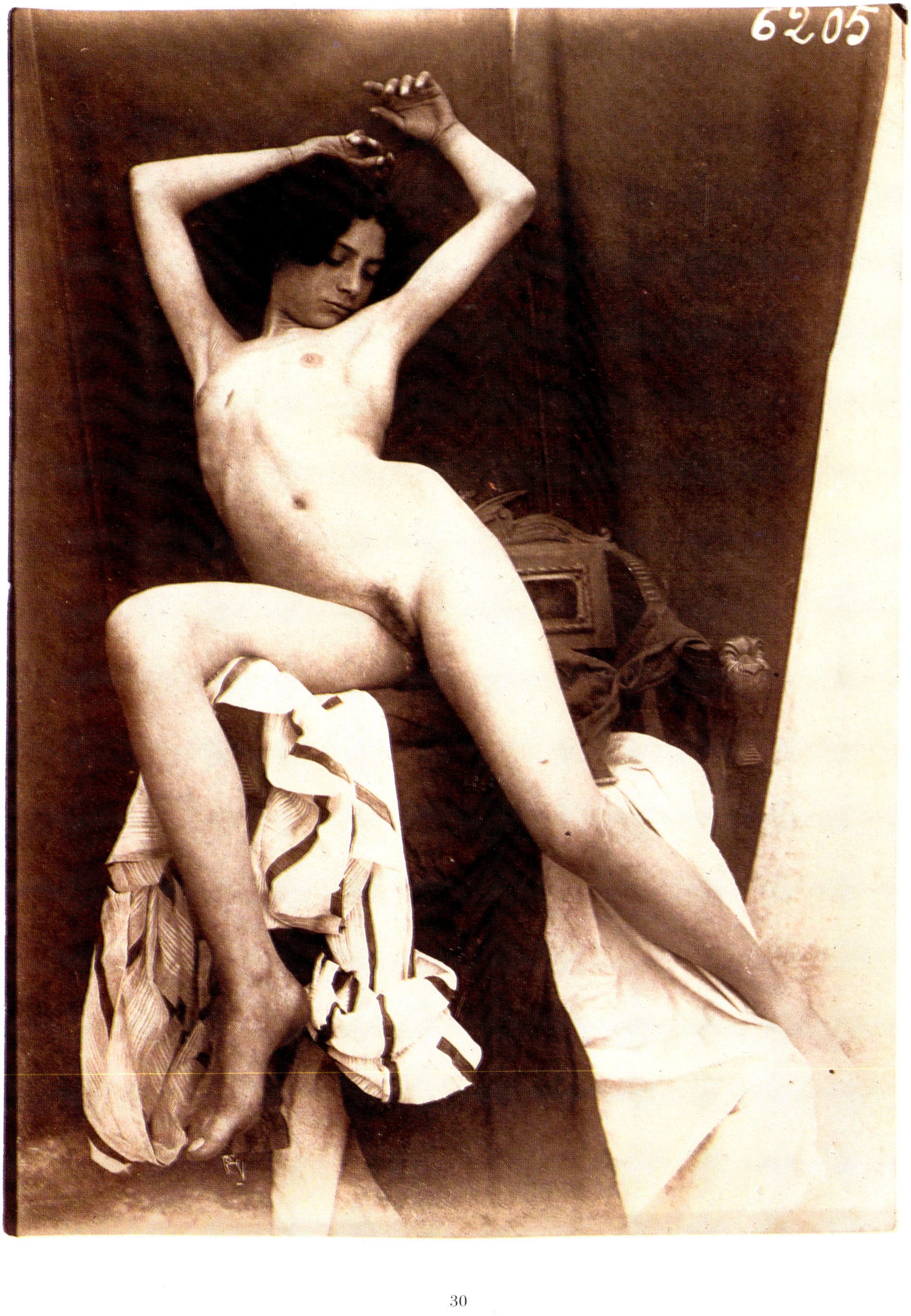
6205

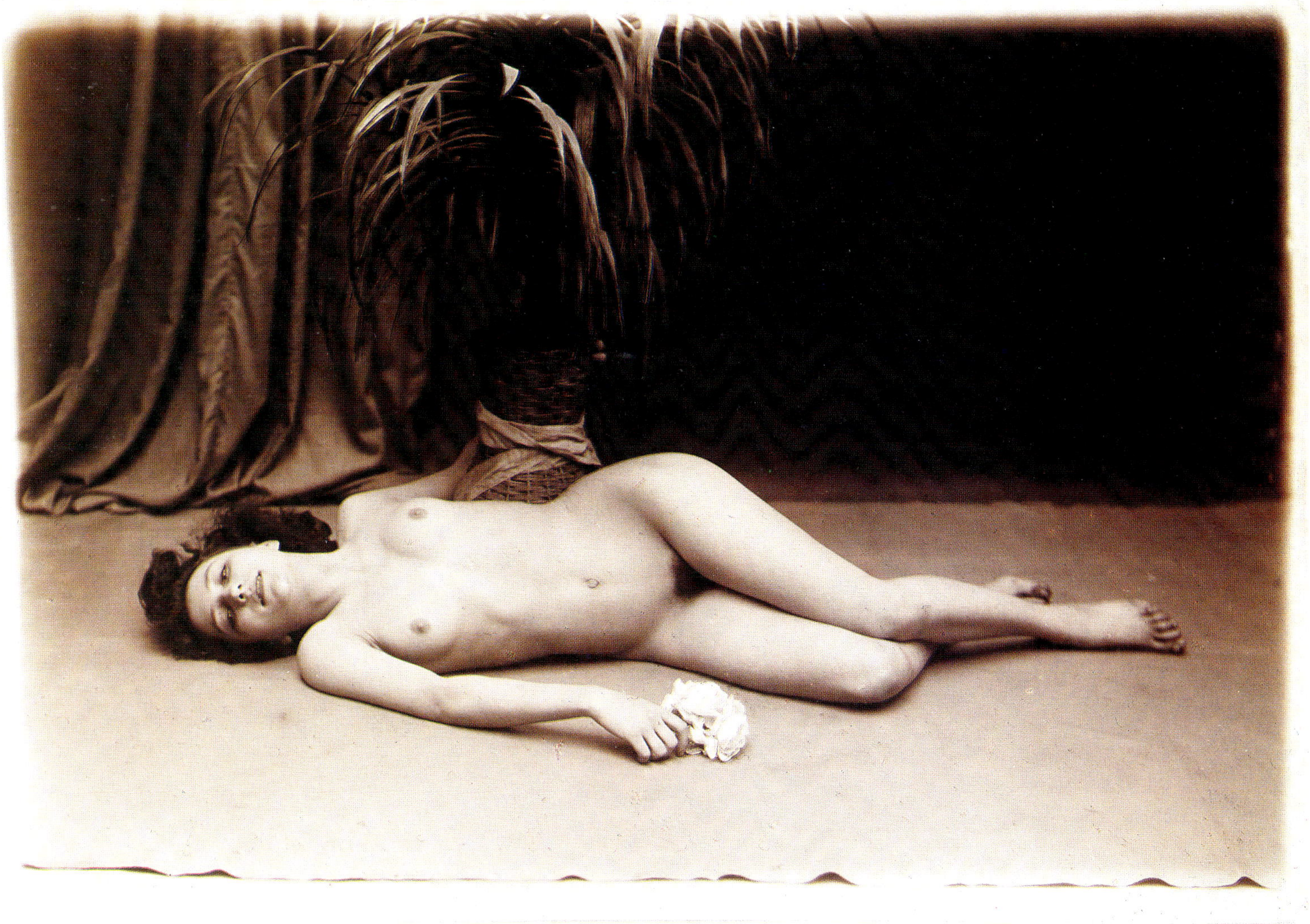

PLATE X (Above)
ANONYMOUS (French)
Untitled c.1900
Joseph Vasta, New York

PLATE IX (Left)
ANONYMOUS (French)
Untitled Nude c.1900
Private Collection

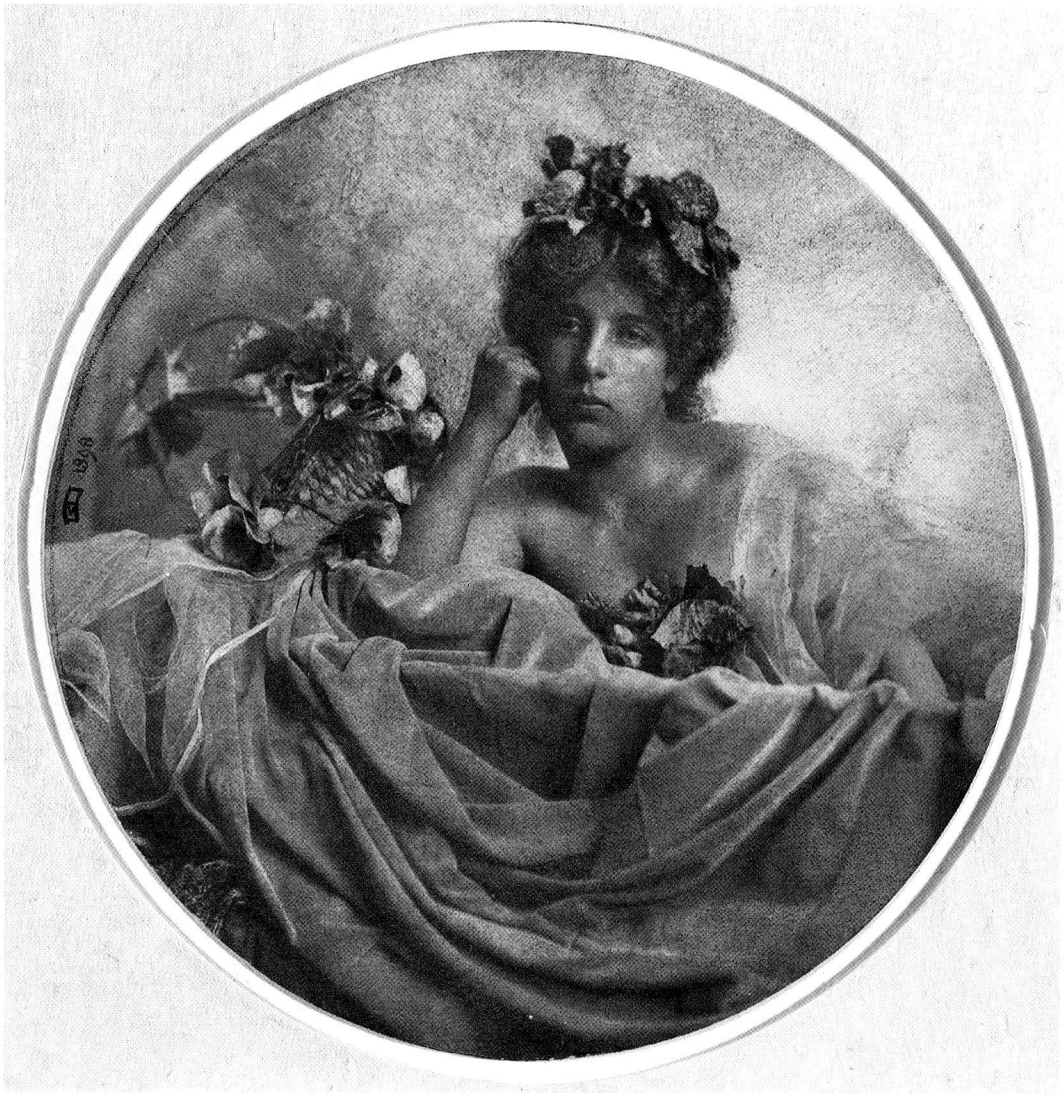

PLATE XI
ROBERT DEMACHY
Panel 1898
GUM BICHROMATE PRINT
The Metropolitan Museum of Art, New York

In 1895, when Demachy first showed gum bichromate prints in Paris, he was instantly accepted as the foremost French Pictorialist photographer. Selecting a subject did not, Demachy felt, make him an artist; but the subsequent manipulation permitted by the gum bichromate process enabled the limitations of the machine-made image to be overcome. In his words, "the essence of Art consists in emphasis and suppression."

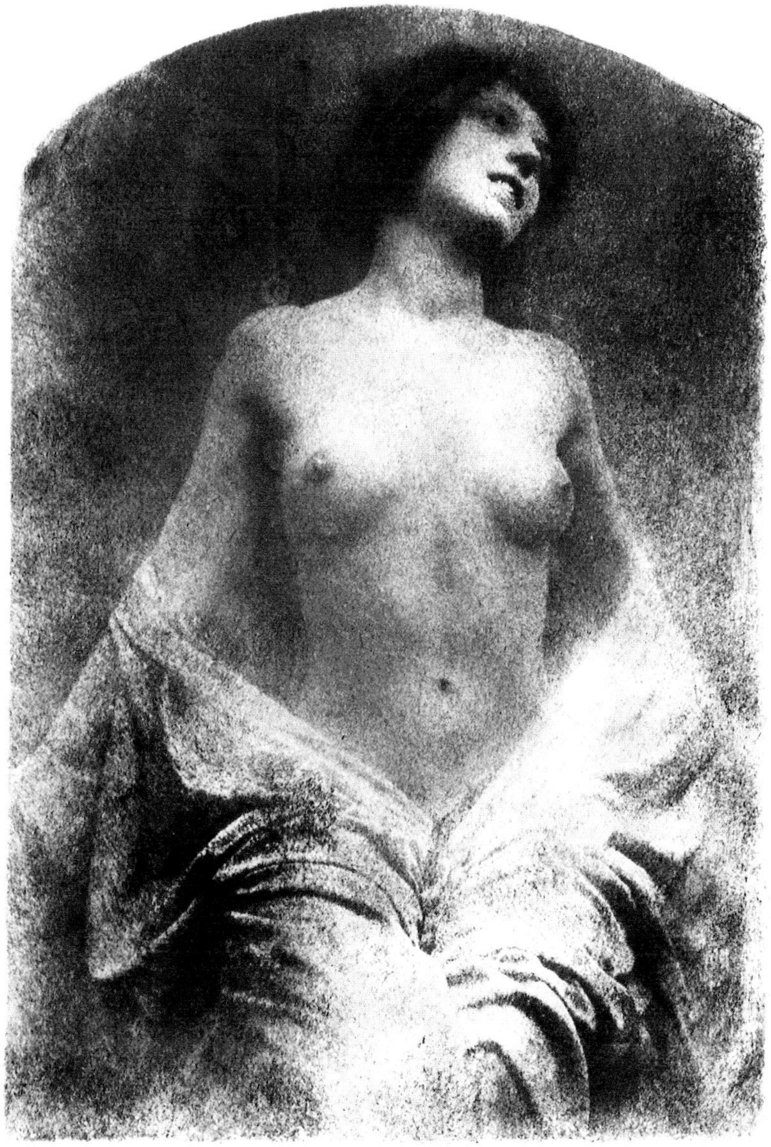

PLATE XII
ROBERT DEMACHY
Untitled
OIL TRANSFER PRINT
Sotheby's, London

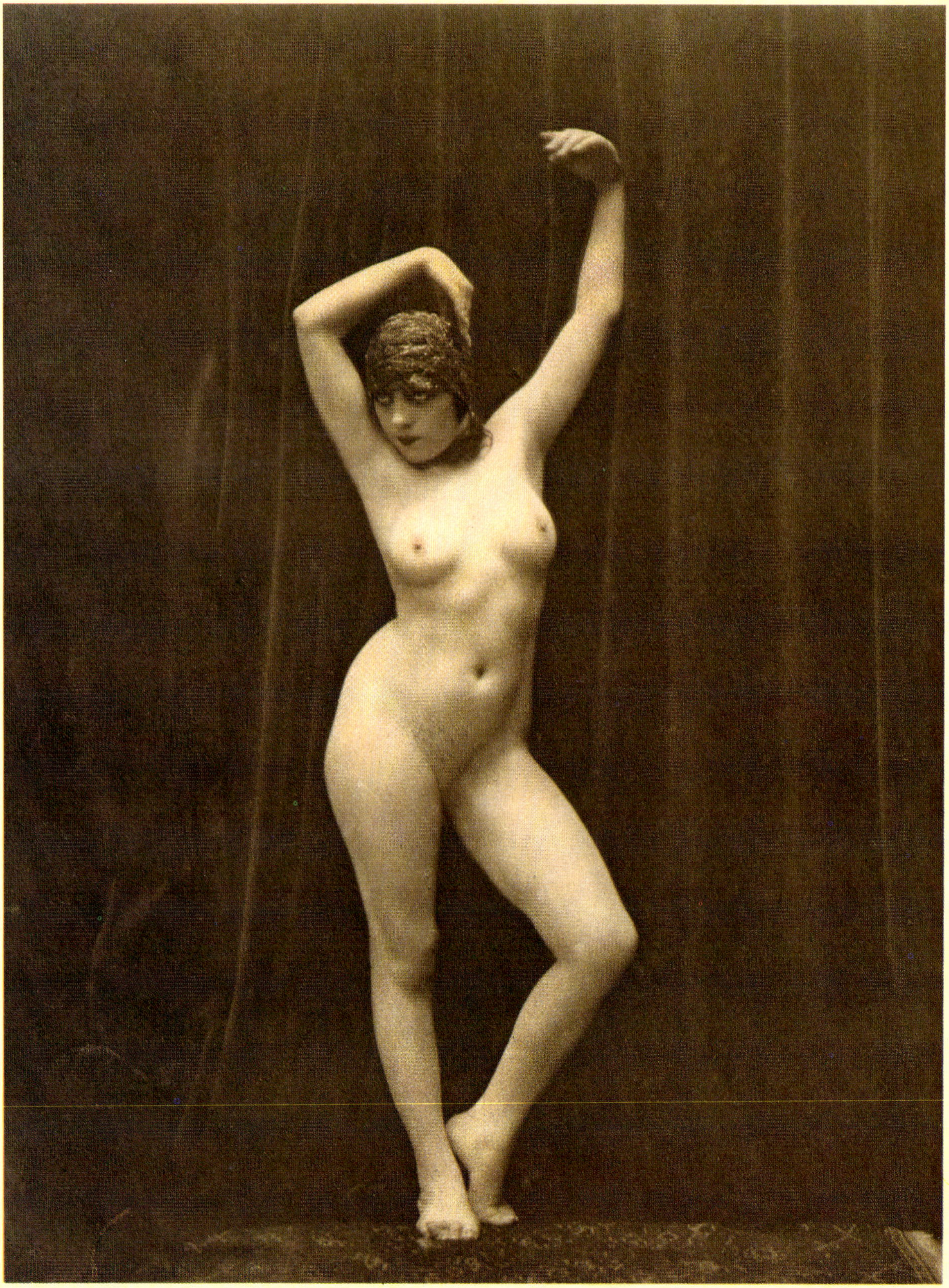

PLATE XIII
ANONYMOUS (French)
Untitled c.1925
David Bailey Collection

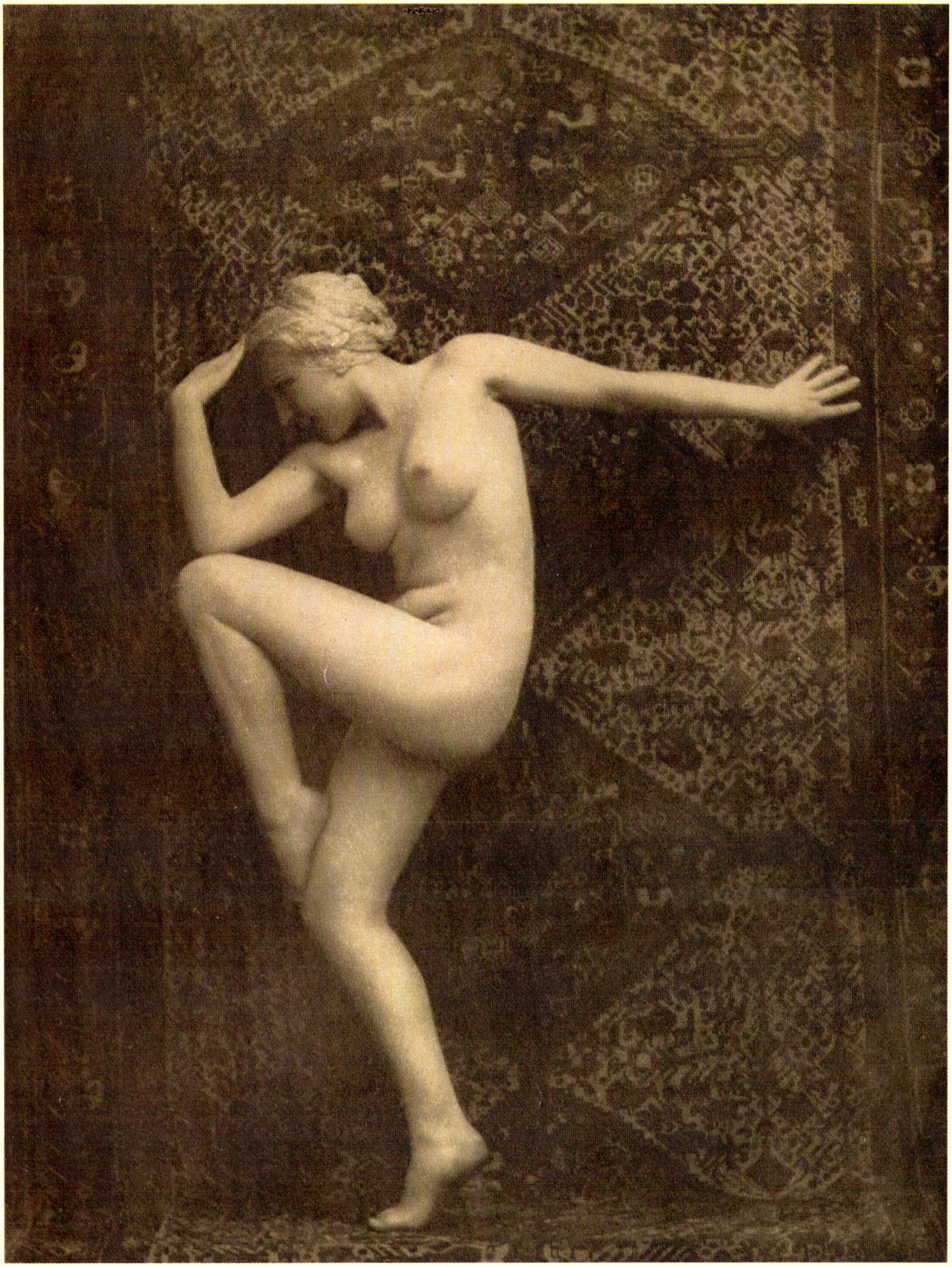

PLATE XIV
ANONYMOUS
Untitled c.1925
David Bailey Collection

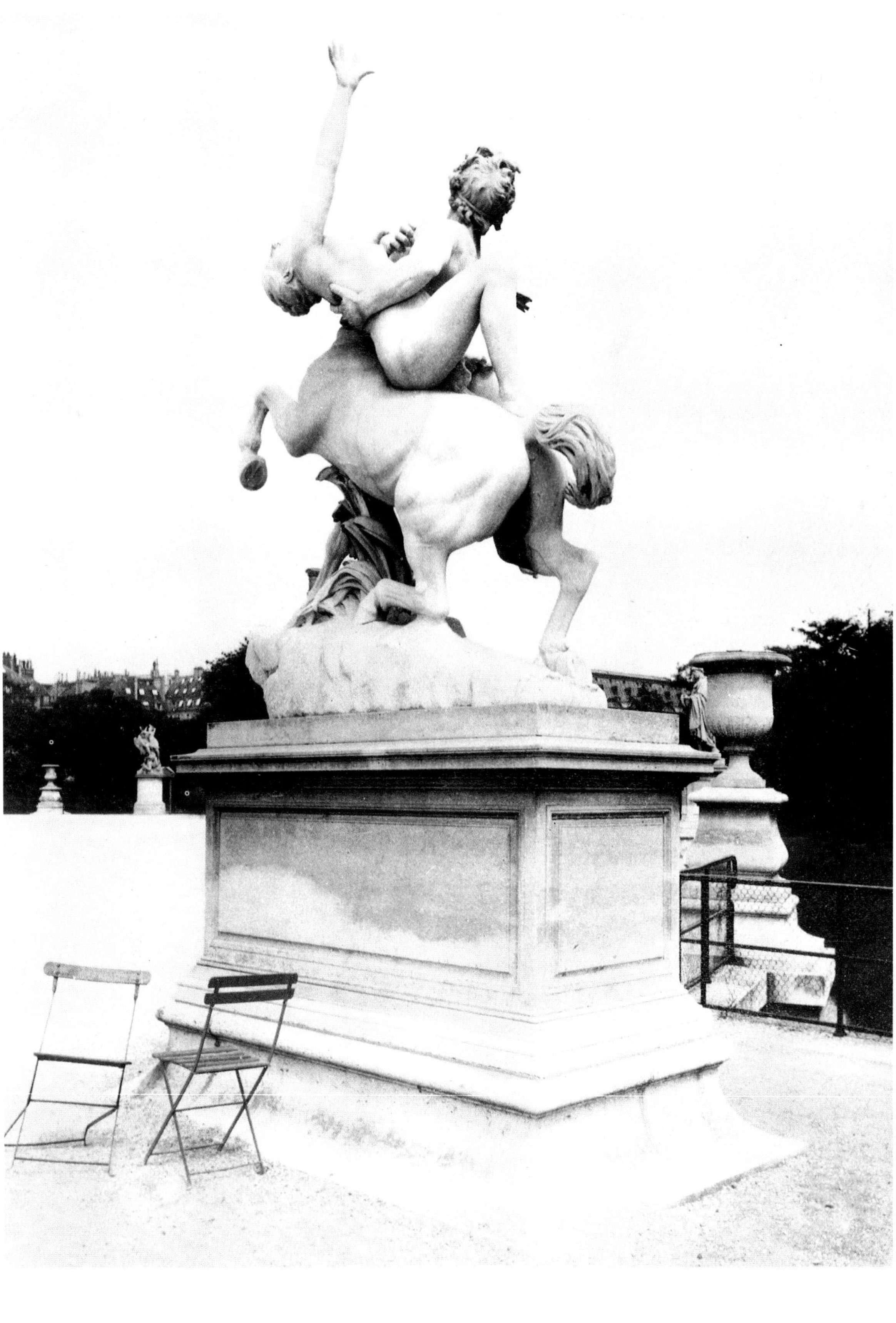

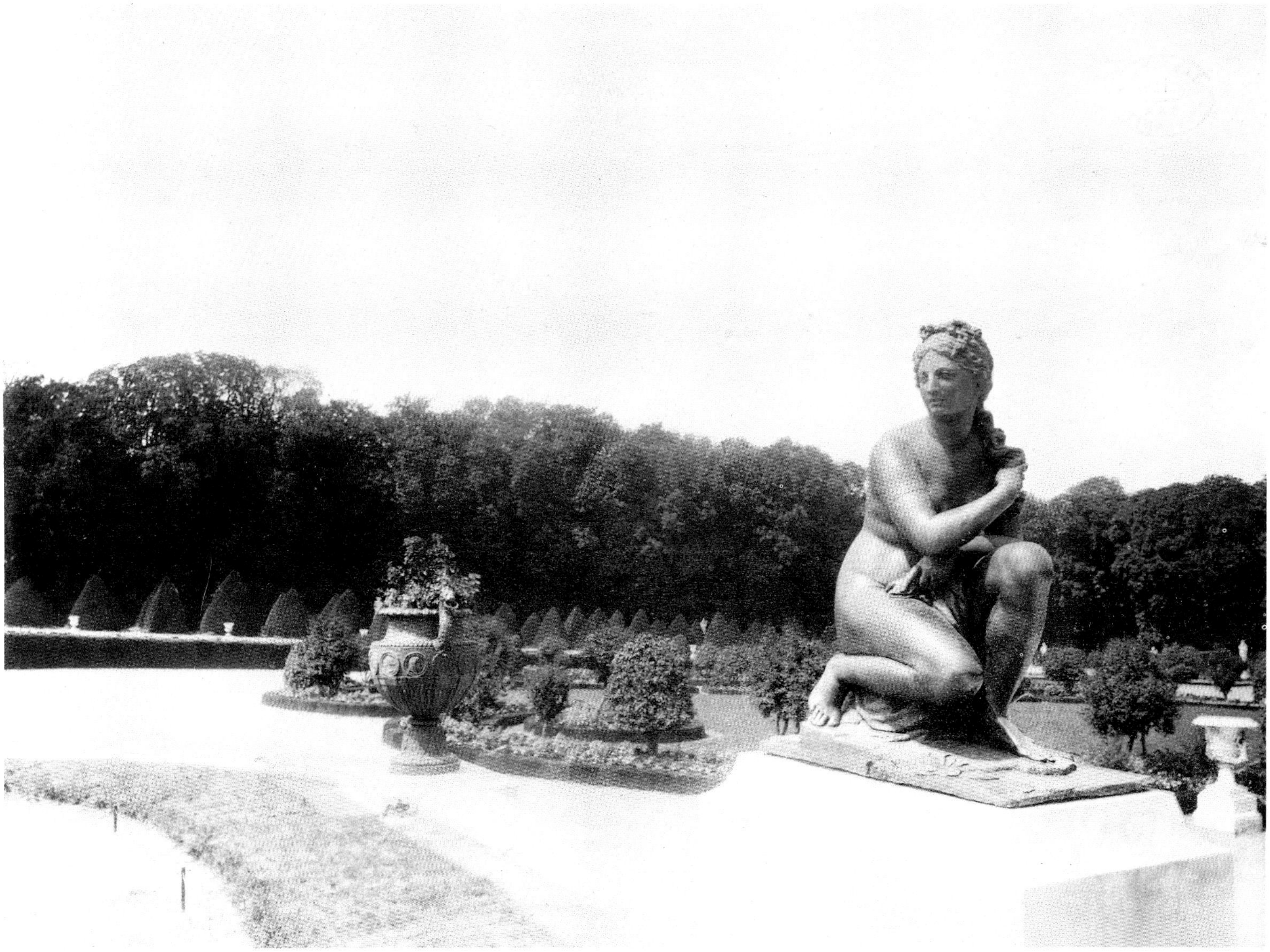

PLATE XVI (Above)
EUGENE ATGET
Statue of Venus, Versailles c.1900
ALBUMEN PRINT
Victoria & Albert Museum, London

The Victoria & Albert Museum purchased these Atgets in 1903 as documents of sculpture, not with astonishing foresight of their future status as photographs. Only later was it possible to describe Atget's oeuvre, as John Szarkowski did, as "wholly poised, reticent, dense with experience, mysterious and true."

PLATE XV (Left)
EUGENE ATGET
The Rape of Deianeira, Tuileries Gardens, Paris c.1900
ALBUMEN PRINT
Victoria & Albert Museum, London

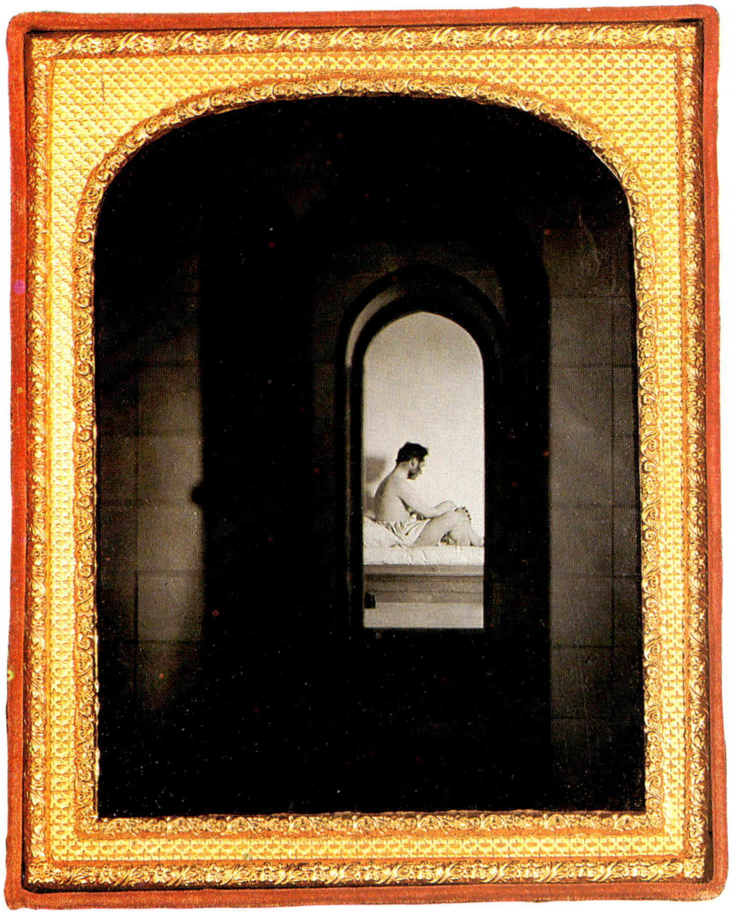

PLATE XVII

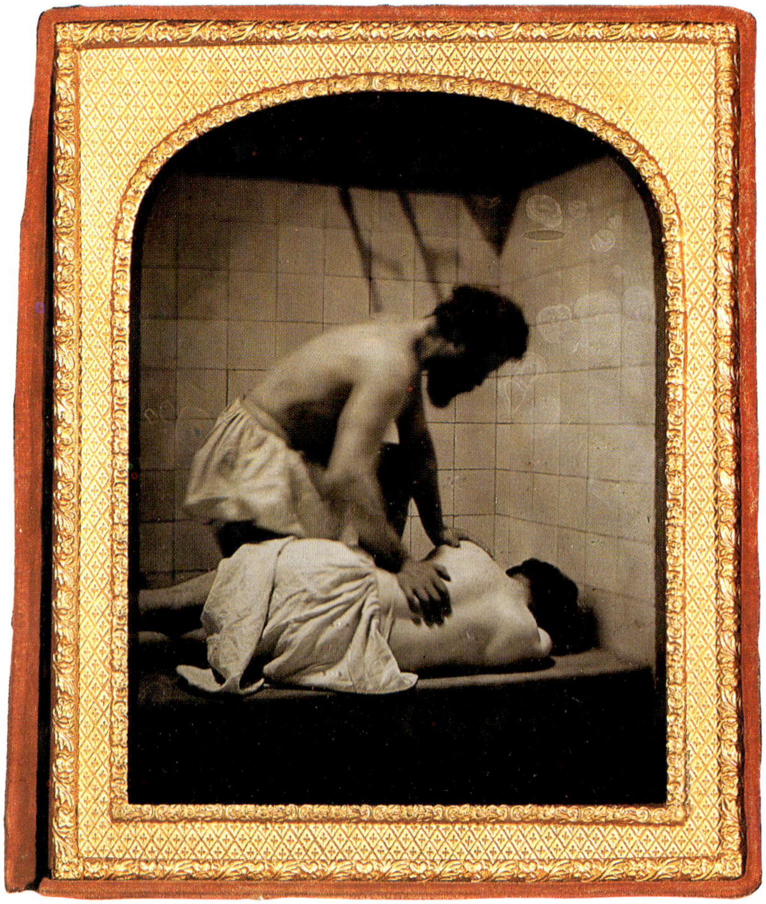

PLATE XVIII

PLATES XVII – XIX
ROBERT THOMPSON CRAWSHAY
Turkish Bath Scenes c.1870
COLLODION POSITIVES
Victoria & Albert Museum, London

These remarkable images are the only known instances where Crawshay used the collodion positive process. They share the sophistication and technical excellence of his albumen prints, the best known of which are large scale genre scenes, enacted by members of his family. Active as a photographer in the 1860s and 1870s, Crawshay became President of the Photographic Society of London, sponsoring a competition held by the society for large scale figure studies. He came from a wealthy family and was the second son of William Crawshay, the "Iron King", from whom he inherited Cyrfarthfa Castle, his home in South Wales. His brother, George Crawshay, significantly, pioneered the introduction of the Turkish bath to Britain.

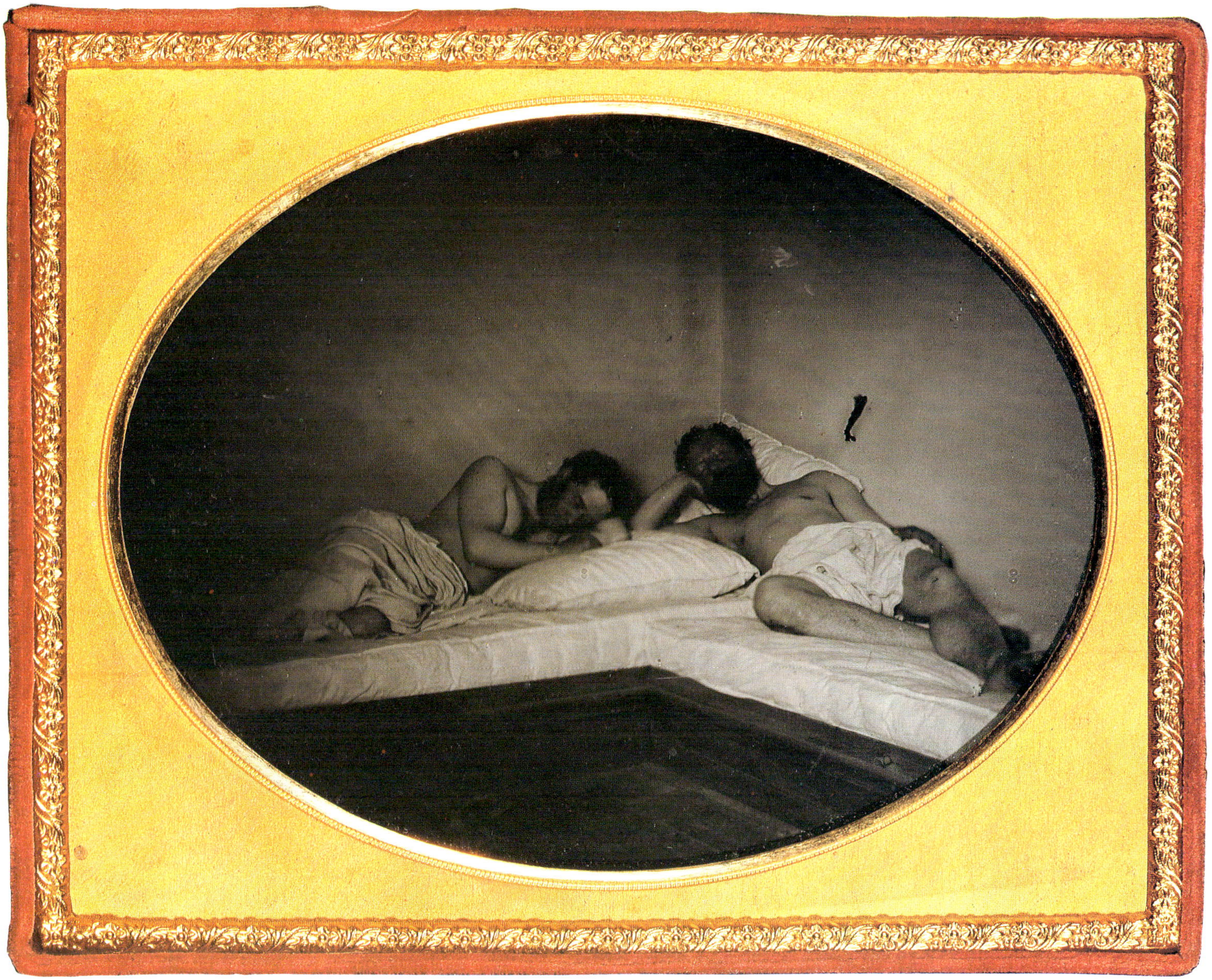

PLATE XIX

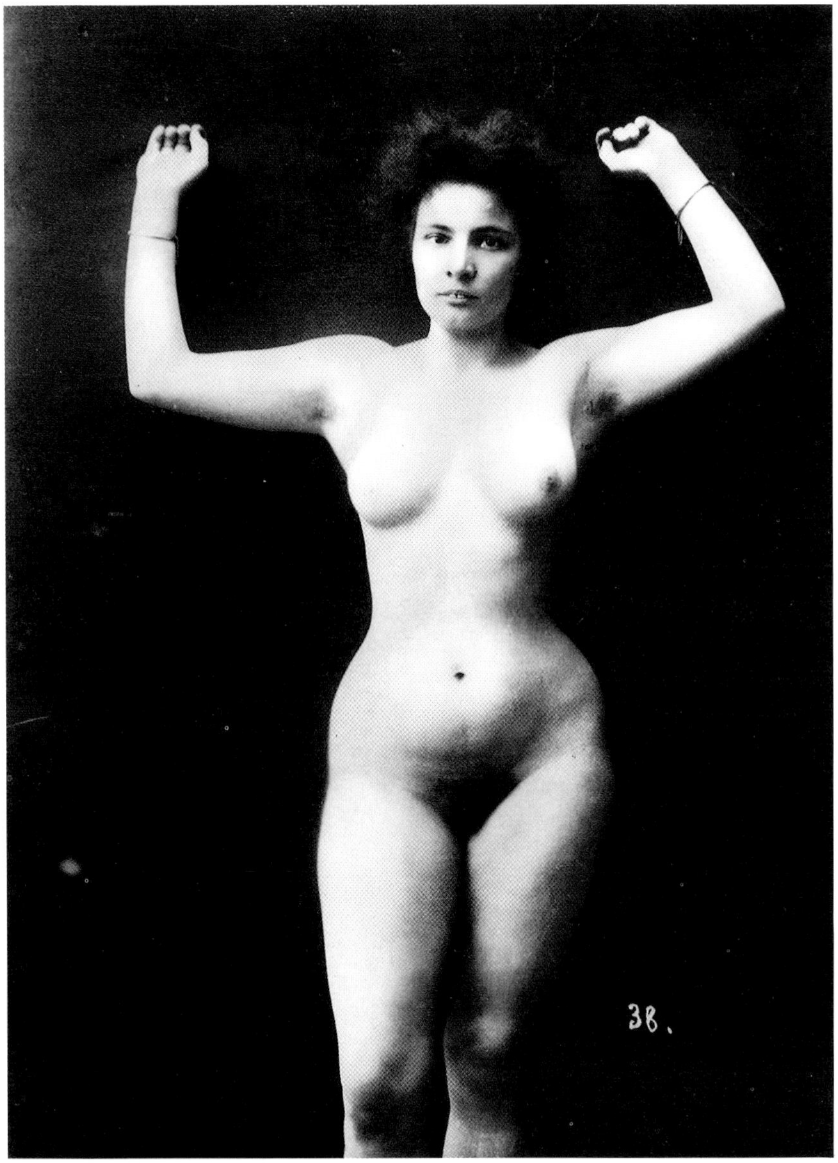

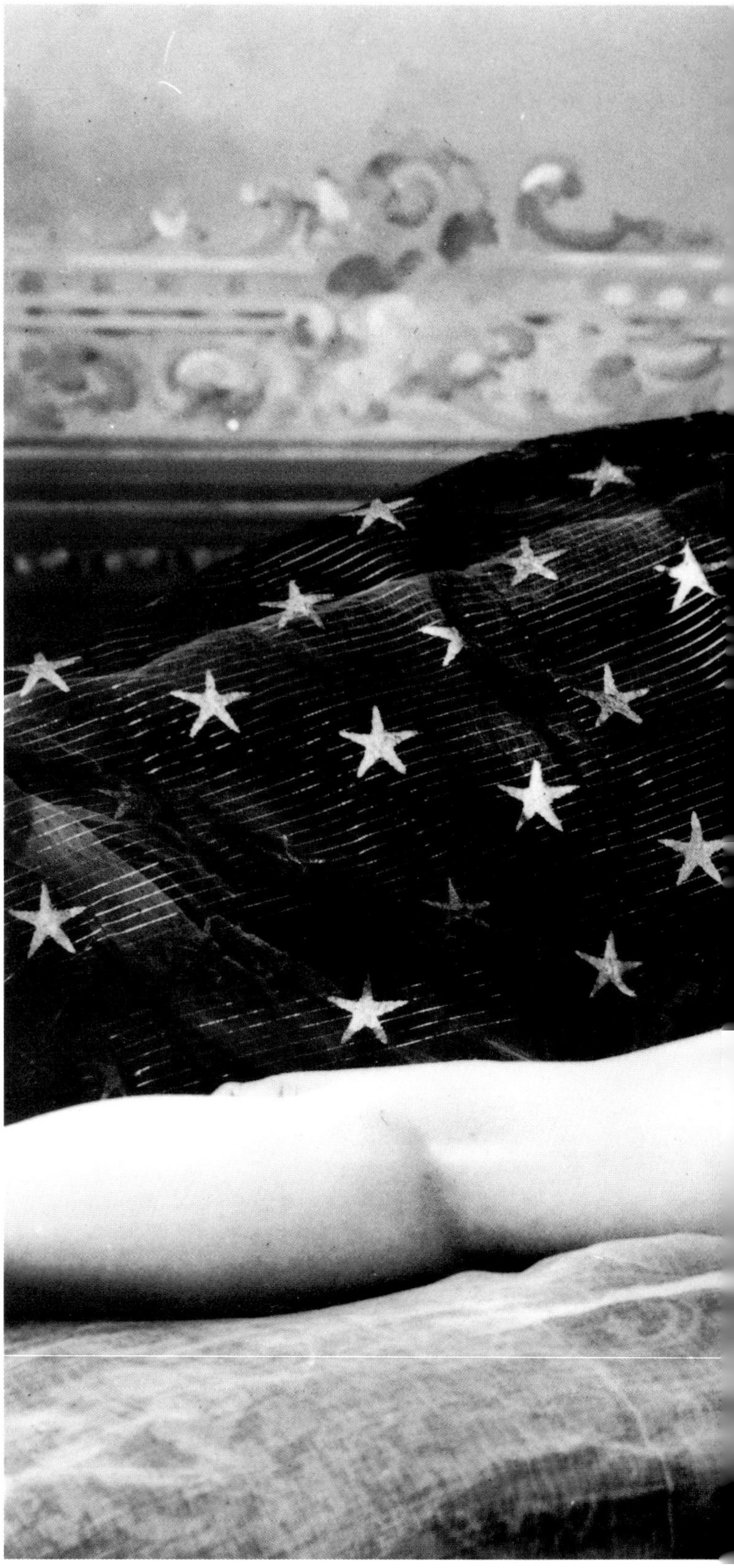

PLATE XX (Above)
ANONYMOUS
(from *Academies*) 1892
Graham Ovenden Collection

PLATE XXI (Right)
ANONYMOUS
(from *Academies*) 1892
Graham Ovenden Collection

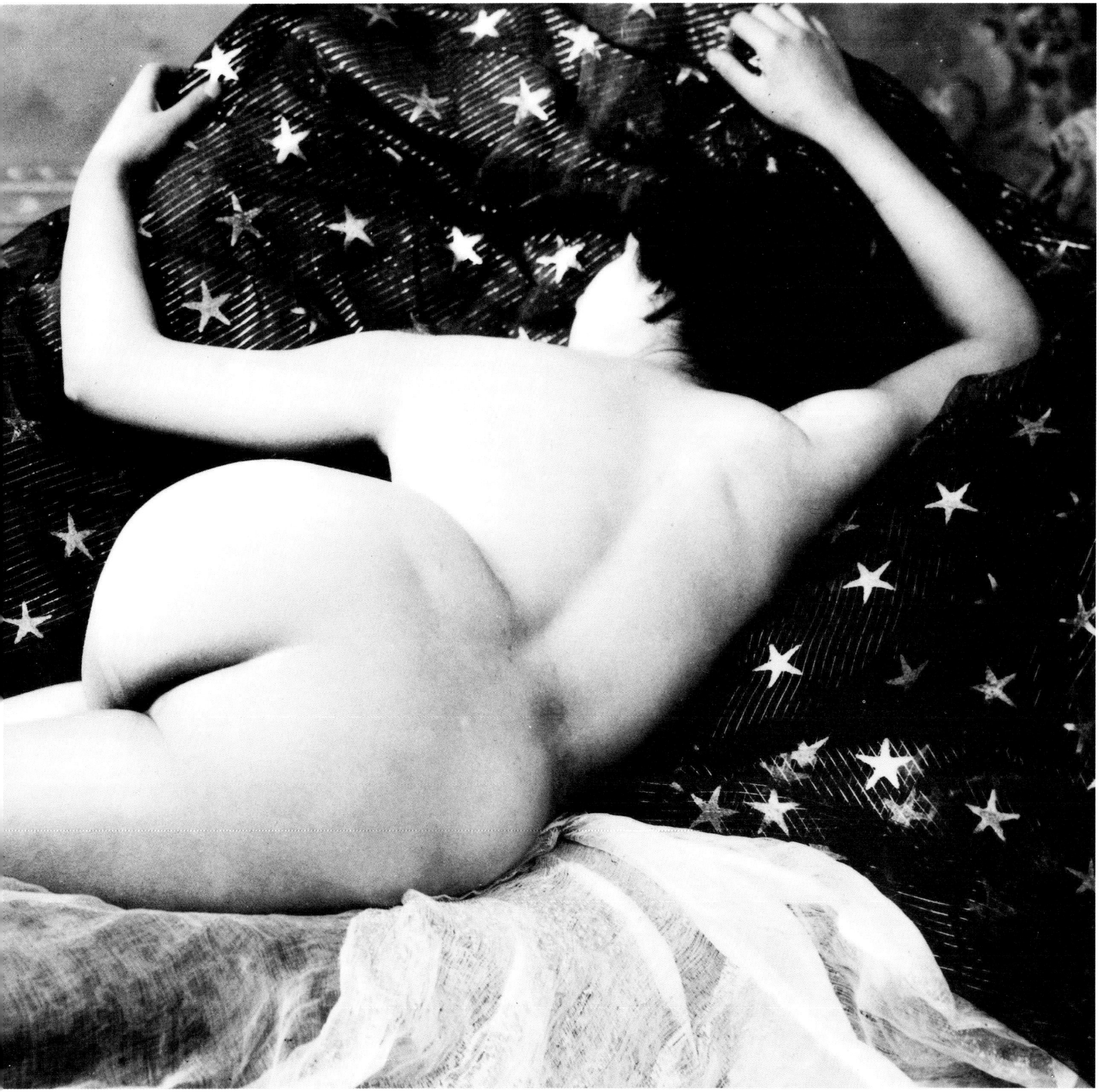

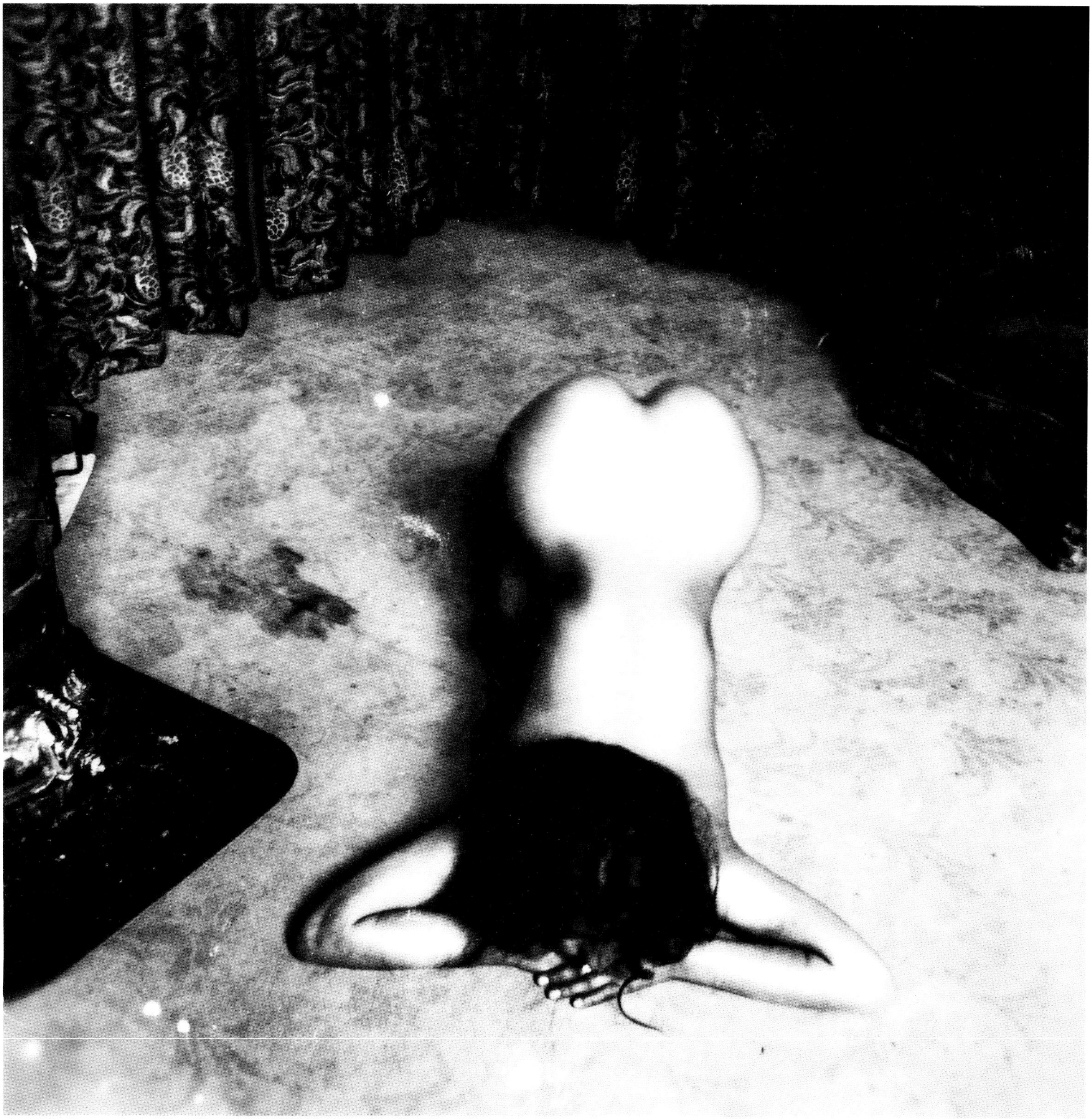

PLATE XXII
PIERRE LOUYS
Untitled 1896
Graham Ovenden Collection

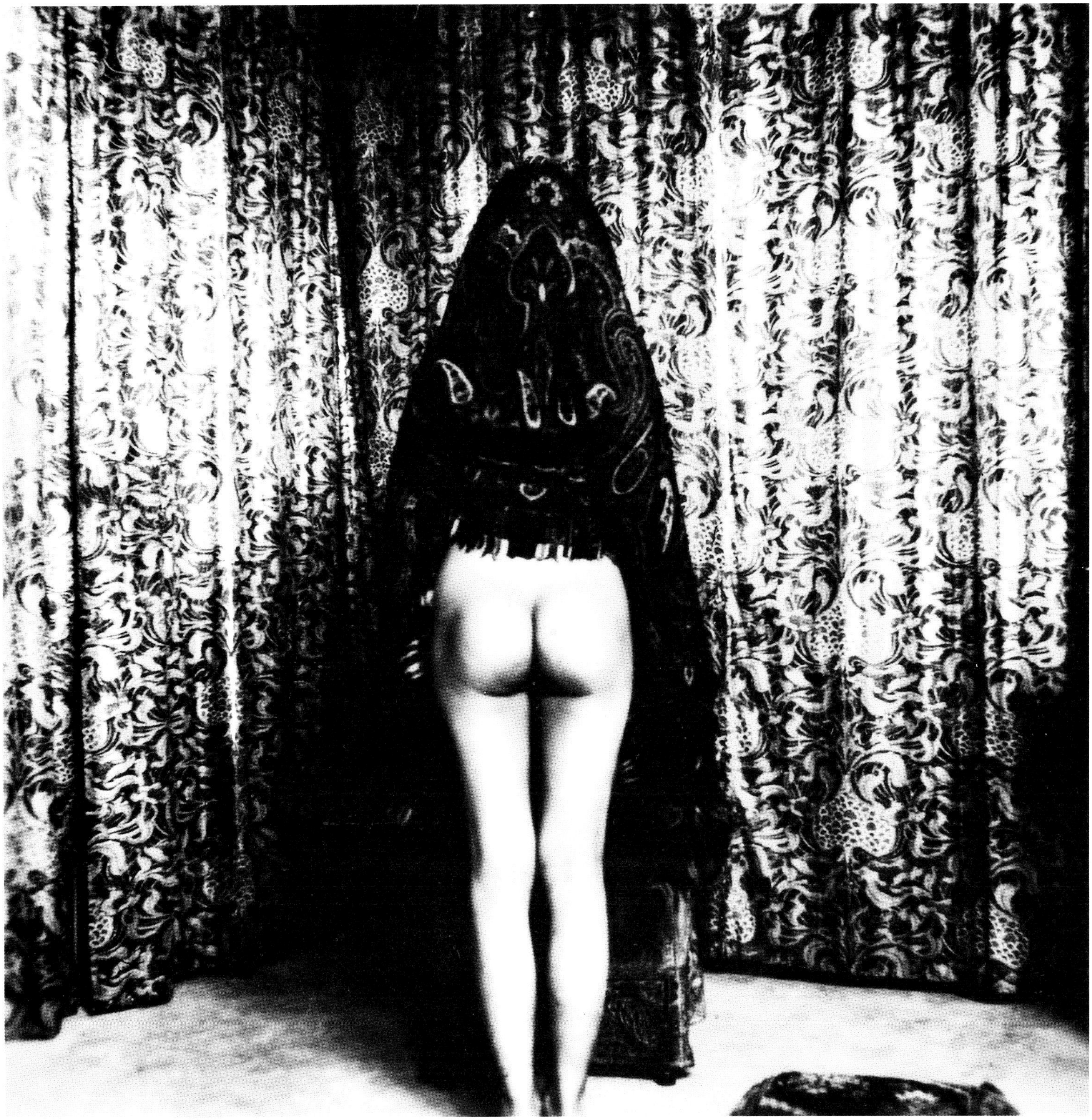

PLATE XXIII
PIERRE LOUYS
Untitled (Amelia Palumbo) 1896
Graham Ovenden Collection

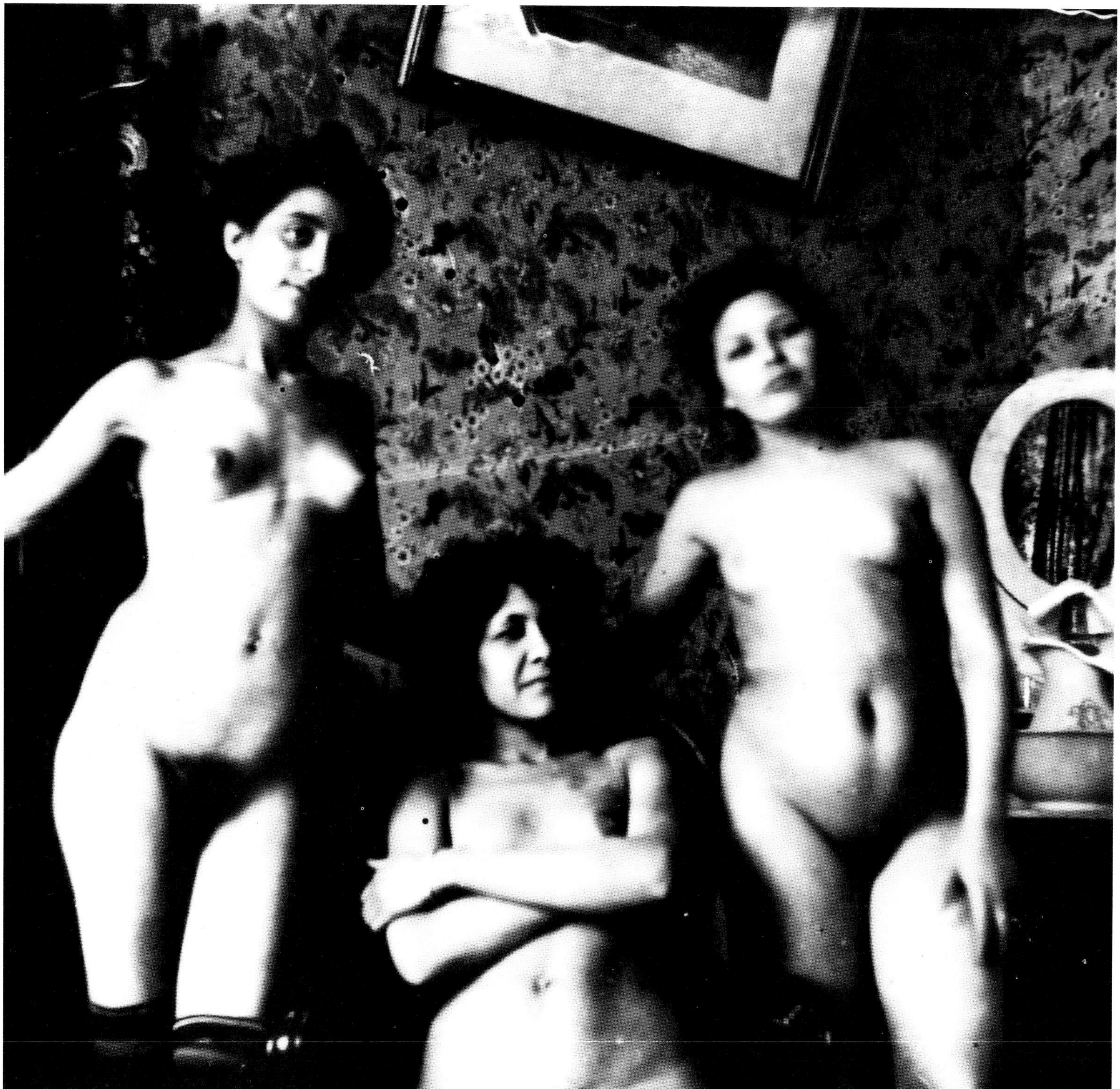

PLATE XXIV
PIERRE LOUYS
Untitled 1896
Graham Ovenden Collection

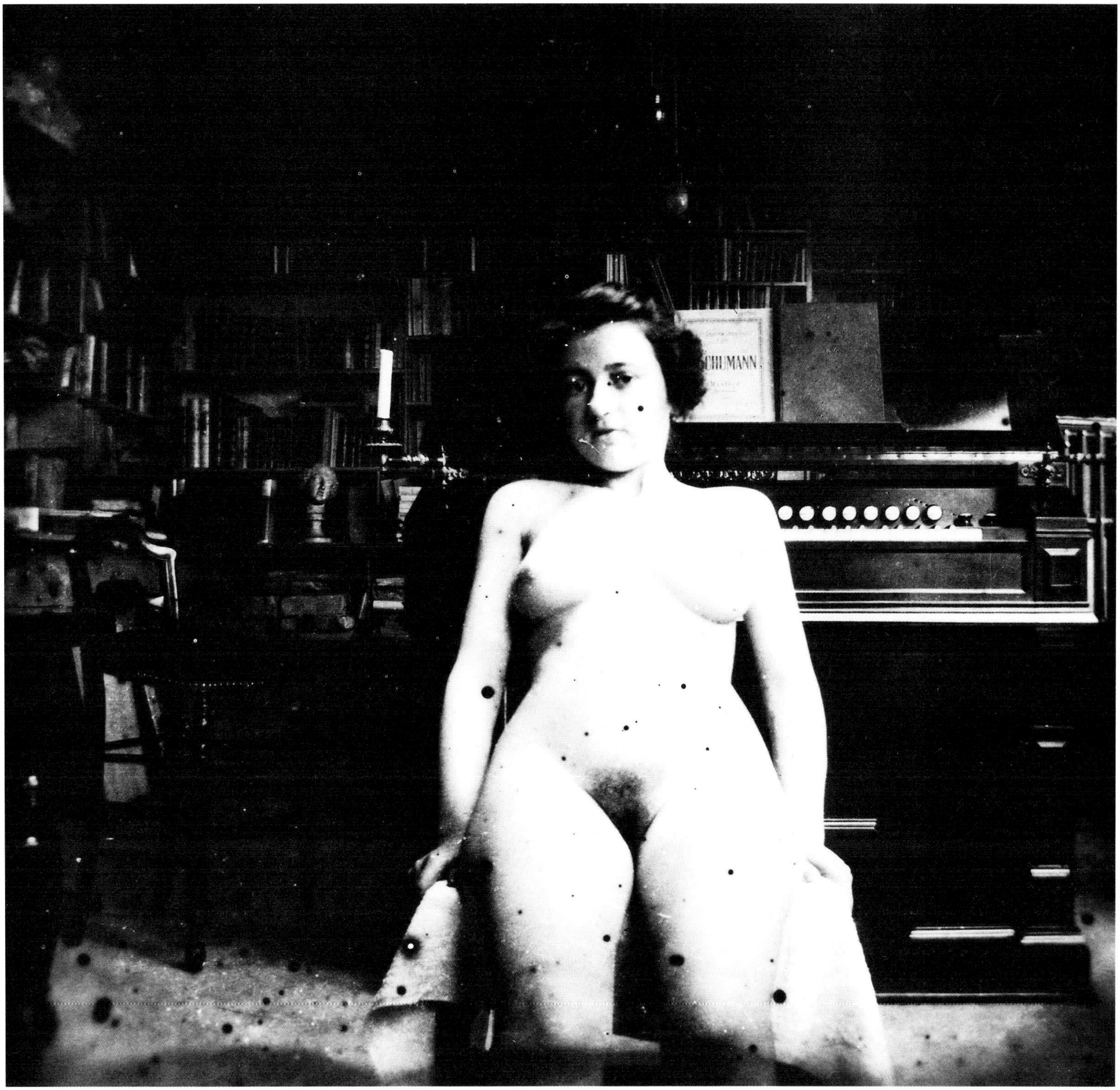

PLATE XXV
PIERRE LOUYS
Untitled 1896
Graham Ovenden Collection

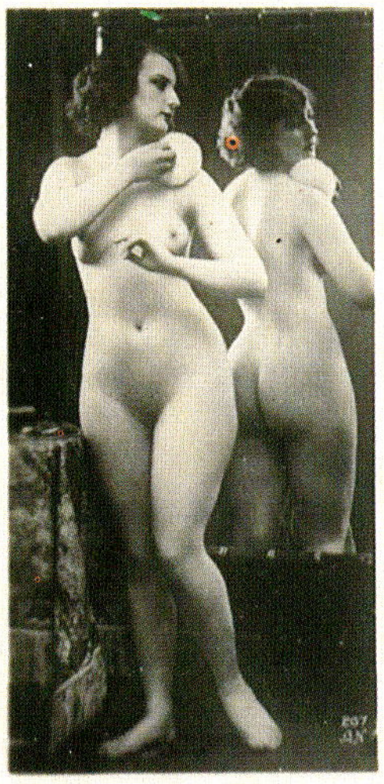
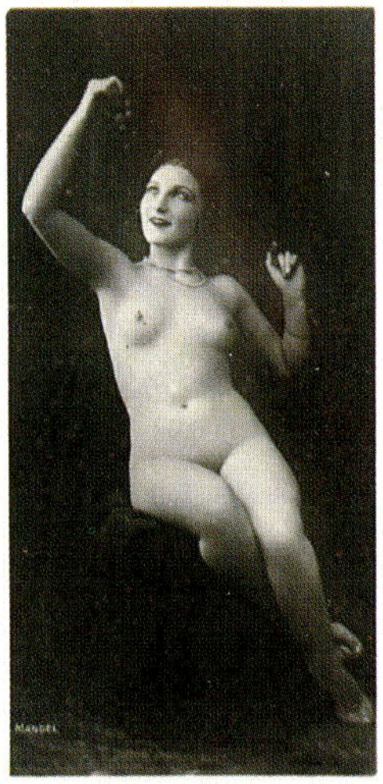
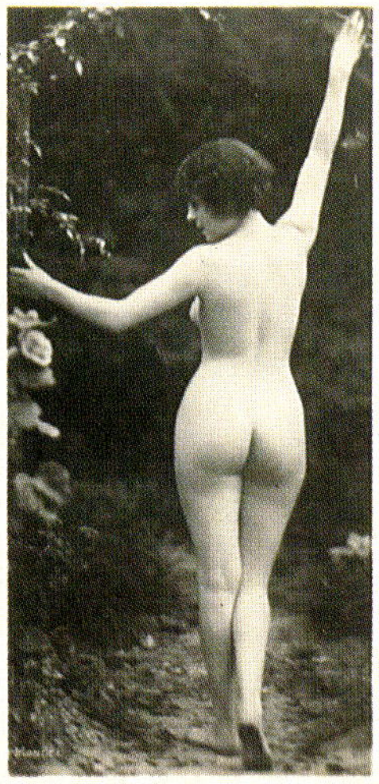
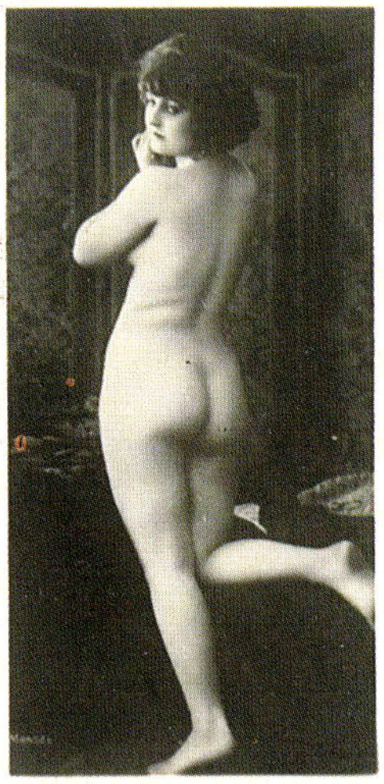
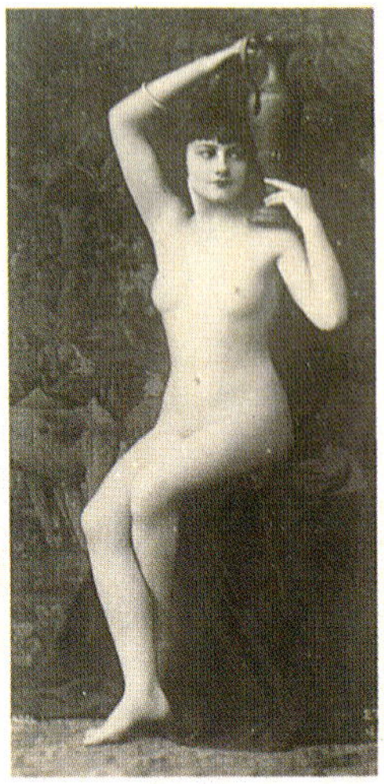
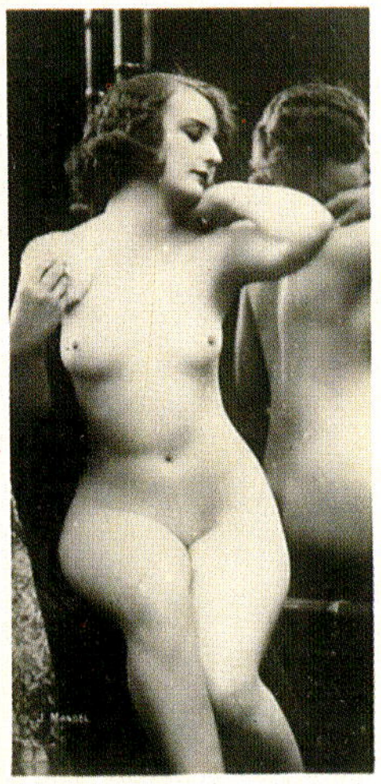
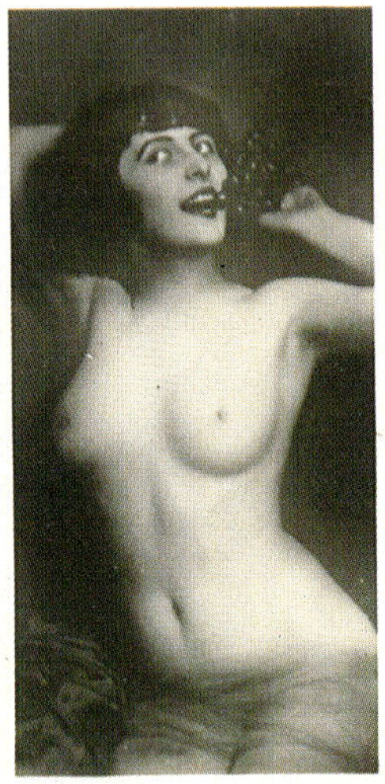
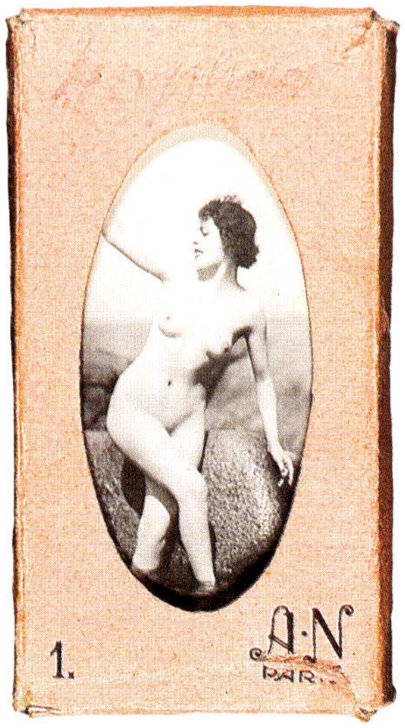
1.
A·N
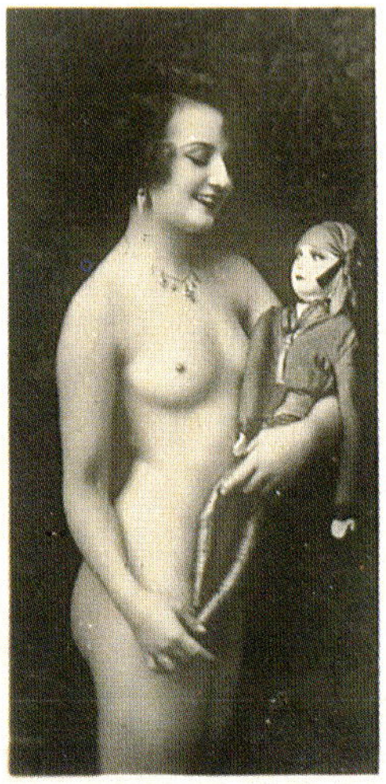
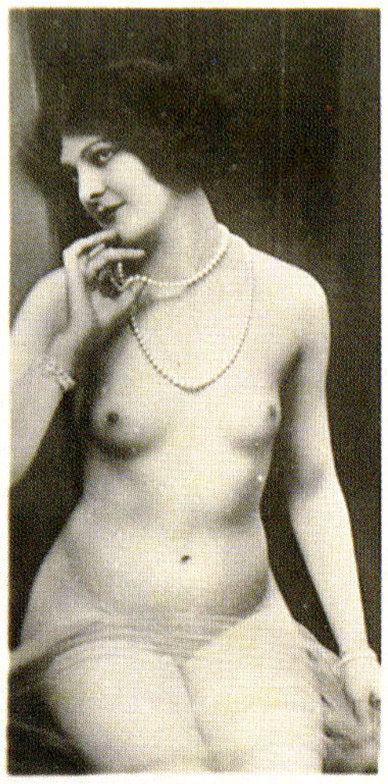
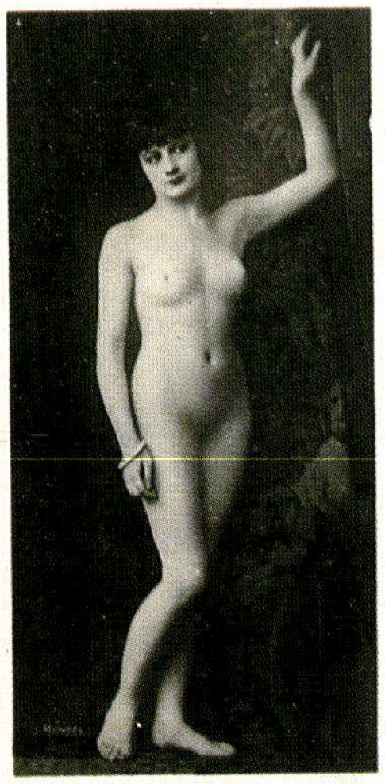
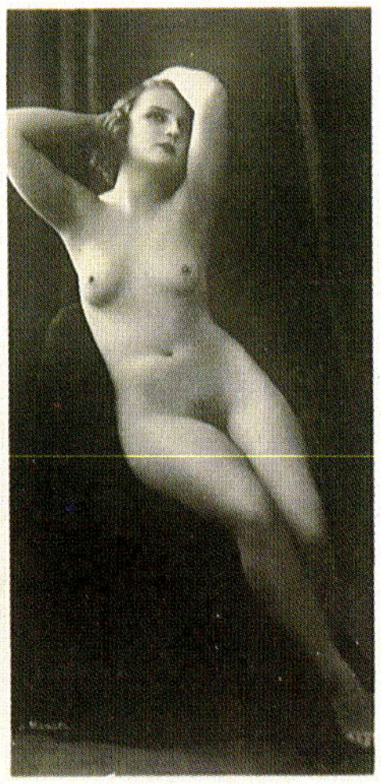
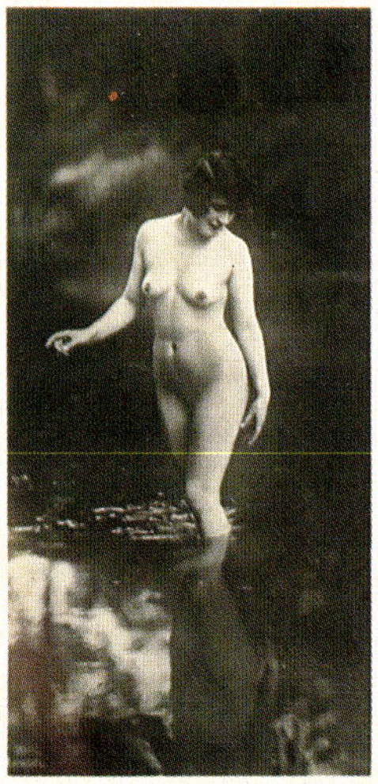
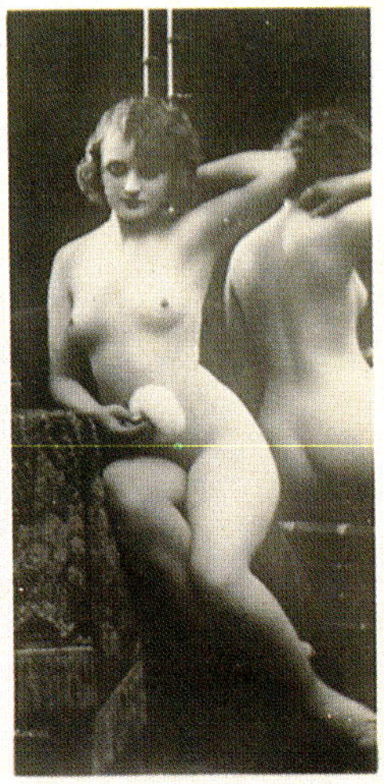
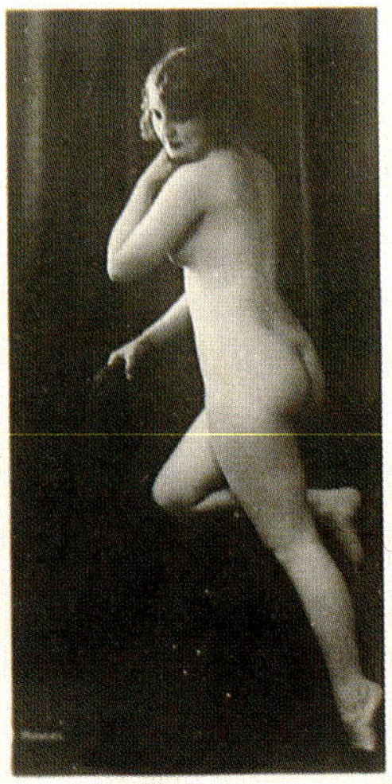

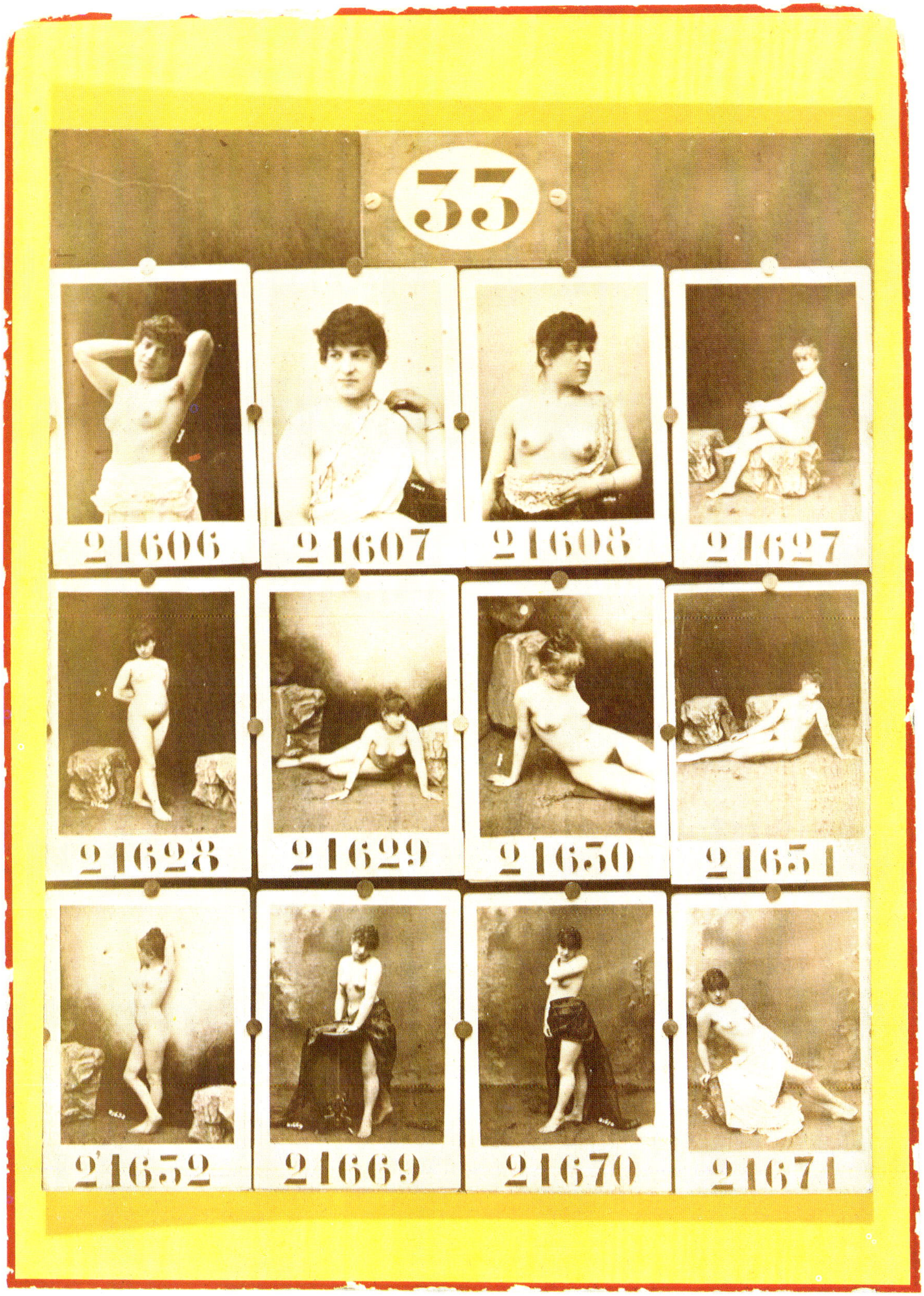

PLATE XXVI (Far left)
ANONYMOUS (French)
Sixteen from a set of forty miniature cards c.1920
Private Collection

PLATE XXVII (Left)
ANONYMOUS (French)
Salesman's display card
c.1900
Joseph Vasta, New York

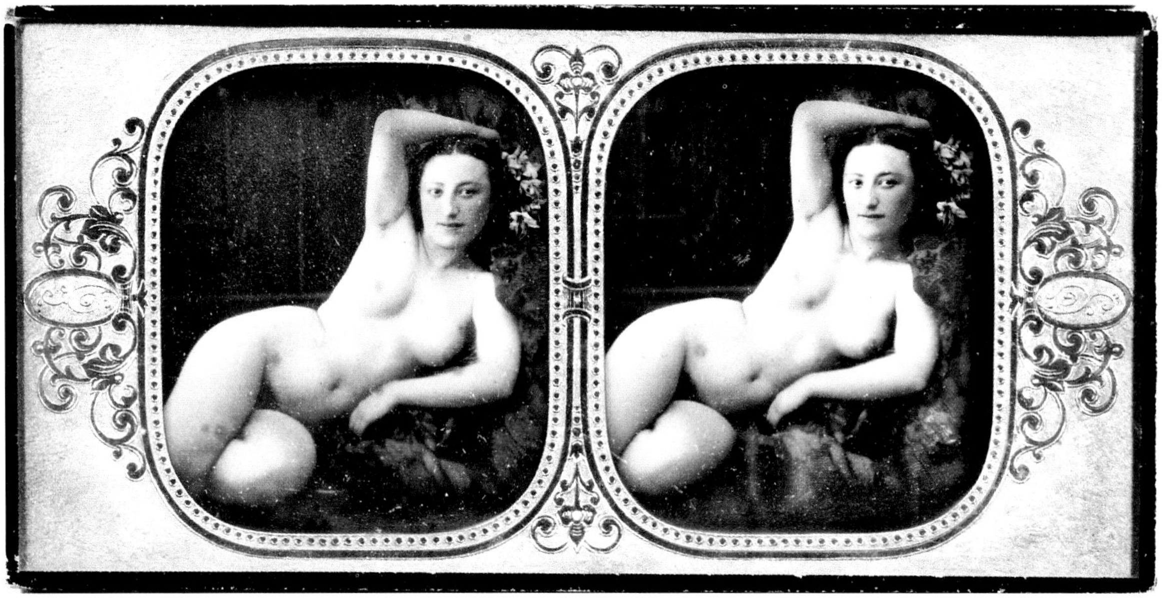

PLATE XXVIII
ANONYMOUS (French)
Stereocard c.1855-60
Sotheby's, London

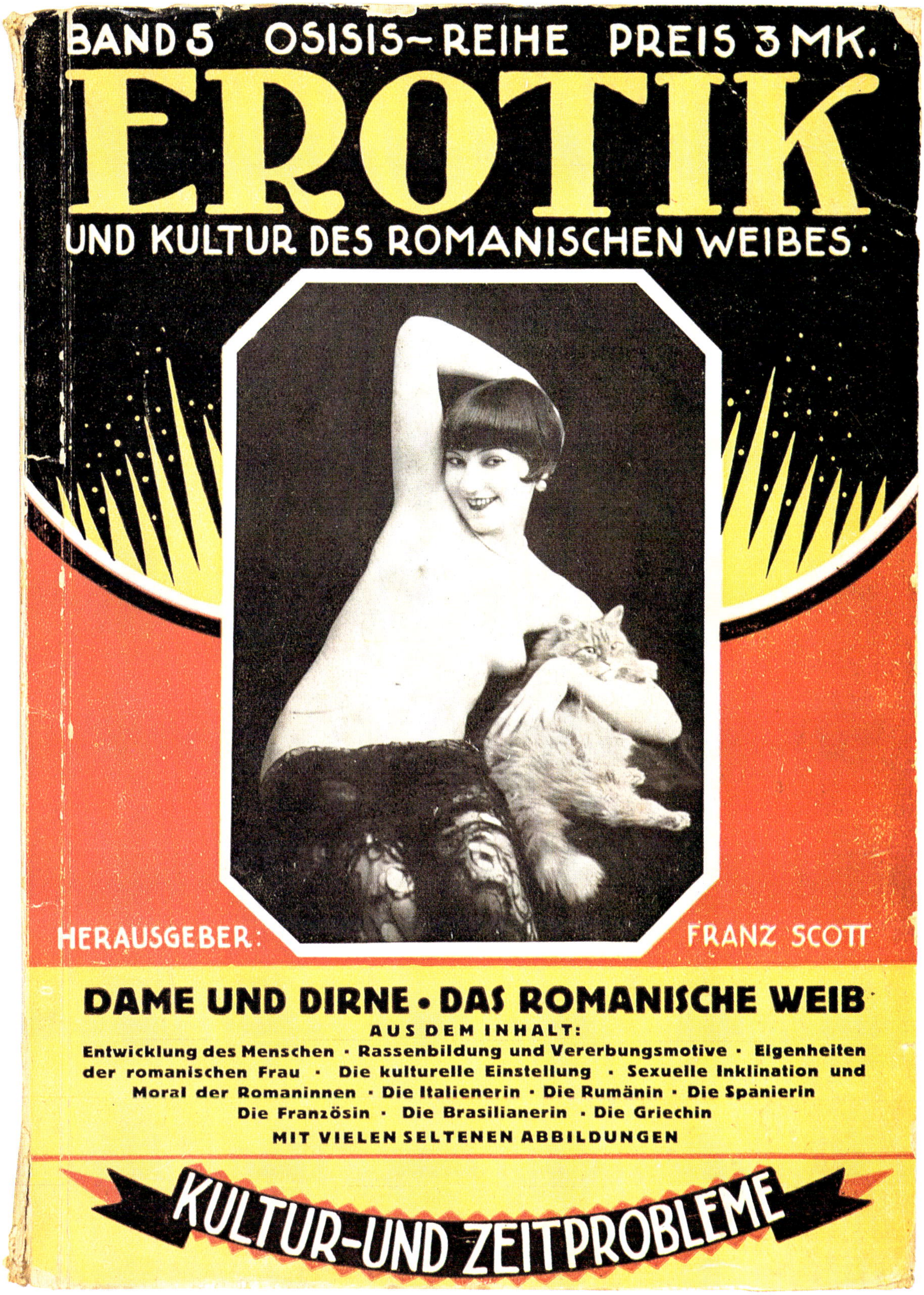

PLATE XXIX
ANONYMOUS (German)
Book cover. *Erotik* 1925
Graham Ovenden Collection

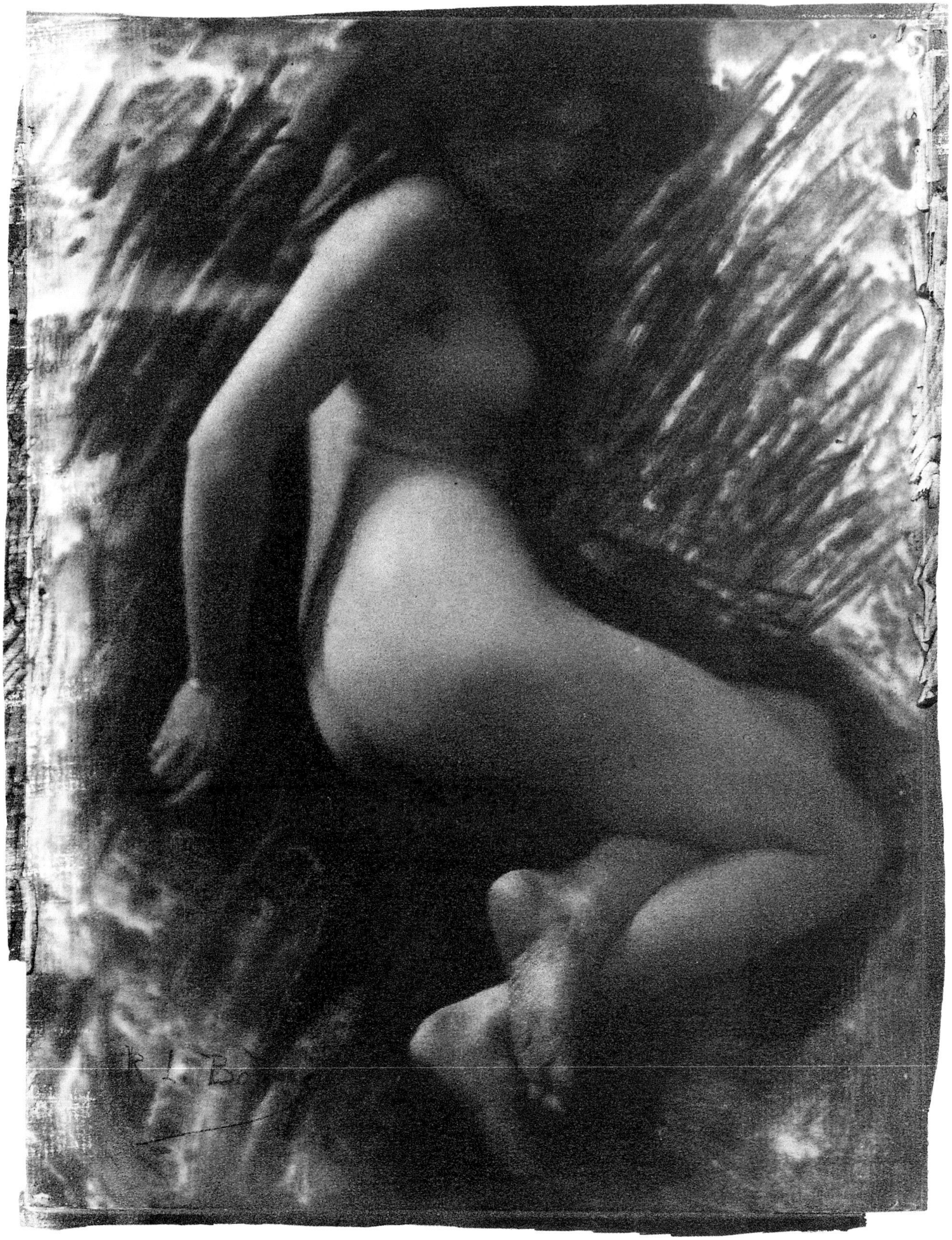

PLATE XXX
RENE LE BEGUE
Academie 1902
GUM BICHROMATE PRINT
The Metropolitan Museum of Art, New York

In 1894, René le Bègue became the first of the French Secessionists to be elected into the British Linked Ring Brotherhood. Not all of his work was as heavily after-manipulated as this example, which affects the appearance of a charcoal drawing.

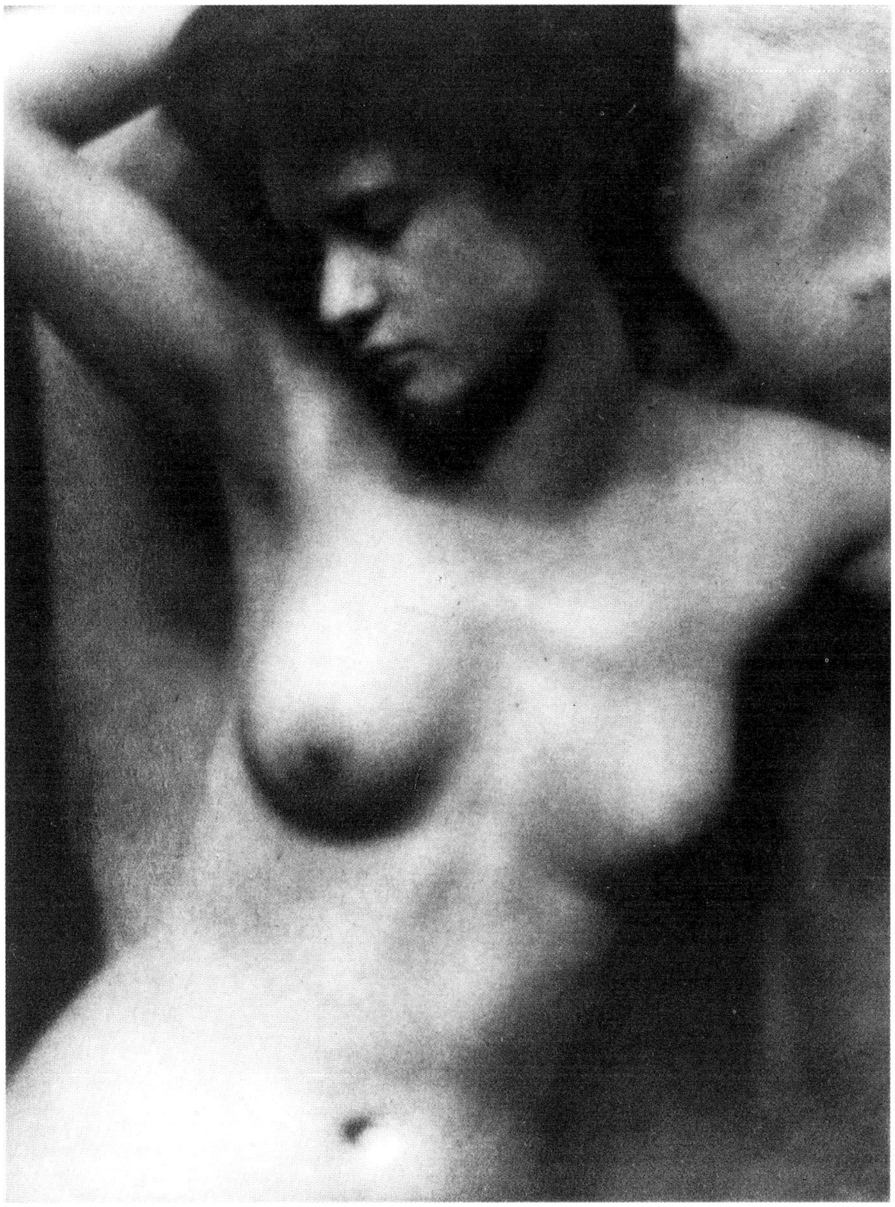

PLATE XXXI
CLARENCE WHITE and ALFRED STIEGLITZ
Torso 1907
PHOTOGRAVURE
Sotheby's, London

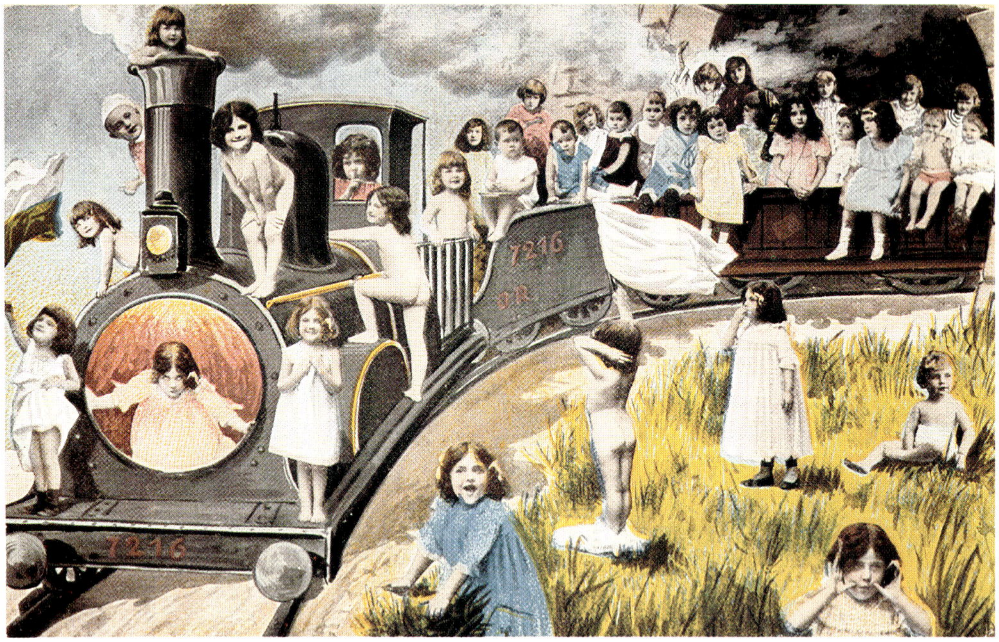

PLATE XXXII

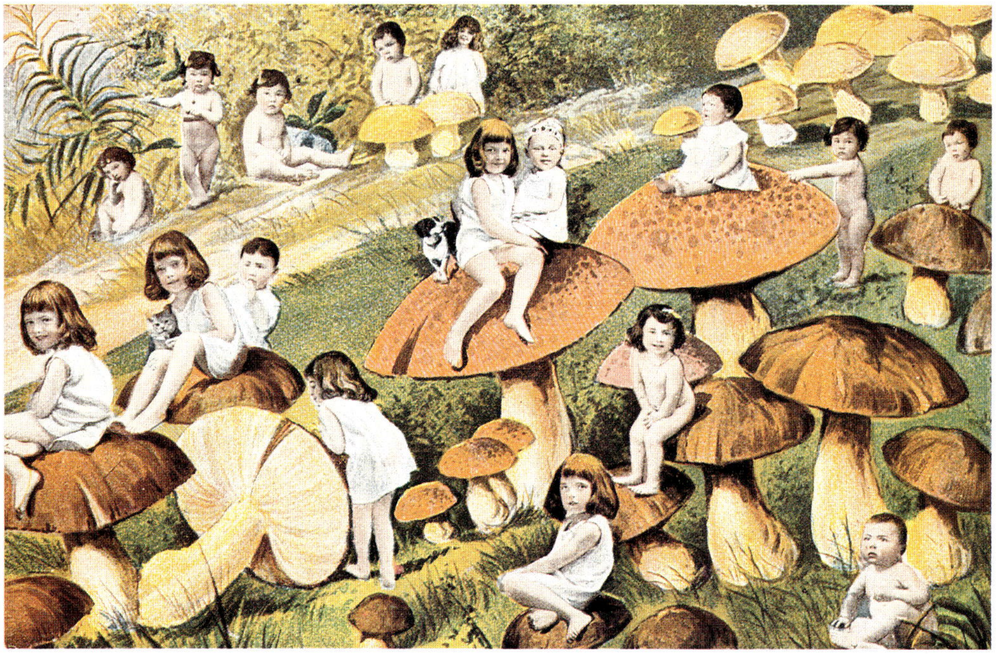

PLATE XXXIII

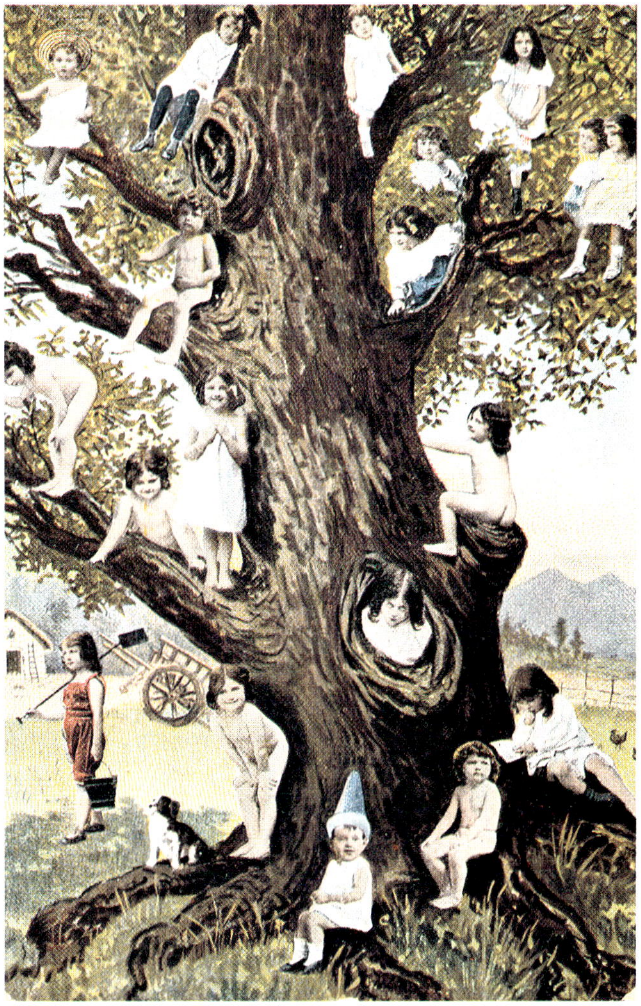

PLATE XXXIV

PLATES XXXII – XXXIV
ANONYMOUS
Children (Collage postcards) c.1904
Graham Ovenden Collection

These bizarre postcards, produced in Germany, enjoyed a brief but widespread popularity around 1905. They accurately identified a widespread belief in the value of procreation, and other versions directly reflected this by showing the children hatching from eggs or being delivered by storks. They also represent the equally short peak of the creative flowering of postcard art, which was all but over by 1910.

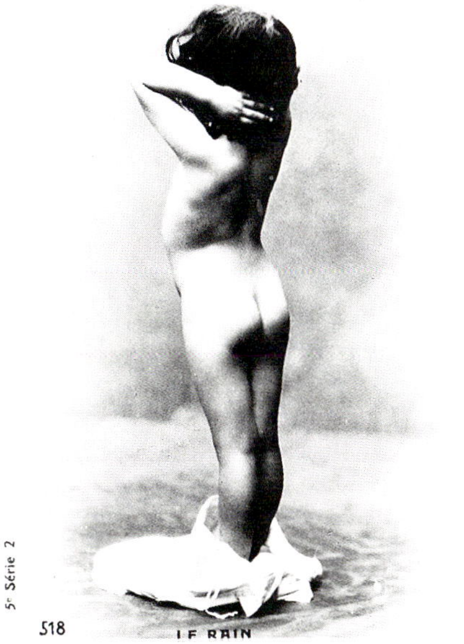

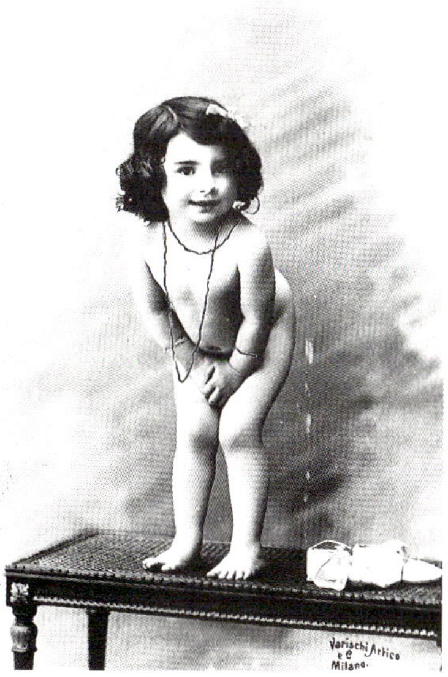

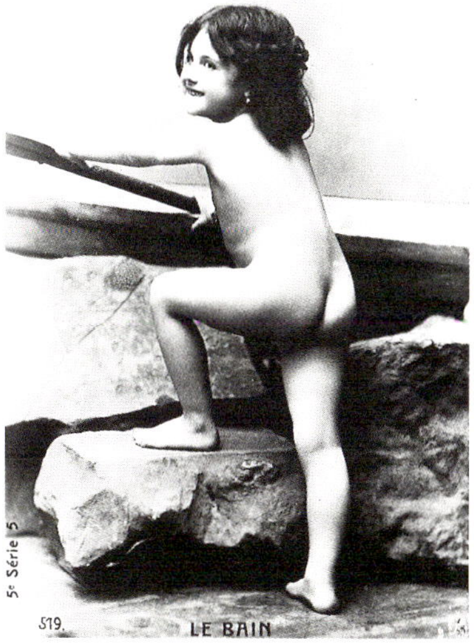

PLATE XXXV (Left)
MONTEBONI OF MILAN
Children (Postcards) 1900
Graham Ovenden Collection

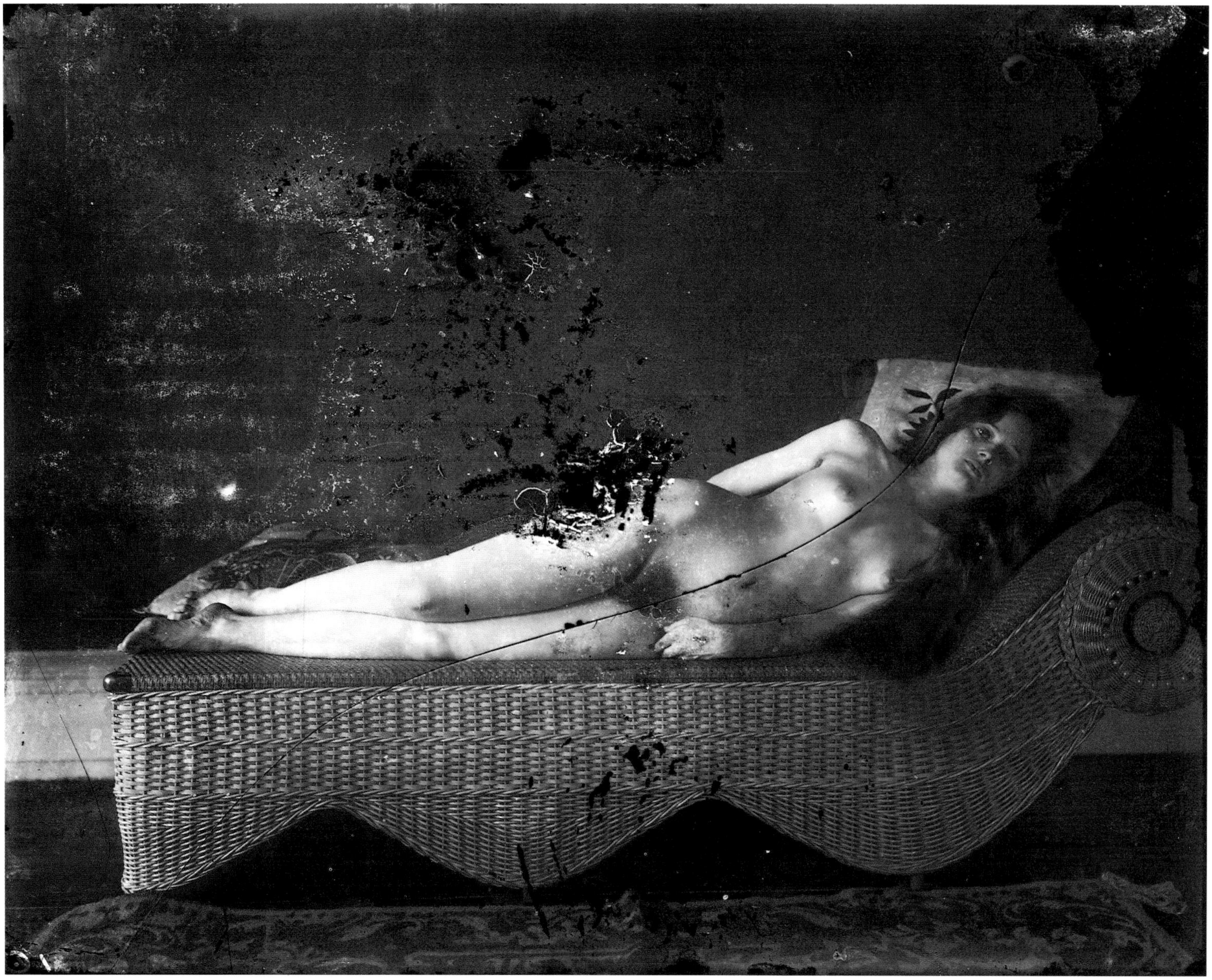

PLATE XXXVI
E.J. BELLOCQ
Untitled c.1912
Courtesy Lee Friedlander

Bellocq's portraits of prostitutes are both sensitive and authentic documents and highly personal (and private) statements. His models appear to have had complete trust in him and together they conspired to create pictures which would immortalize both subject and photographer.

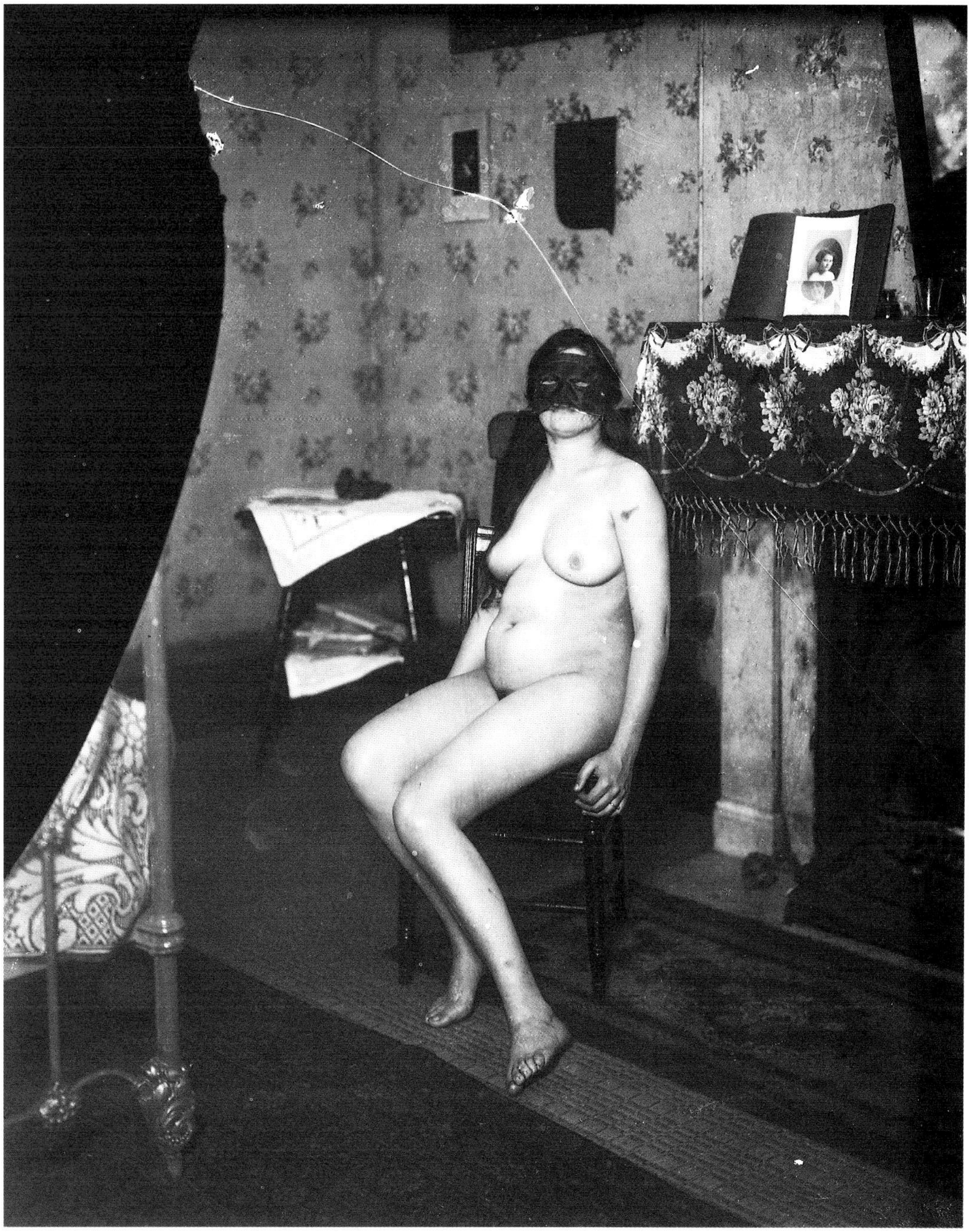

PLATE XXXVII
E.J. BELLOCQ
Untitled c.1912
Courtesy Lee Friedlander

The often cluttered domestic settings Bellocq used as backdrops for his portraits only add to the strangely relaxed and informal quality of his pictures. Even when his sitters are masked, we are persuaded of his sympathy for, and understanding of them.

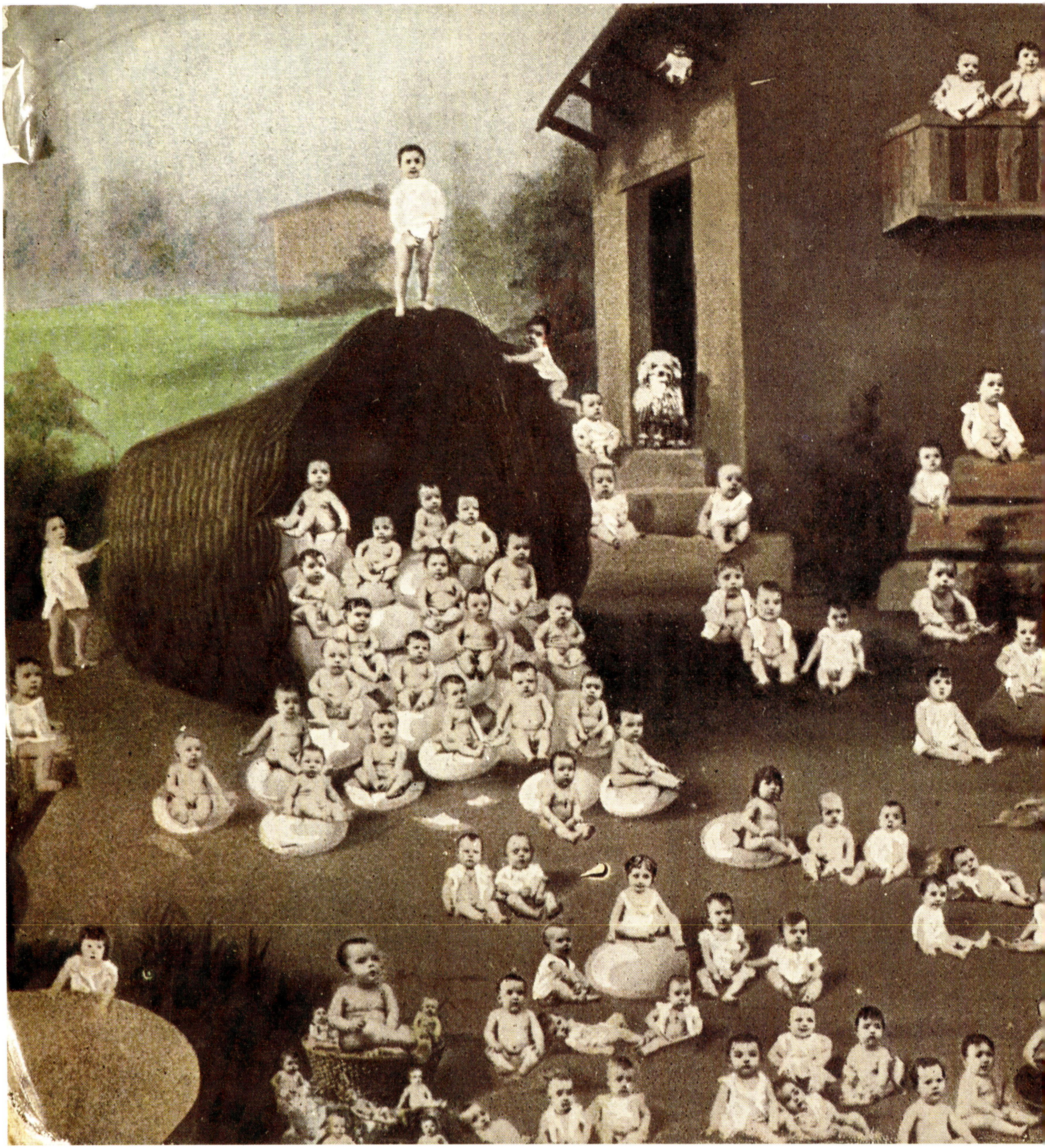

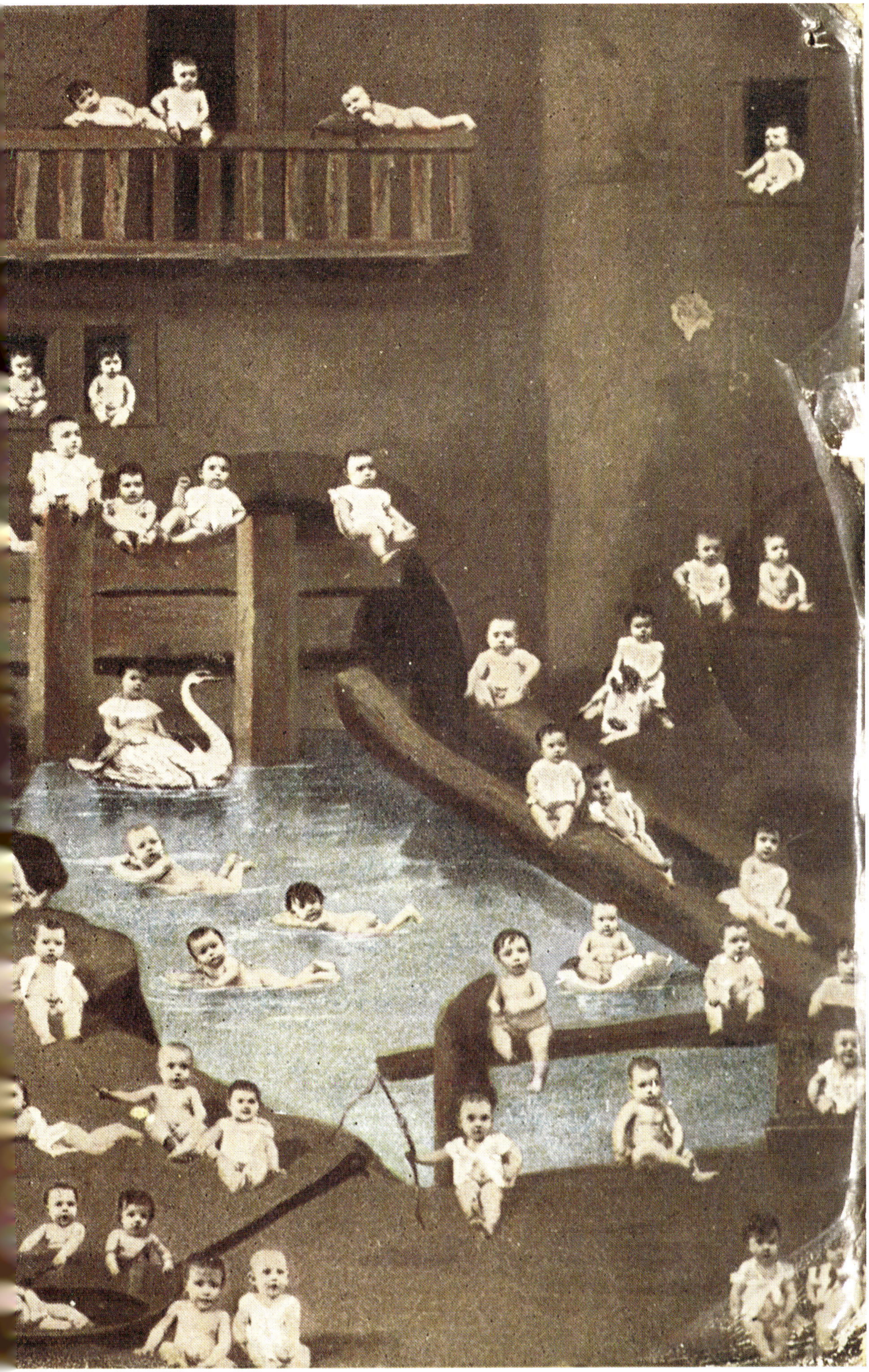

PLATE XXXVIII
ANONYMOUS
Babies (Collage postcard) c.1904
Graham Ovenden Collection

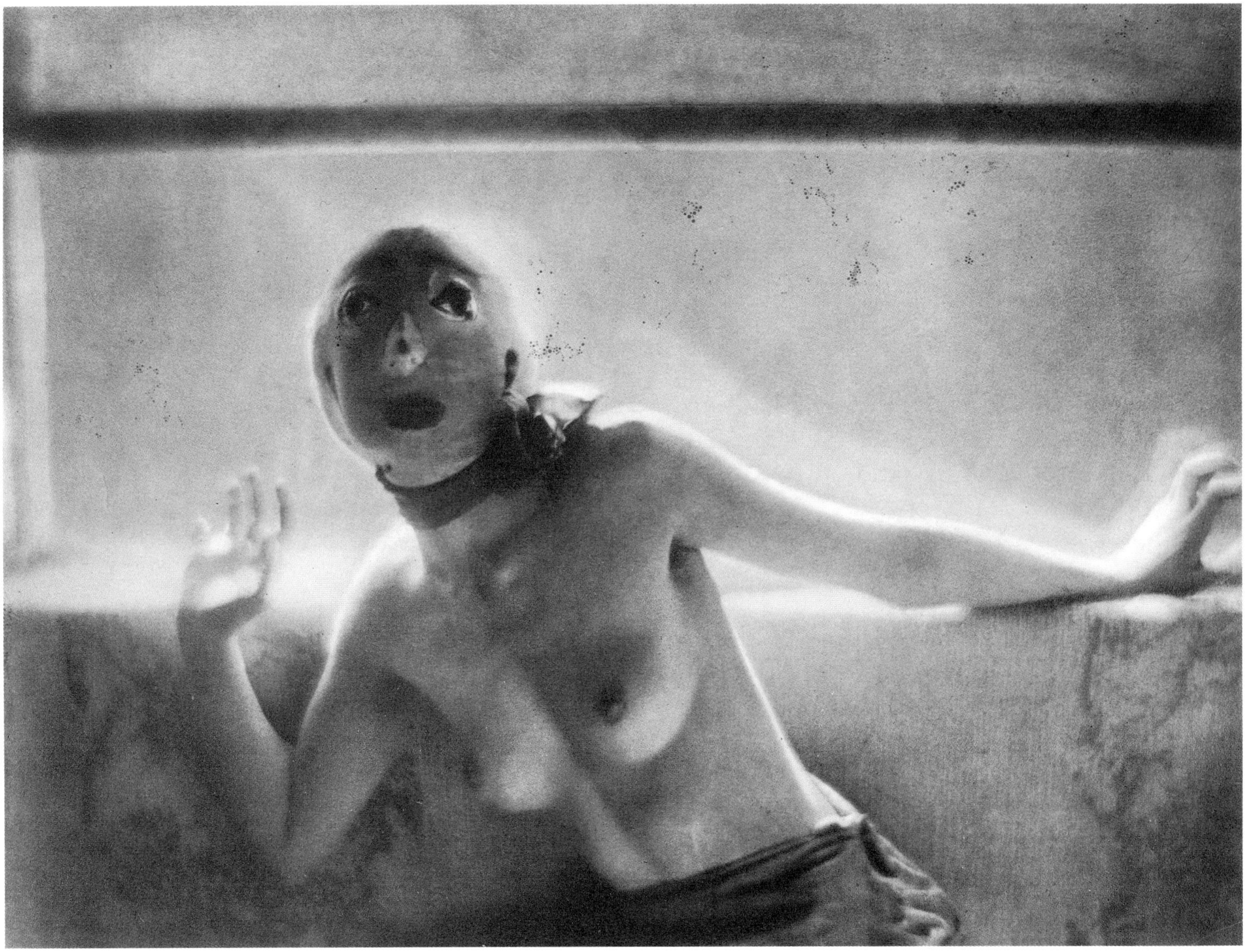

PLATE XXXIX

BARON ADOLF DE MEYER

Dance Study c.1912

The Metropolitan Museum of Art, New York.

Cecil Beaton described De Meyer as "the Debussy of the camera," no doubt having in mind De Meyer's dazzling skill with contre-jour lighting and his impressionistic use of the soft-focus lens. This extraordinary photograph also has a sense of movement and drama not usually associated with De Meyer's work.

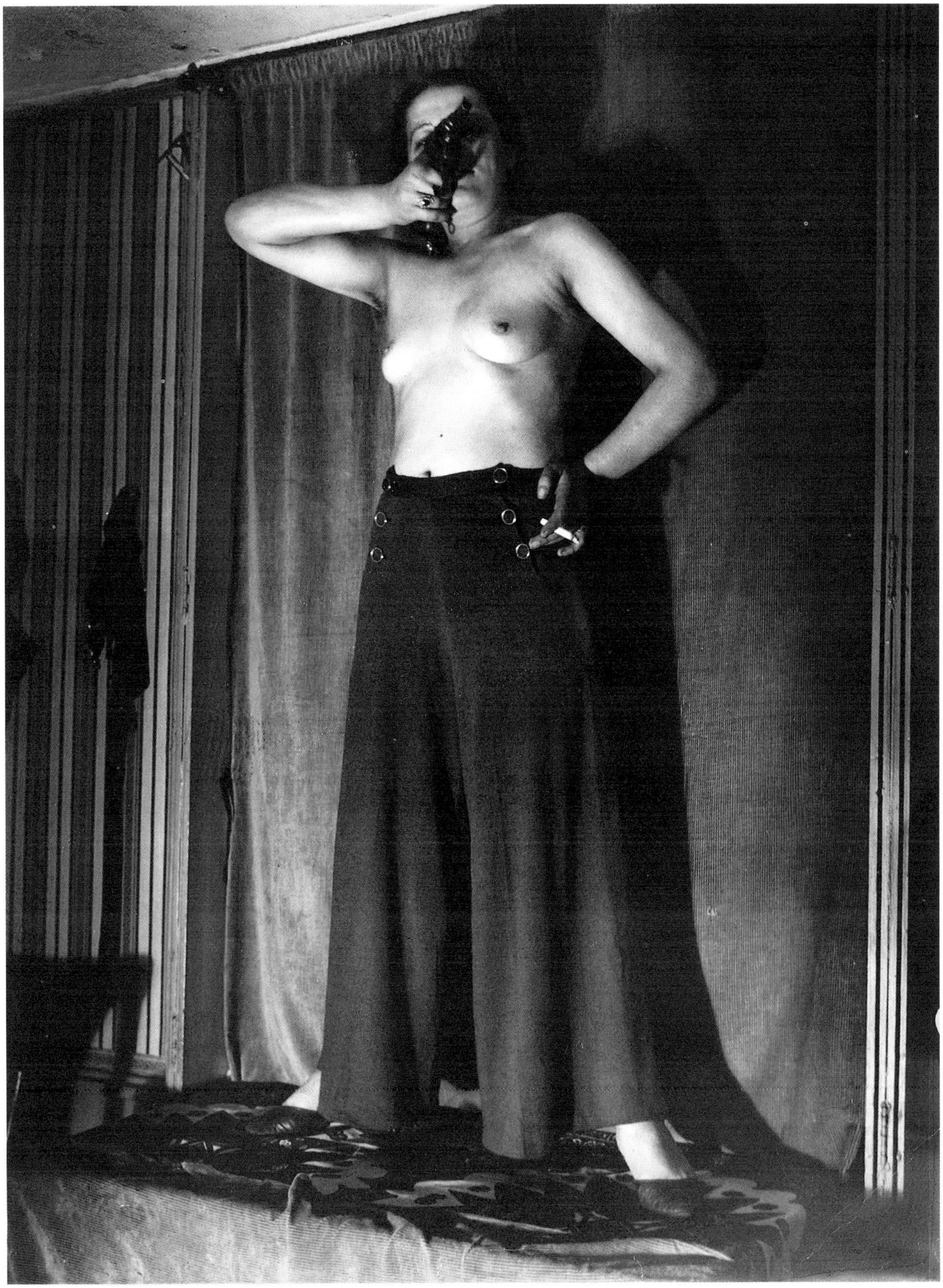

PLATE XL
ANONYMOUS (French)
Woman with Gun c.1930
Joseph Vasta, New York.

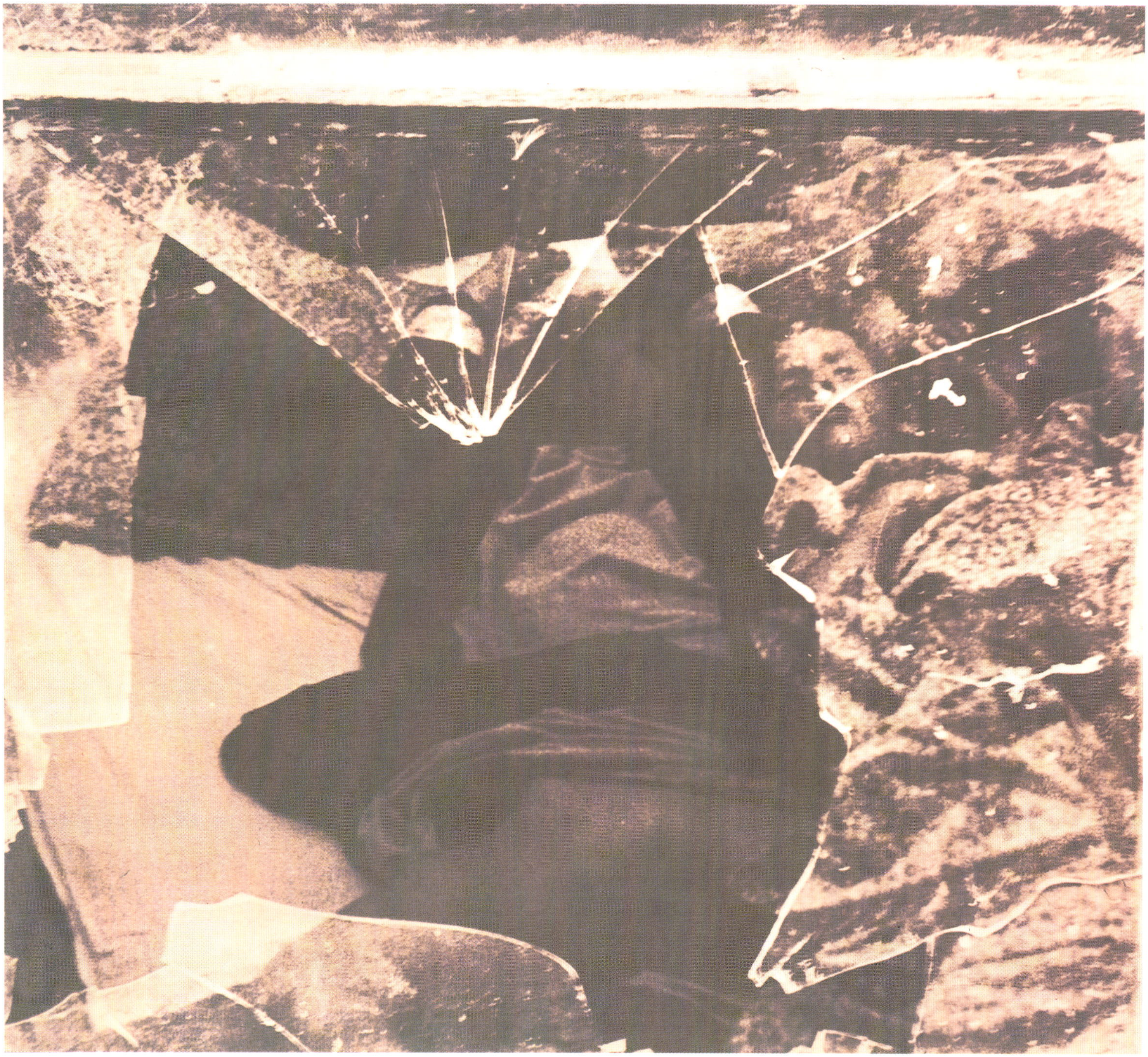

PLATE XLI (Above)
GRAHAM OVENDEN
Broken Window, Stepney 1958
PRINT-OUT PRINT
Courtesy the photographer

PLATE XLII (Right)
PAUL BARKSHIRE
Messagio d'Amore, Merchant Taylors Hall, London
David Bailey Collection

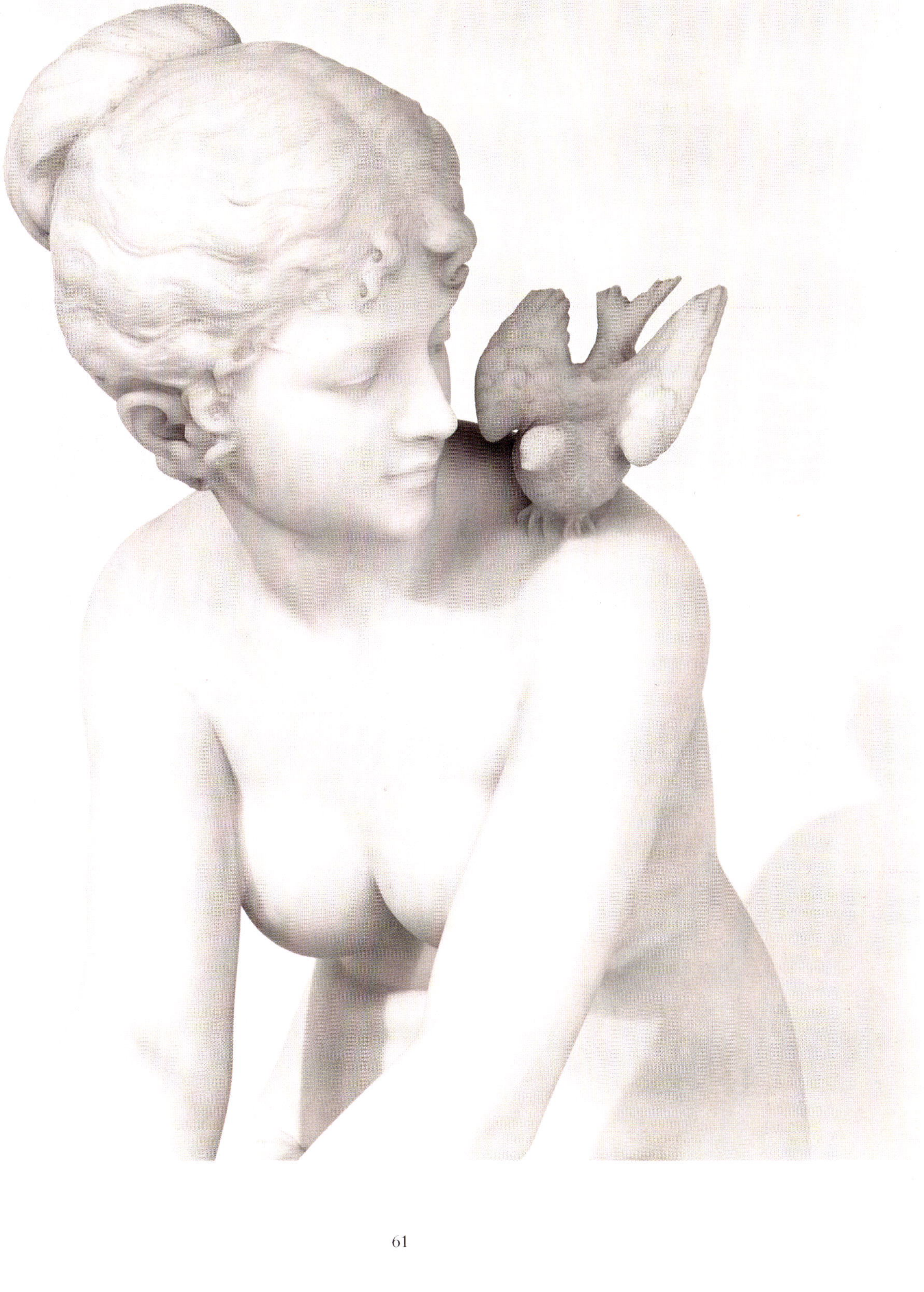

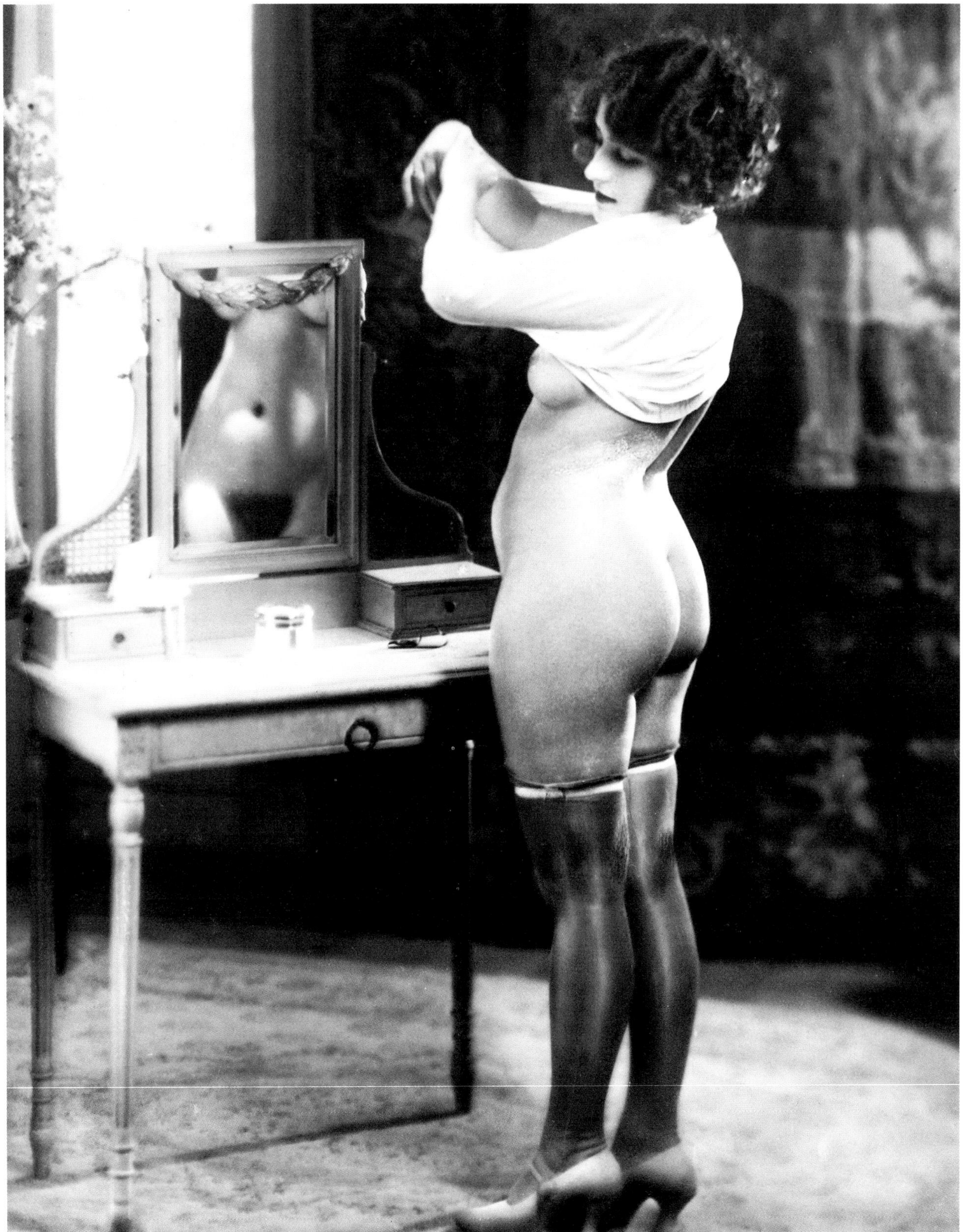

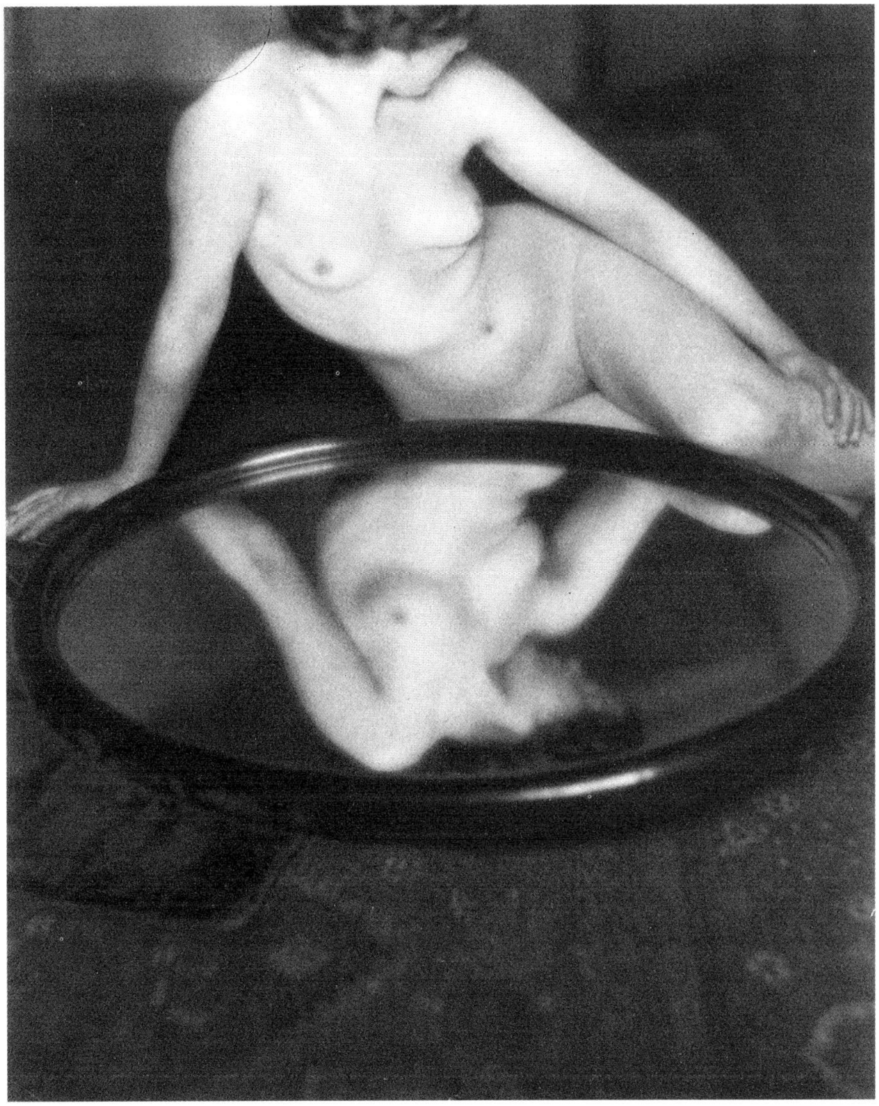

PLATE XLIV (Above)
CLARENCE WHITE
Reflected Nude 1909
PLATINUM PRINT
Robert Miller Gallery, New York

White's photographs were the most delicate, feminine and intimate of all the American Secessionists. His gentle visions were underpinned by his refined spatial sense and strongly influenced by his admiration for Japanese prints (which he collected) and the paintings of Whistler.

PLATE XLIII (Left)
WYNDHAM (Paris)
Woman in front of Mirror c.1920
Julian Hartnoll Collection

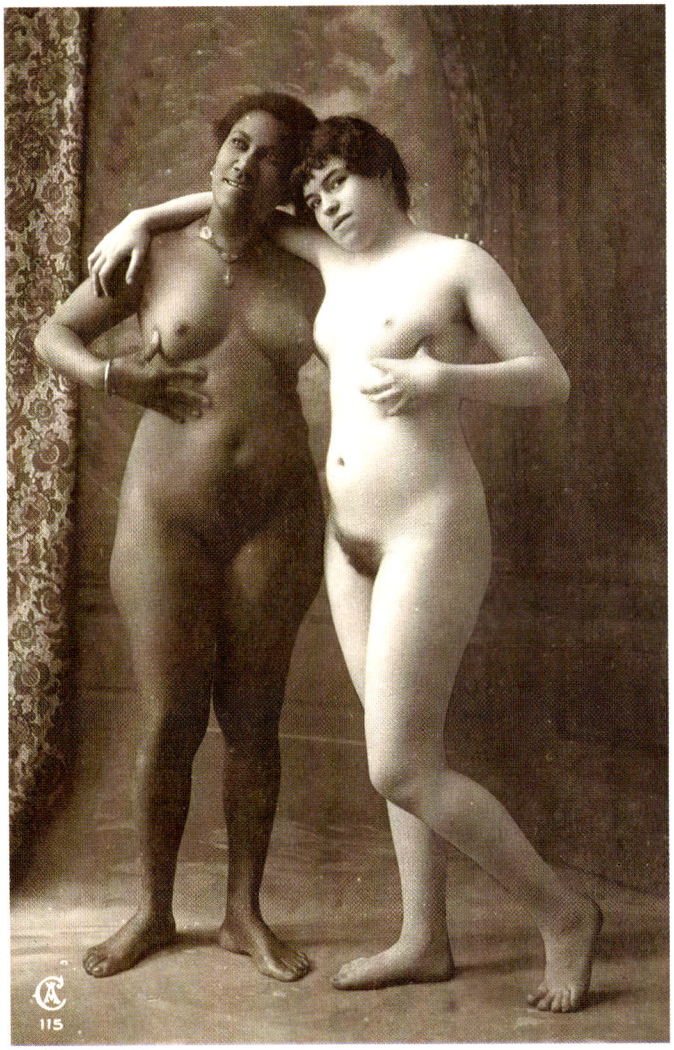

PLATE XLV
ANONYMOUS (French)
Black and White Women (Postcard) c.1910
Private Collection

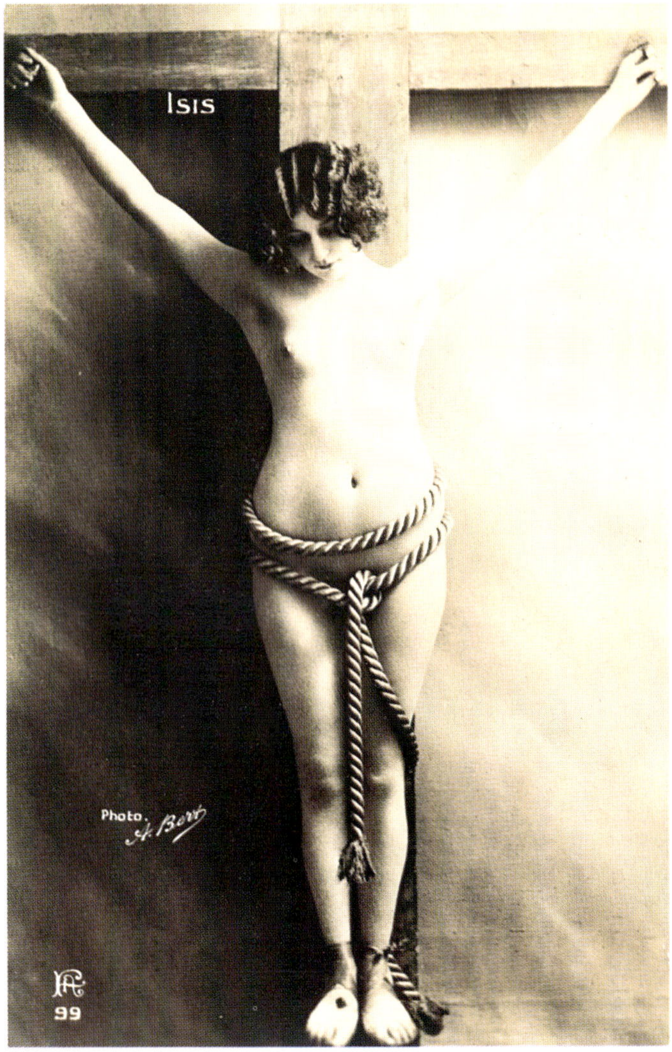

PLATE XLVI
ANONYMOUS (French)
Woman on Cross c.1905
Private Collection

PLATE XLVII (Right)
ANONYMOUS
Plate from German ethnographical book 1900
Graham Ovenden Collection

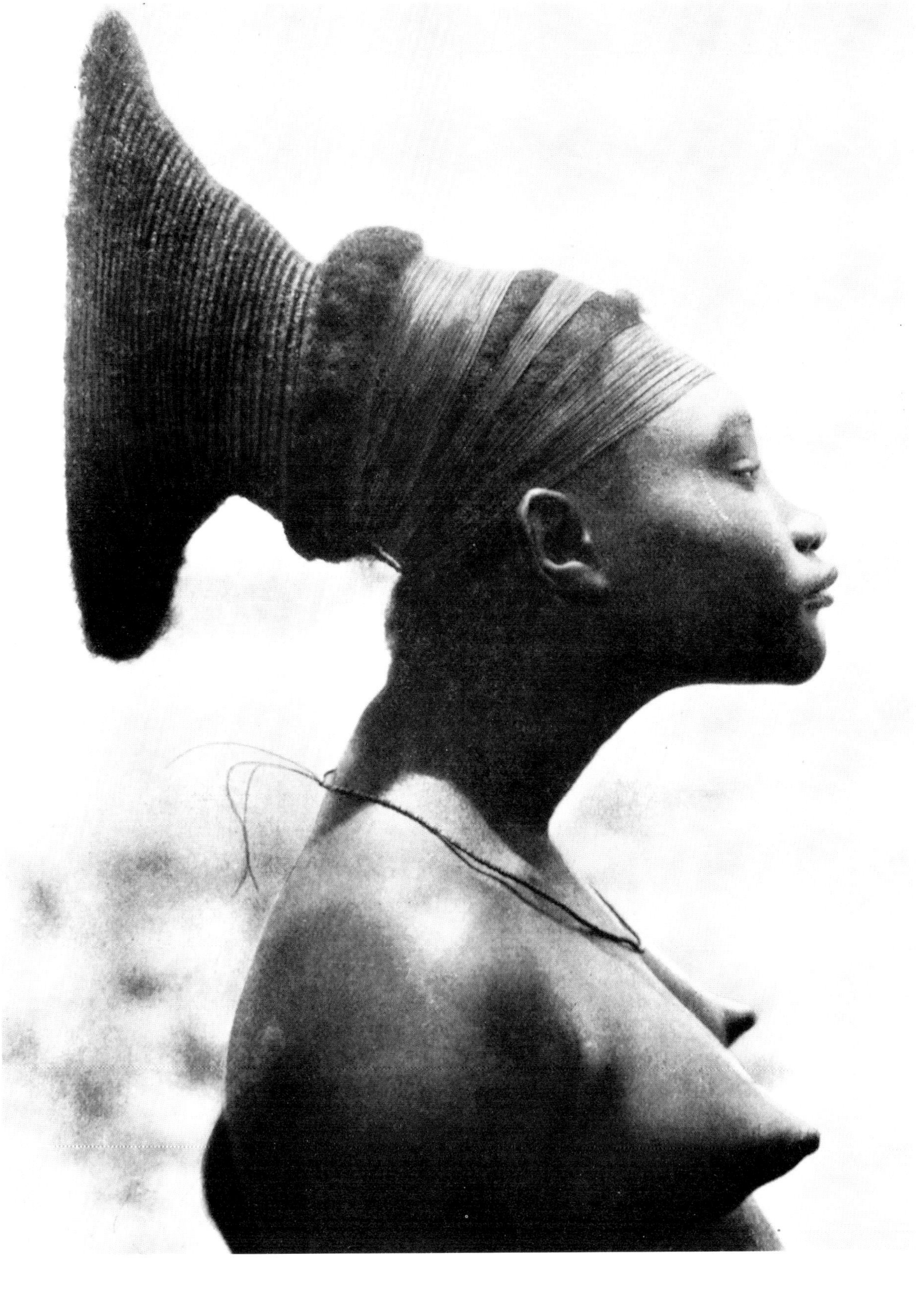

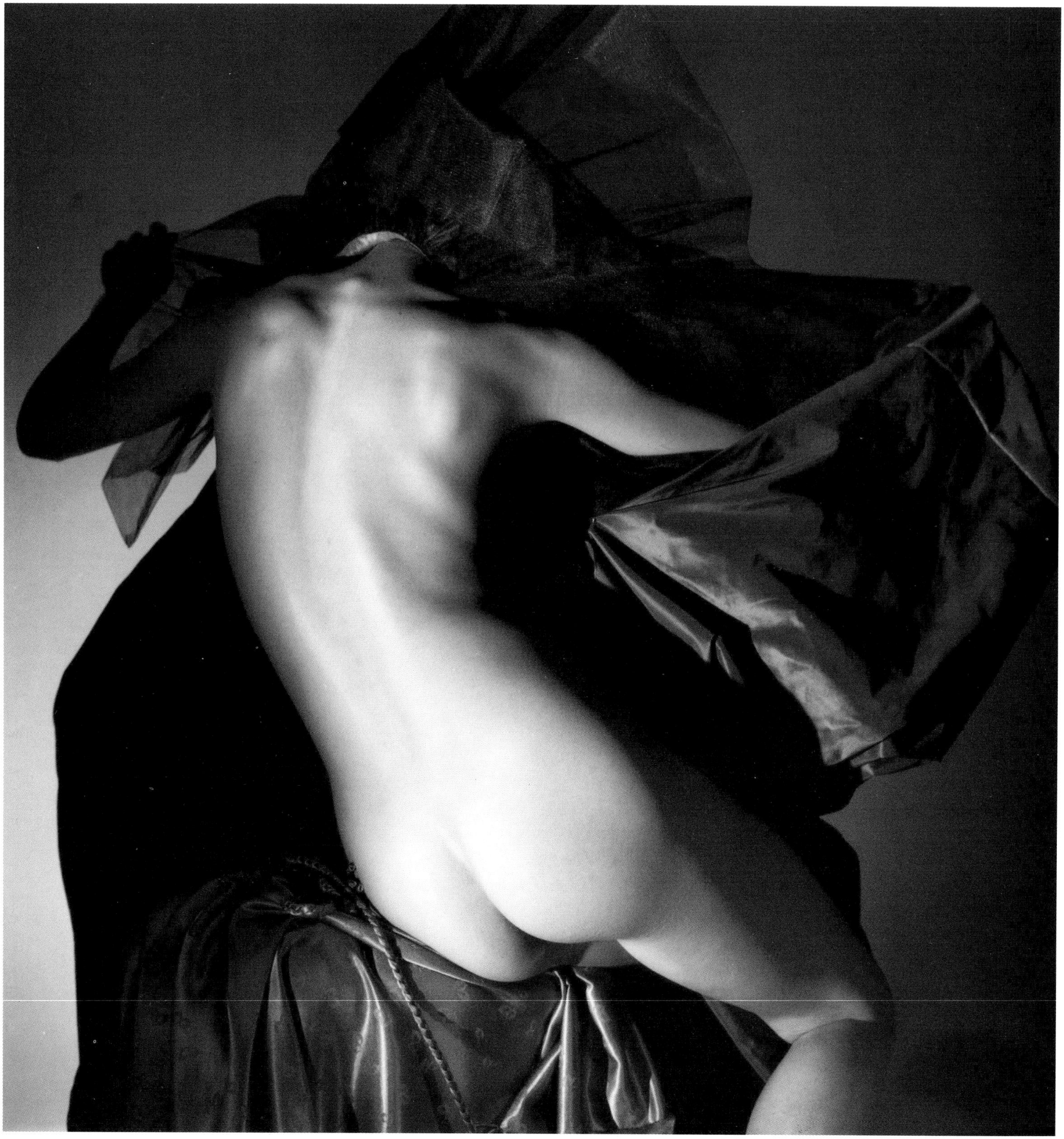

MODERN NUDES

The year in which Frederick Holland Day gave up photography, 1917, provided another significant change of emphasis in the medium. *Camera Work*, the influential magazine started by Alfred Stieglitz in 1903 as [illegible] platform for the Photo-Secession, last appeared in 1917. It was an event that symbolized the end of pictorial photography and a growing acceptance of the purist approach. The last photographs published in *Camera Work* were made by a newcomer, Paul Strand. Stieglitz wrote of them: 'The photographer has added something to what has gone before. The work is brutally direct. Devoid of all flim-flam; devoid of trickery and any [illegible]'. In a [illegible] which accompanied an exhibition of his own photographs in 1921, Stieglitz started with a telling sentence: 'This exhibition is the direct result of an idea.' From now on, straight photography, with sharp, clear, uncomplicated, untouched prints, would reassert itself.

Among the first photographs Stieglitz made in this new direction were a number of intimate [illegible] portraits of his lover, the artist Georgia O'Keeffe [illegible]

PLATE XLVIII
HORST P. HORST
Nude 1982
Staley-Wise Gallery, New York

The length and fruitfulness of Horst's career, which spans six decades, is well illustrated by comparing one of his earliest nudes (PLATE LXII) with the undiminished vigour and panache displayed in this recent composition.

catalogued as "*A Woman: One Portrait*." "For me," says Bailey, "these are the first pictures which clearly indicate a warmth and intimacy in the model-photographer relationship."

Partly under Stieglitz's influence, EDWARD WESTON also turned to straight photography in 1922. Weston's nudes, with their technical clarity and the forthright nature of his vision, make most earlier twentieth century photographs appear timid and inhibited by comparison. Weston's first major nudes were those he made in 1924 of his current belle, the photographer and communist activist, Tina Modotti. They were taken at a crucial moment in his career, when he was reacting violently against what he saw as the "dishonesty" inherent in the smudgy Secessionist approach of his earlier work. As such, they tend towards a treatment of the female body in terms of abstract form, as opposed to flesh and blood, and clearly show the influence of contemporary abstract painting, which he first encountered in about 1915. But by the 1930s Weston, while losing none of the eloquence of the formal virtues of his compositions, combined with this some noticeably warmer, more human qualities. He ceased, for example, to employ the radical cropping of the human form which had suggested an exercise merely in abstract elegance. In his search for an intensity of vision through objective seeing, it was as if the nude had at first been rendered on terms no different from those which he applied to his famous studies of peppers and shells. But in his later work it is evident that the woman in front of his lens is held not only in affection but also in respect, both as a woman and as his equal.

The most completely satisfying nudes Weston took in the 1930s were those of Charis Wilson, a beautiful young woman some twenty-eight years his junior. In Bailey's opinion "the great thing about Edward Weston is that he was the first of the really great photographers to do nudes where the woman

inspire, evincing the attitudes of an individual who has lived his life through photography. If his purist camera technique has been largely eclipsed in recent years then the influence of his spartan but bohemian way of life lives on. It is evident, for instance, in the work of another American photographer, BRUCE WEBER.

Weber became a favourite of Bailey's on the strength of his first fashion photographs, which were published in *Vogue* in 1981. Here was a highly original talent operating in what had become for Bailey (who knows it well) a jaded field. A great eclectic, Weber nevertheless succeeds in combining and integrating his wide-ranging historical enthusiasms into a completely personal approach. The nudes he takes are, more often than not, photographed on fashion sessions. Sometimes a fashion sitting turns into a nude sitting and the photographs selected by Bailey (PLATES XLIX and L) were produced in just this way. The models were being photographed in archery clothes, in colour, and Weber continued to shoot in black and white for his own satisfaction. The colour shots appeared in *Vogue*, the striking black and white images were featured in Weber's highly acclaimed touring exhibition, *Athletes*. For Bruce Weber there are no hard and fast boundaries in his photography: if he feels that a fashion picture will convey more of the essence of its message minus clothes, then that is the way he will take it. He feels he is creating an image of a way of living as opposed to merely documenting a dress or suit, an uncompromising attitude as a result of which he is only hired by a relatively small group of sympathetic magazine editors and advertisers. The nudity in his pictures evokes a kind of new naturalism, a conscious antidote to the style, wealth and artifice epitomized by the modern America of television's *Dallas*.

Edward Weston's contemporary, MAN RAY, was also an American, which is just about all they had in common. By the time Man Ray emigrated to Paris, in 1921, he was a fully paid-up member of the American avant-garde: he had already adopted the airbrush technique he would use all through his painting career, had begun his first experiments in photography and, with his friend Marcel Duchamp, had founded a New York branch of the Dada movement.

Like Weston, Man Ray tended to center his production of nude photographs on the woman who was his lover at the time, starting with Kiki de Montparnasse and including Lee Miller, Nusch Eluard and his wife, Juliet. But whereas Weston continued earnestly along the path of Stieglitz's modernism, the more urbane Man Ray maintained a broader philosophy, a willingness to experiment and take risks which freed him to encompass in his work qualities of wit and subversion that would have been quite foreign to Weston's seriousness. The irreverence which Man Ray claimed to hold for photography reflected a defensiveness on his part, an inability to reconcile himself to the obvious truth that his photographs were more resolved manifestations of his creativity than his rather contrived paintings. This irreverence did nevertheless allow him to take liberties with the medium that would be denied to the more timid: in his first year in Paris he gave to photography the Rayograph, or cameraless image, and in 1923 he invented the technique of solarization, subsequently adopted by many other photographers with surrealist leanings.

Bailey met Man Ray towards the end of his life. In 1968 he spent two days in London with him and took the well-known portrait of the older man with his walking cane and spectacles. Bailey found him "grumpy and self-opinionated" – which the tenor of Man Ray's autobiography, *Self Portrait*, would seem to bear out – and, while he has the greatest respect for Man Ray's work, added: "his intelligence was in his eyes rather than his mouth." Bailey chose the photographs of Kiki and Meret Oppenheim (PLATES LXXVIII and LXXXI) "because I wanted to avoid the more obvious and well-known pictures such as the solarizations; the photograph of Kiki is a straightforwardly erotic record of his lover, and that of Meret Oppenheim qualifies as surreal by her presence in those odd surroundings, rather than by any technical tricks."

PAUL OUTERBRIDGE is a photographer whose work, and his nudes in particular, has only been rescued from obscurity since the publication of a major monograph in 1980. He had dabbled in photography while serving in the United States Army in 1918 and, having married into money in 1921, was able to attend a course at the Clarence White School of Photography in New York to pursue this interest. White's pictorialist style was an anachronism by this time, but Outerbridge found him "a great inspiration." Outerbridge's early photographs were inspired by Cubism, still lifes printed (despite its cost and scarcity) in platinum. With the exception of "Ethiopian Form" (PLATE LXXI) the nudes he made in this period reflected the influence of Clarence White's romantic diffuseness. In 1922, Outerbridge attended a lecture given by Alfred Stieglitz and two years later met him again and talked with him at length. The following year Outerbridge and his wife sailed, via London, for Paris, where they stayed for the next four years.

In Paris, Outerbridge soon struck up a friendship with Man Ray, who, like Stieglitz in New York, was sought out by many aspiring young photographers. Outerbridge also studied books on eroticism and fetishism, which bore fruit in the colour photographs he made between 1935 and 1939. Bailey feels that the refined still life product shots that Outerbridge made in the 1920s are "the acceptable face of commercialism," but contemporary morality and legal problems ensured that his later nudes were anything but commercial (PLATES LXIV and LXV). In 1935, Outerbridge took up colour

contact with the person viewing the picture. Have a lovely nude model look directly at the camera, especially with a provocative smile or an inviting glint, and you have usually crossed the border between the nude and a particular girl without her clothes on." Particularly abhorrent to him were the mass of photographs by those who "unfamiliar with the subject matter offered up a lot of ludicrous posturing of naked girls masquerading as studies of the nude." But, in spite of Outerbridge's efforts to raise the standards of serious nude photography, this aspect of his career was forced by convention into obscurity. In 1945 he married a young fashion designer, Lois Weir, and in later years his energies were largely directed into making a success of their fashion business. He died in 1958, duly recognized for his consummate skills as a colour technician, his nudes all but forgotten.

ERWIN BLUMENFELD was born and raised in Berlin, where as a young man he was associated with the Berlin Dadaists, including Richard Huelsenbeck, George Grosz and Paul Citroen, who had been a friend since childhood and whose cousin Blumenfeld married. Blumenfeld moved to Amsterdam in 1919 where he and Paul Citroen were made honorary leaders of the non-existent Amsterdam branch of the Dada movement by Huelsenbeck. Meanwhile, Blumenfeld was trying to make a living by running an unsuccessful leather goods shop. But, as he related in his autobiography: "What I really wanted: to be a photographer, just that, art for art's sake, a brand new world, so successfully discovered by the American Jew Man Ray." In 1936, he joined the migration of artistic talent to Paris. Through photography he could now pursue what have been described as his three main obsessions, women, death and sex.

Although Blumenfeld had his work published in annuals such as *Photographie* and *Arts et Metiers Graphiques*, and in the prestigious new journal *Verve*, he was not making enough money to support his wife and three

Bruguière and Fuller settled in London in 1928 and the multiple exposure he made of his lover with a cello dates from their early years there (PLATE LI). In his book *Photography* (1951), Cecil Beaton recalled the impact of Bruguière's work in London, suggesting that his photographs were a "marriage of the camera and the essence of light . . . even today most of Bruguière's work remains remarkably dramatic in effect and timeless in quality."

DOROTHY WILDING was a highly successful portrait photographer established by the mid-1920s in a flourishing studio in London's fashionable Old Bond Street. Bailey was attracted to the nude portrait (PLATE LXIII) and the comparable shot of Josephine Baker by Wilding's Parisian counterpart MADAME D'ORA (PLATE LXXII) for the same reason: "They both sum up perfectly the period: you think of jazz in Paris, of Art Deco—even the poses suggest a cross between Egyptian art and the Russian Ballet, two of Art Deco's sources."

The photograph by MAURICE BECK (PLATE LXVIII) was included by Bailey "because again it's typical of the period and obviously English, but simply the best example of its kind I've ever seen." It certainly is a remarkably accomplished photograph, combining an oiled-bodies sensuality with a balanced yet dynamic composition. Beck worked together with Helen MacGregor in the 1920s, making portraits of Bloomsbury personalities, many of which were published in *Vogue*. MacGregor continued to specialize in theater and fashion portraits in the 1930s, while Maurice Beck became official photographer for Shell-Mex and British Petroleum, working in a manner derived from the German *Neue Sachlichkeit* (New Objectivity).

The Czechoslovakian photographer FRANTISEK DRTIKOL trained as a portrait photographer, setting up his own studio in Prague in 1910, but his

Bailey has long been acquainted with Horst's fashion photographs, and has a preference for his 1930s pictures. Bailey only became aware of the Horst nudes he has selected relatively recently (PLATES XLVIII and LXII), but it is the same qualities of impeccable handling of studio lighting and control of form and space which Bailey finds appealing in them. Horst's delicacy of touch would suggest that images might be termed "fashion nudes," photographs calculated not to upset the propriety of fashion magazines at a time when frontal or other more blatant nudes would have been unpublishable in this context.

The most influential and widely admired British photographer of the nude is undoubtedly BILL BRANDT. After moving to London in 1931 Brandt concentrated mainly on documenting different aspects of English life during a period of rapid social change in which marked inequalities still prevailed. After the war, he felt a less urgent call on his camera as a political tool and began a more inward exploration by way of the nude. He also made many perceptive and dramatic portraits, in addition to some of his most powerful and enduring landscape photographs, but it is difficult not to believe that, for Brandt, it was his nudes which were of the greatest personal, as well as photographic, significance.

He had begun to feel that the camera might be coerced into revealing more than was apparent to the human eye, or at least to perceive things in a radically different and illuminating way. His search to convey meanings beyond surface reality, "transcending the ordinary" as Brandt put it, can be partially traced back to the three-month period he spent in Paris in 1929, working in the studio of Man Ray. Here, at the center of Paris Surrealism, he encountered not only Man Ray's work but also such key Surrealist films as Dali and Bunuel's *L'Age d'Or* and *Un Chien Andalou*, as well as photographs

and Bailey feels that Brandt's pictures frequently resemble "clips from old movies: you feel you are seeing part of a story – I can never help wondering what's going on in that house where the maid is pulling down the window-blinds."

Two photographers roughly contemporary with Bailey who both openly acknowledge their indebtedness to Bill Brandt are Ralph Gibson and Eikoh Hosoe. Technically, RALPH GIBSON's procedure for making photographs is very different from Brandt's. He came up through the Robert Frank "from-the-hip" school and shoots rapidly and intensely, using a hand-held 35mm camera. In his mastery of developing and printing techniques he is able to force up the contrast of his pictures to achieve a dramatically reduced tonal range, redolent of Brandt, emphasizing Gibson's favourite "big solid blacks." Gibson has described photographing the nude in terms of an exercise in investigating the "mystery and tension between the body and the spirit . . ." He says, à propos Bill Brandt: "When I look at his *Perspective of Nudes*, which is a tremendous book, I begin to see that he is concerned with an entirely different set of mysteries from mine. Perhaps our relationship with Surrealism may have some similar characteristics but other than that he seems to me to relate more to the phenomenon of the figure as opposed to the woman herself. And I consider this merely different but definitely not more or less valid."

Bailey and Ralph Gibson have been friends for ten years now and consequently Bailey knows Gibson's work pretty well; the two photographs included here (PLATES LIII and LXXXIII), both of which appeared in Gibson's recent portfolio of nudes, *L'Anonyme*, were selected because Bailey feels they represent departures from Gibson's earlier work. Bailey is particularly intrigued by the "wilfulness" of shooting the figure out of focus and keeping the background sharp in PLATE LIII.

Contemporary Japanese photography is, in general, surprisingly under-publicized in the West. One of the few photographers whose work has broken through this intangible barrier to communication is EIKOH HOSOE. Over the last twenty-odd years Hosoe has concentrated on the nude as his principal subject matter, majestically spanning the divide between the spirit and the flesh. He has stated: "I am not interested in pattern photographs or making designs. I am interested in photographing human beings with sex. That is all I want to say. I would like to express Love in my nude photographs."

Hosoe's first book of nudes, *Man and Woman*, was published in 1960. On completing this he immediately began work on another project, *Embrace*. The following year he saw Bill Brandt's *Perspective of Nudes*; he wrote, as Mark Holborn revealed, "shattered by Brandt's mastery of the distorting lens and the sculptural, voluminous qualities of Brandt's bodies on the beach. Hosoe abandoned the nudes on which he was working and has never published this early work from *Embrace*. Ten years later he started the series again in the studio." *Embrace* eventually appeared in 1971, together with the awesome portrayal of Yukio Mishima, *Ordeal by Roses*; it remains his best-known and most perfectly realized body of work. Butler [illegible] Hosoe [illegible] Olympus [illegible] Nudes in 1984 [illegible] Hosoe's work from the obvious sensuousness and sincerity as a photographer has a sense of humour. He reasoned that it would be perhaps more interesting to include recent Hosoe's more recent photographs which incorporate the [illegible] side of his nature (PLATES XXI and XXII).

The BRASSAÏ photograph of Matisse with his model brings together a photographer and an artist both greatly respected by Butler (PLATE XXIII). Brassaï's most renowned photographs are those he made of the nightlife of the Paris underworld in the 1930s, but Butler is especially enthusiastic about

Brassai's book *The Artists of My Life*, published only two years before his death in 1985. "It shows," says Bailey, "that Brassai was not only an incredible photographer but had an incredible photographic memory. He writes, as well as photographs, so brilliantly, that this book is one of the best guides to Paris in the 1930s."

Shortly after this book appeared Bailey travelled specially to the South of France to photograph Brassai. He made a highly effective portrait of the old man leaning on the balcony of his house with a darkly dramatic sky as a backdrop. He had, for many years, wanted to talk with the man who stood at the center of Paris culture at a point of great fascination, not least because of the close friendship between Brassai and Bailey's hero, Picasso. For many years, Brassai was Picasso's "official" photographer, despite the artist's dismay that he chose to pursue photography instead of painting. The unhindered directness and clarity of Brassai's vision more than justified his decision.

In the 1930s, Brassai was asked to take fashion photographs for *Harper's Bazaar*. He refused, but was given a much more conducive brief to make portraits of artists. He recalled: "Alexey Brodovitch, the magazine's art director, never gave me any directives, but he liked my photographs very much and his layouts reflected the feeling of the photographs."

Another photographer who might be described as a protégé of the influential Brodovitch is PAUL HIMMEL. He worked for Brodovitch as a fashion photographer in New York, and was one of the first to attempt this kind of work from a photo-reportage angle, shooting in the streets of New York in everyday situations. Himmel became fascinated by the possibilities of showing movement in photographs. His book, *Ballet in Action*, published in 1954, was a highly effective experiment in registering action in blurred images, recalling Brodovitch's own book, *Ballet*, of 1945. Paul Himmel gave

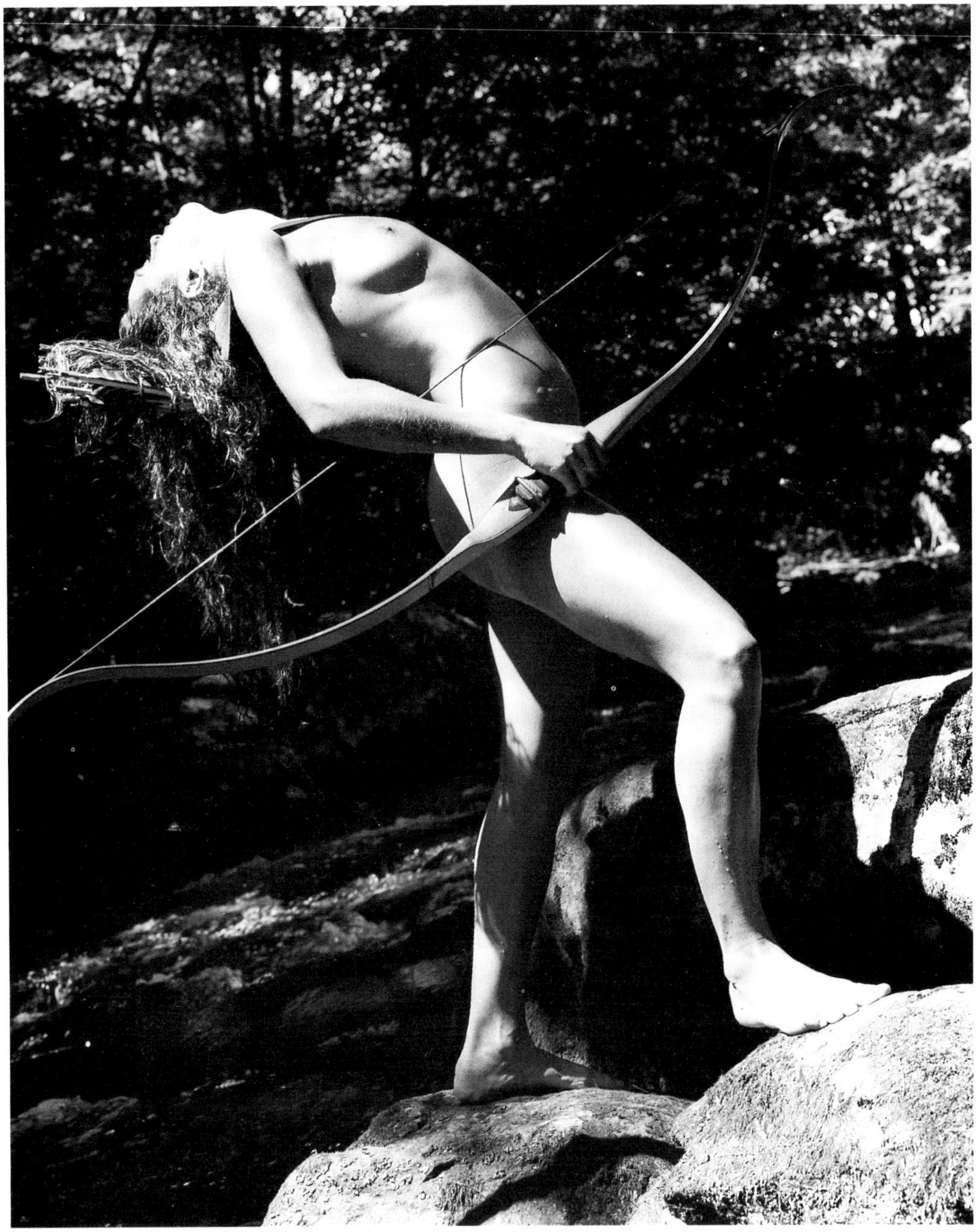

PLATE XLIX
BRUCE WEBER
Liz (Upper Saranac Lake) 1983
Courtesy the photographer

Photographed on a sitting for British *Vogue* in one of his favourite locations, the Adirondacks, these pictures eventually featured in Weber's first major publication, *Athletes*. His strong sense of design is combined with an invigorating naturalism.

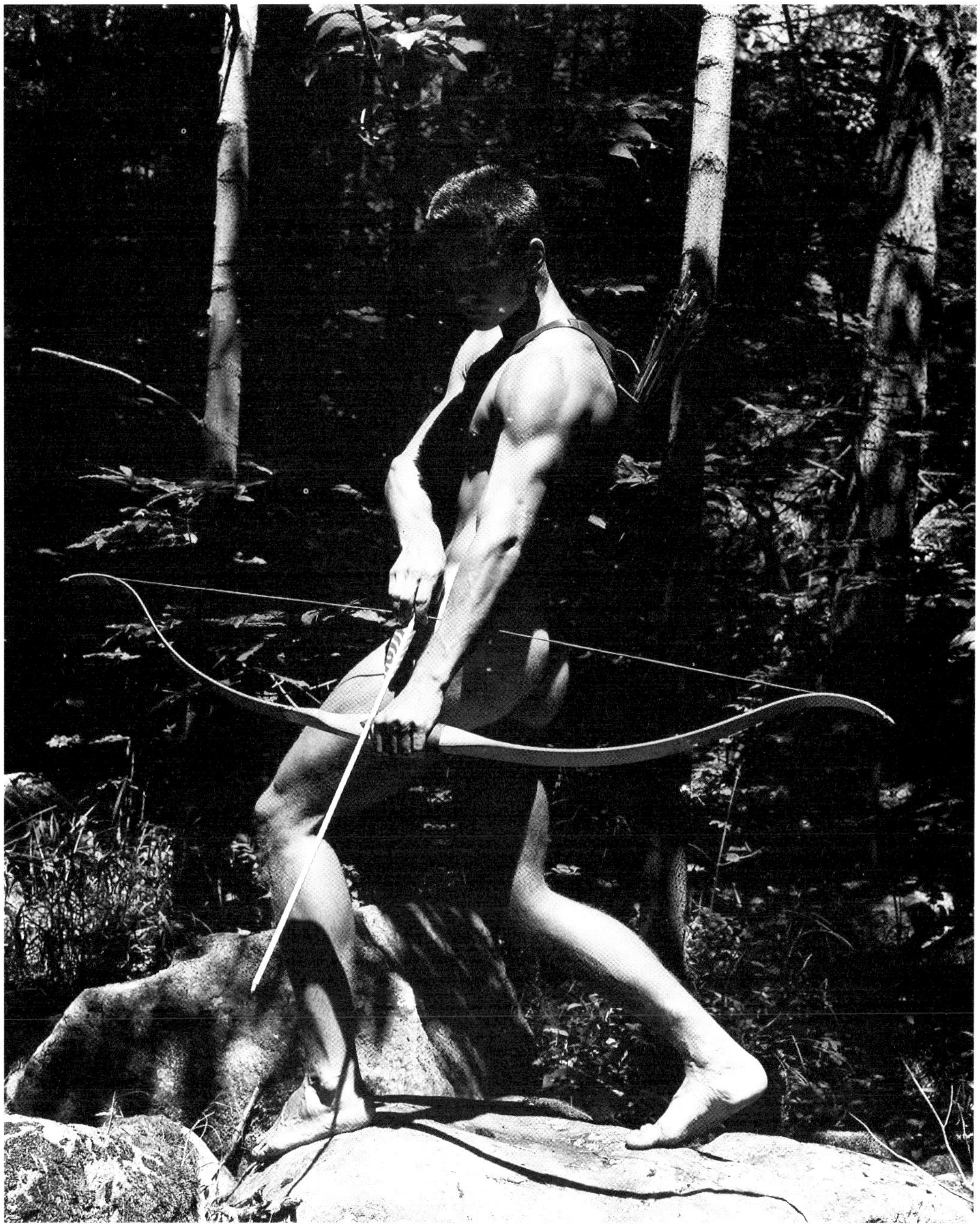

PLATE L
BRUCE WEBER
George (Upper Saranac Lake) 1983
Courtesy the photographer

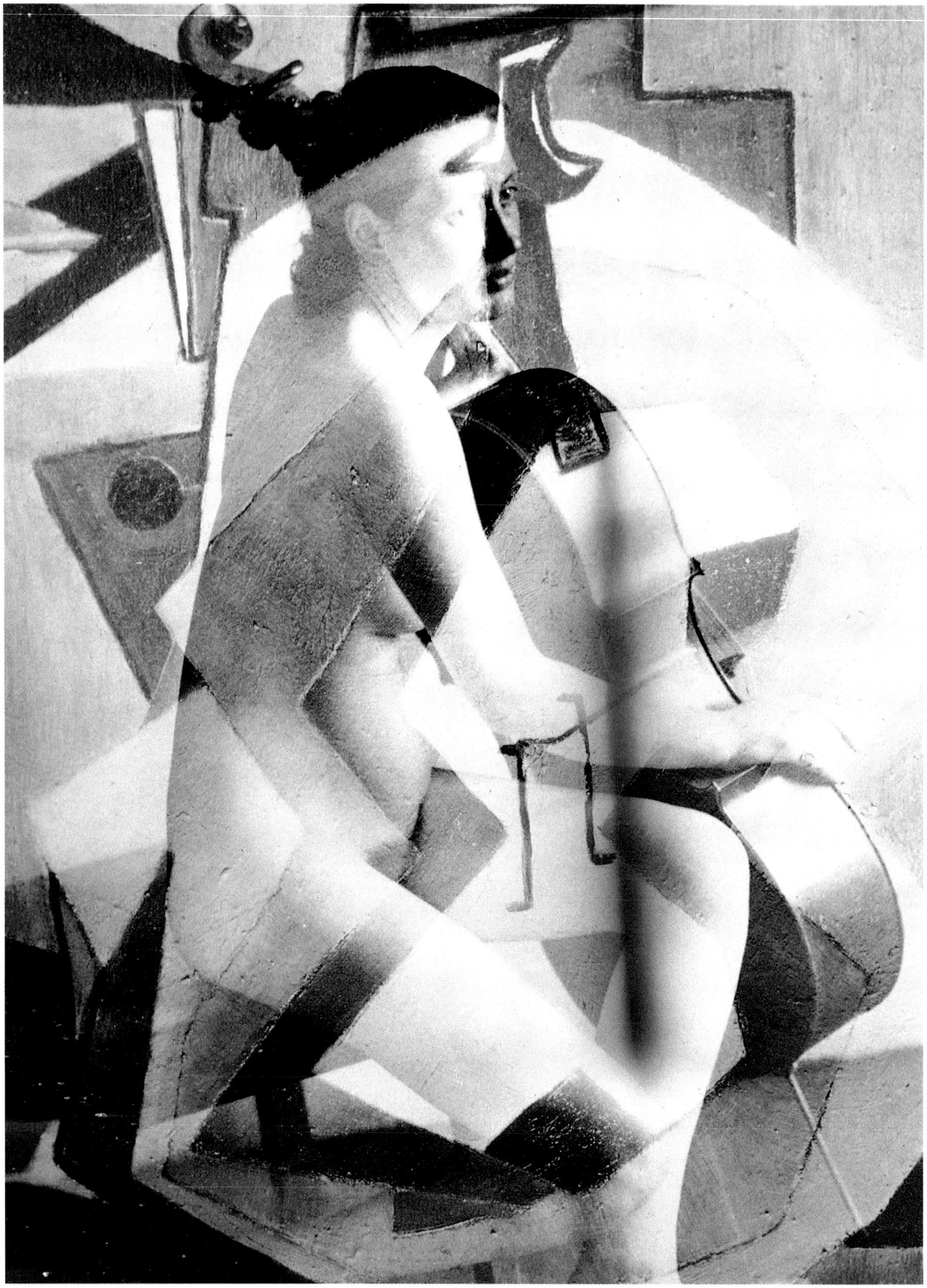

PLATE LI
FRANCIS BRUGUIERE
Rosalinde Fuller and Cello
1930
Robert Miller Gallery, New York

Bruguière was a pioneer investigator of abstract photography (and film) and this image bears a close relationship with his own paintings, which shared the concerns of Cubism and Synchronism.

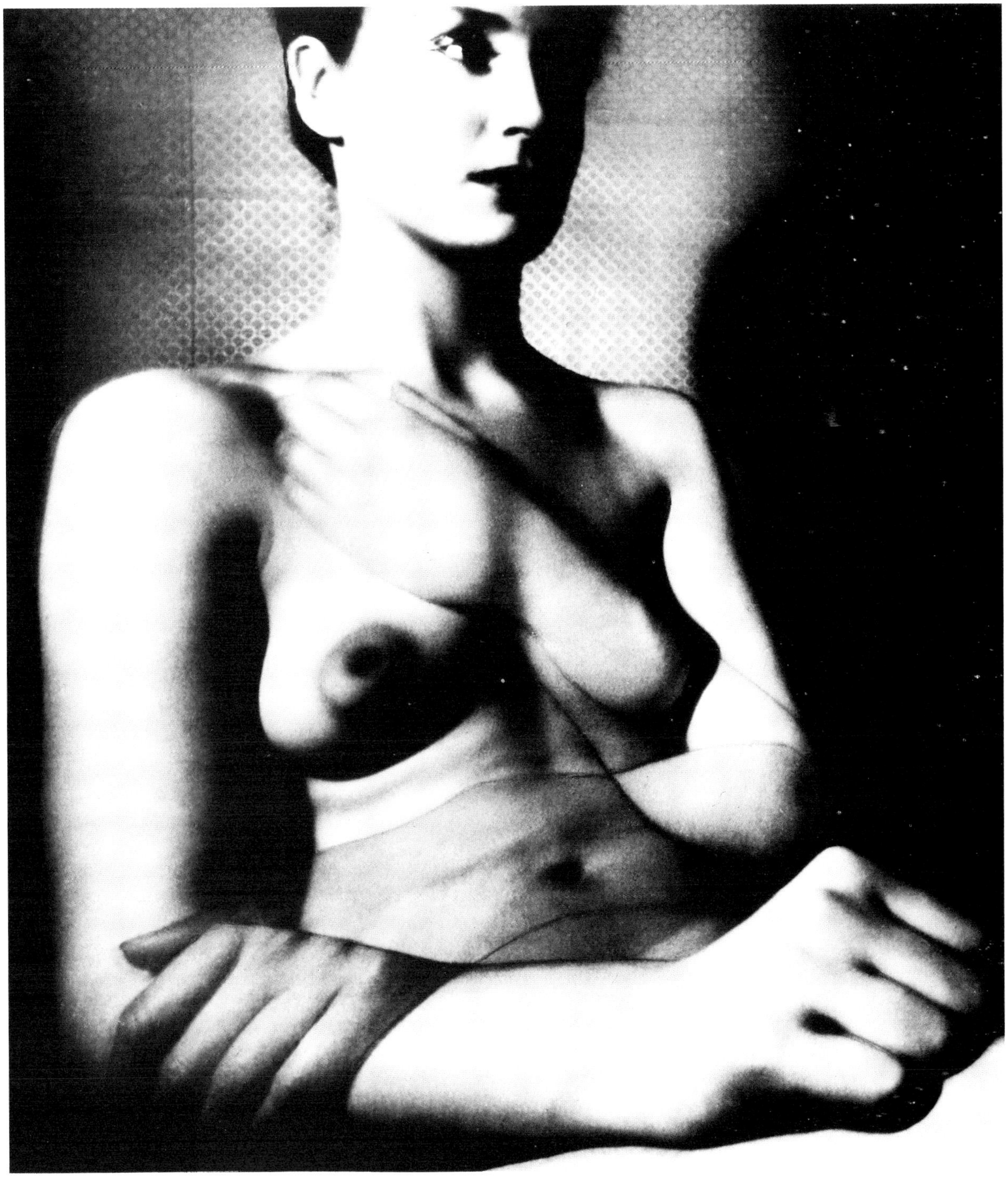

PLATE LII
BILL BRANDT
London 1956
Victoria & Albert Museum, London

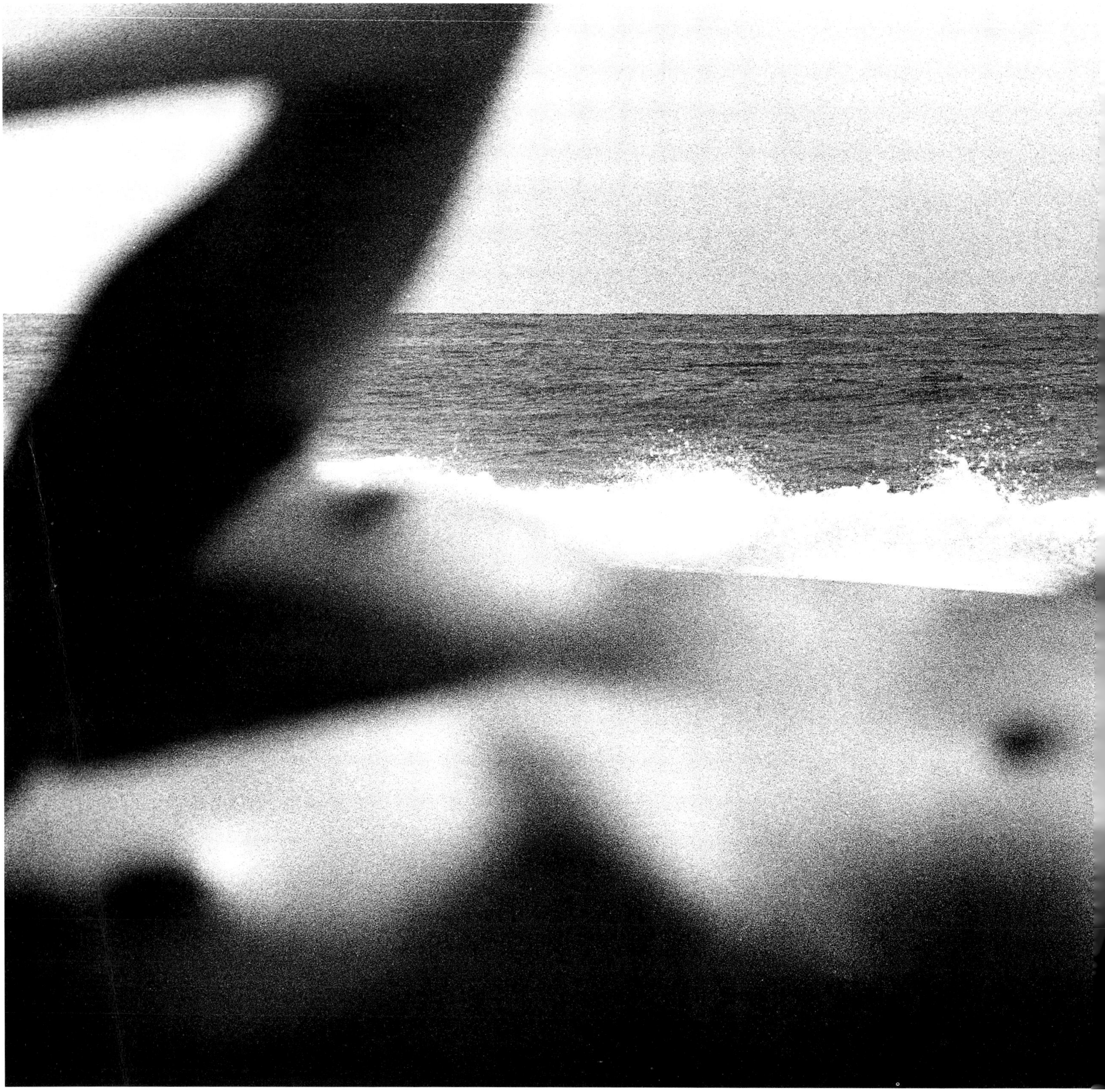

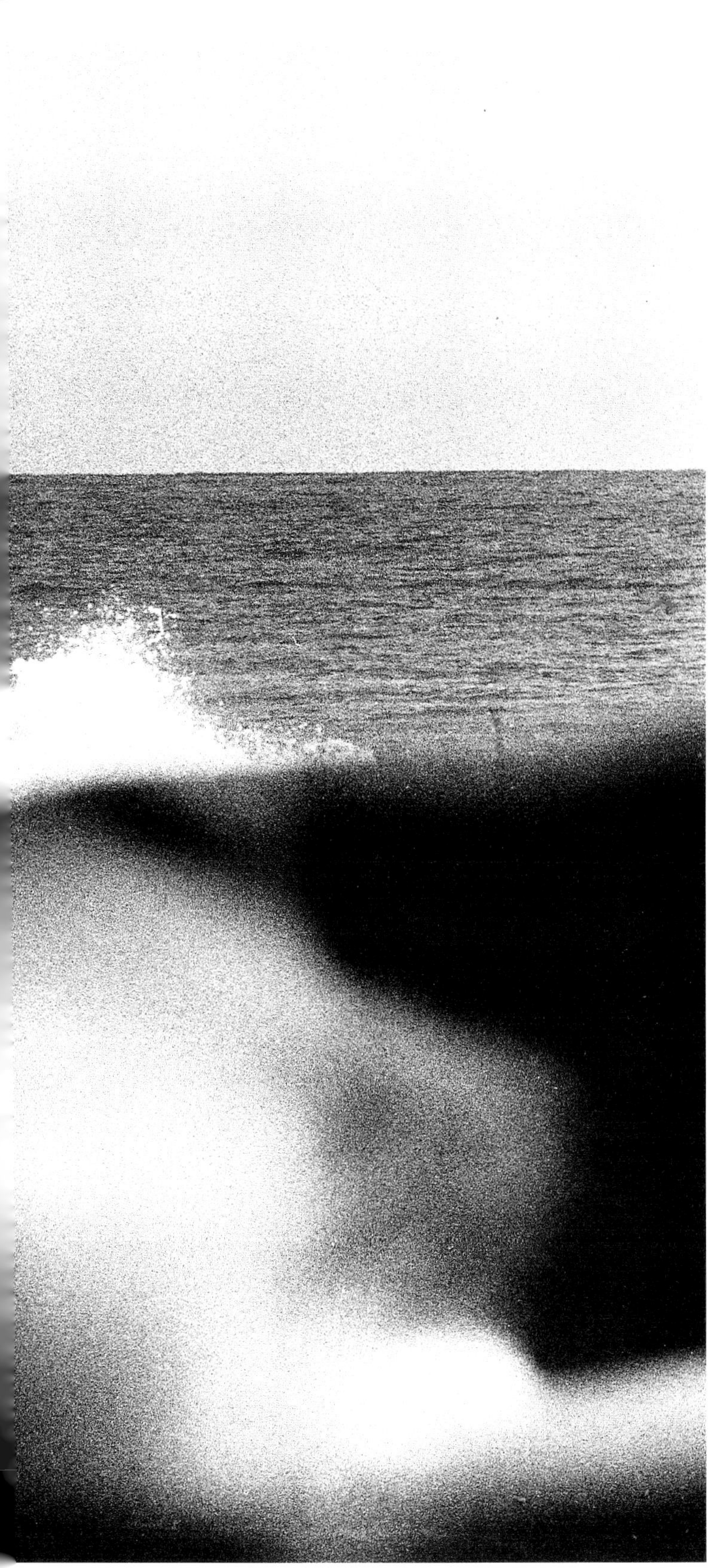

PLATE LIII

RALPH GIBSON

Untitled 1986

Courtesy the photographer

Ralph Gibson, unlike most contemporary photographers, has combined an interest in narrative, often autobiographical narrative, with his pursuit of formalism. The nude has been a constant preoccupation and offers a perfect vehicle for exploring the relationship between form and meaning.

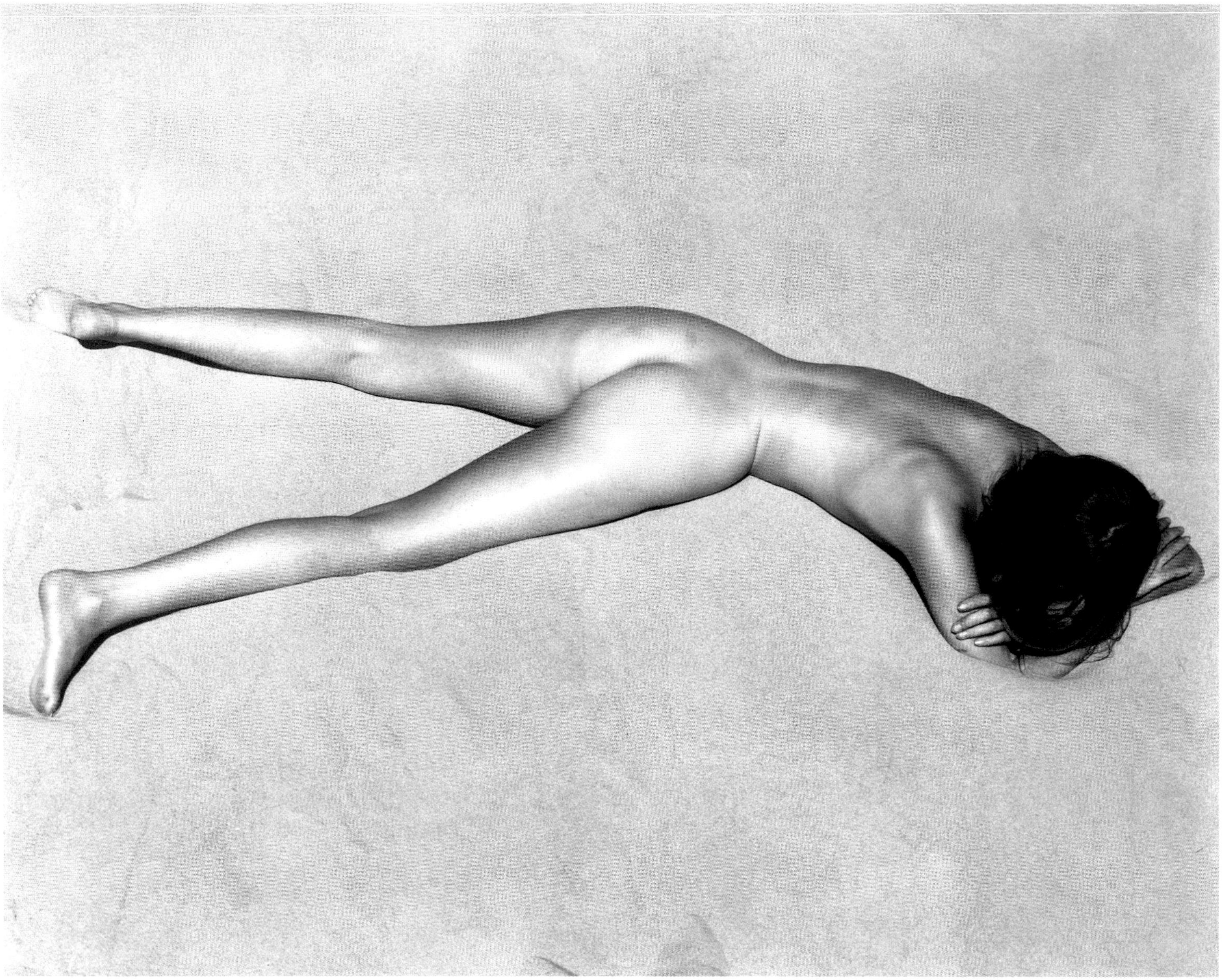

PLATE LIV
EDWARD WESTON
Nude 1936
© 1981 Arizona Board of Regents Center for Creative Photography

It is instructive to compare Weston's treatment of these two nudes. In PLATE LIV the figure is elegantly posed as a component of an overall abstract pattern, while the approach in PLATE LV is more direct, concentrating on the woman herself.

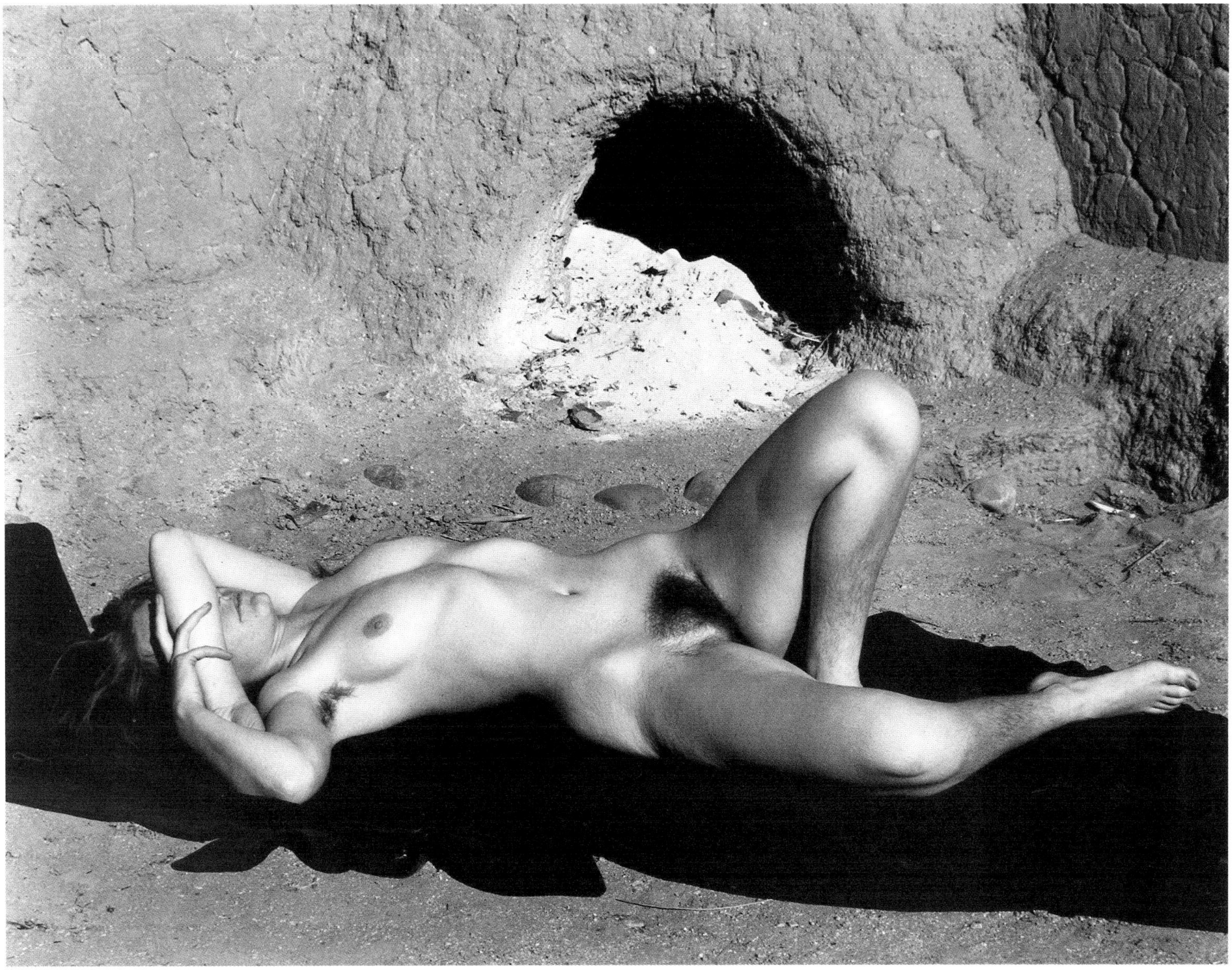

PLATE LV
EDWARD WESTON
Nude, New Mexico 1937
© 1981 Arizona Board of Regents Center for Creative Photography

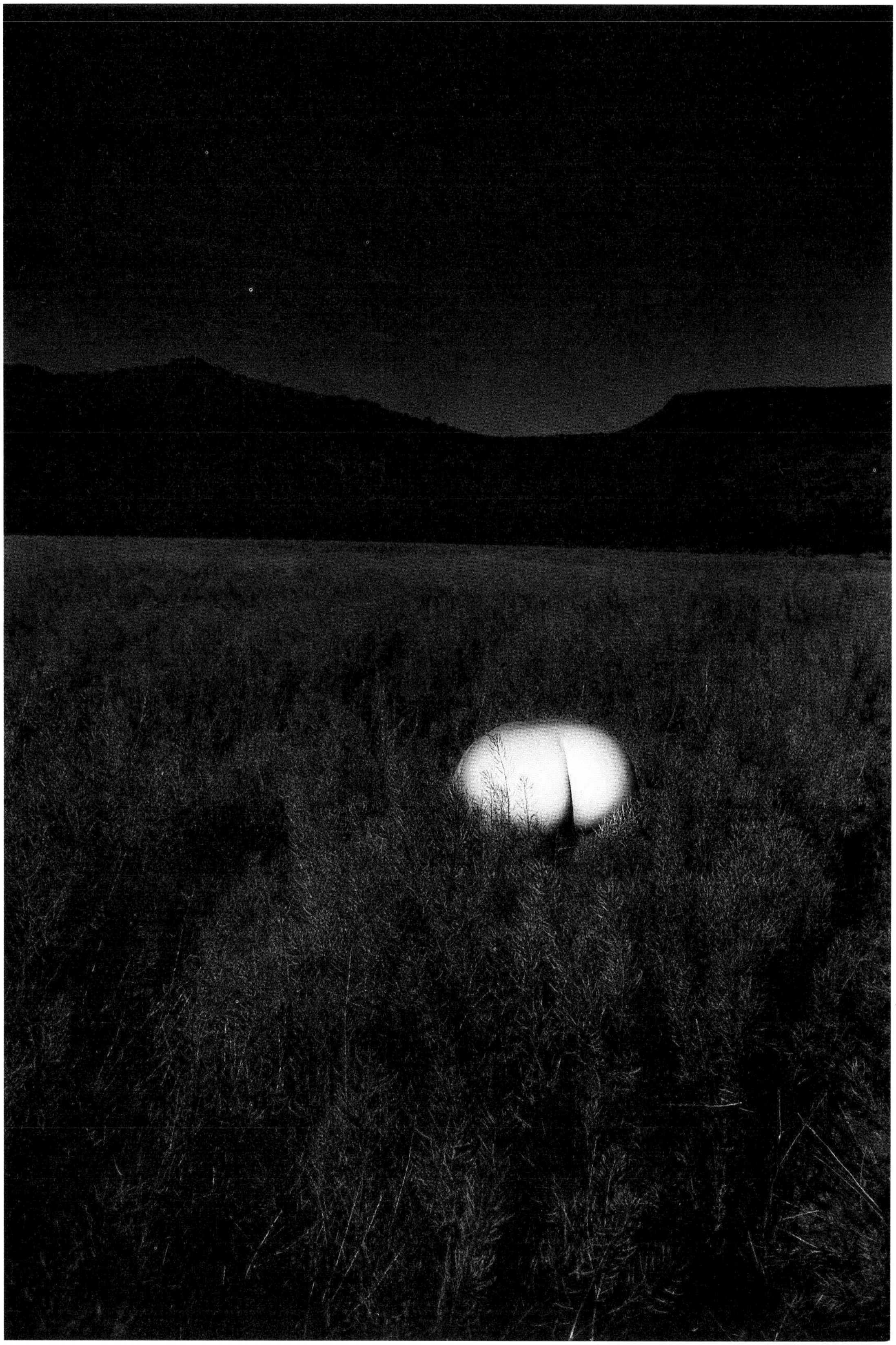

PLATE LVI
EIKOH HOSOE
Moonrise in Arizona 1983.
Courtesy the photographer

His reputation as one of the great photographers of the nude ensures that Eikoh Hosoe is frequently invited to teach at photography workshops and seminars. These events also afford him opportunities to make his own pictures, which are usually more light-hearted than his more extended, serious projects.

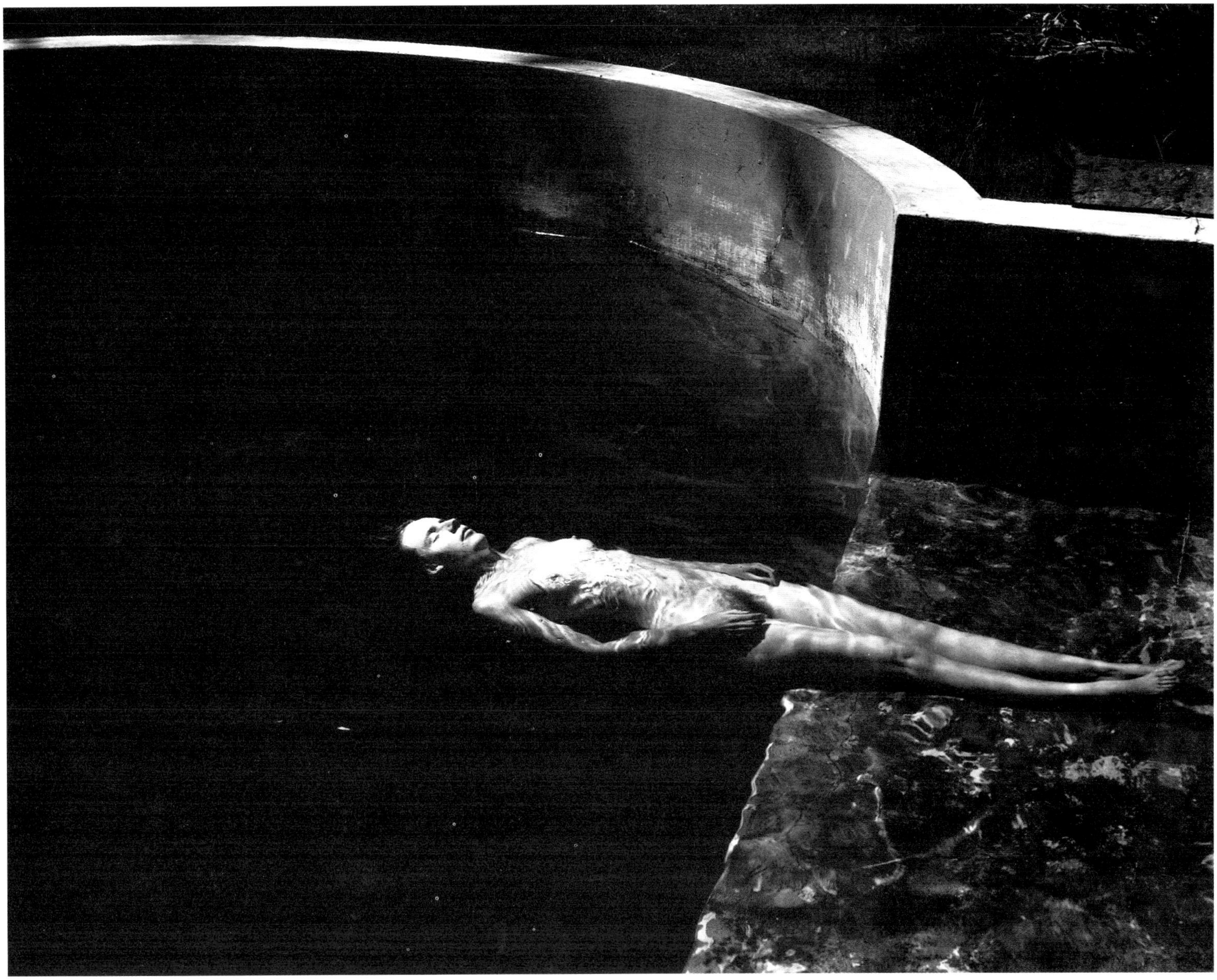

PLATE LVII
EDWARD WESTON
Nude Floating 1939
© *1981 Arizona Board of Regents Center for Creative Photography*

Weston's conception for this nude relates to a 1917 photograph made in Hungary by André Kertész, "Man Diving," though it is highly unlikely Weston would have been aware of this. Weston's photograph, in turn, anticipates the similar treatment adopted for a famous Helmut Newton nude made in St Tropez in 1975, an example of Newton's continuing preoccupation with swimming pools as backdrops.

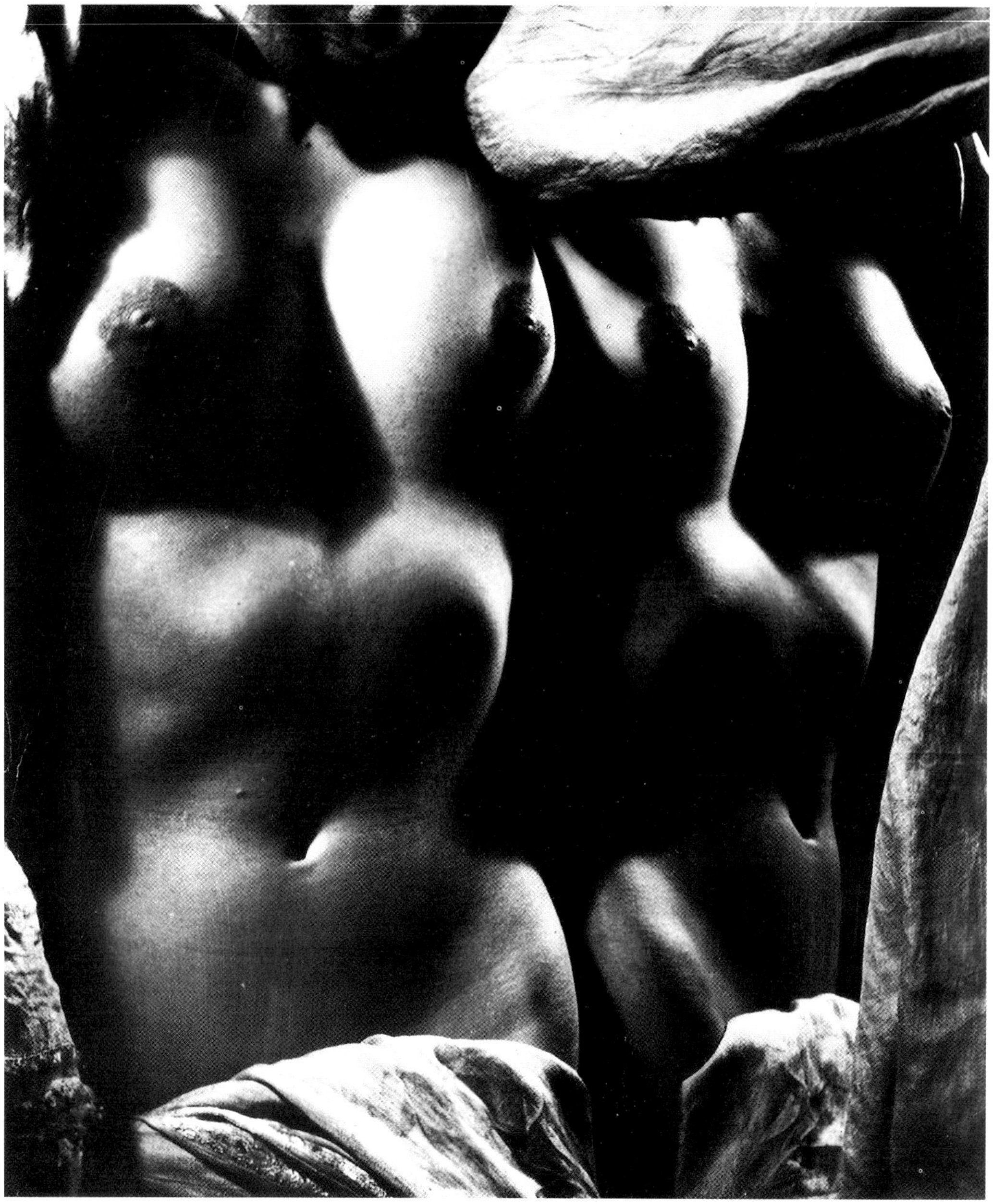

PLATE LVIII (Above)
ERWIN BLUMENFELD
Untitled c.1937
Private Collection

PLATE LIX (Right)
ERWIN BLUMENFELD
Wet Veil II (Published in *Verve*) 1937
Sotheby's, London

At the age of nine, Blumenfeld was taken by his governess to a studio where he watched a model put on a filmy chiffon dress and "There was born in me the desire to see through transparency." He was equally moved by the veiled women in Cranach's paintings and it was these effects he seems to have been recreating here.

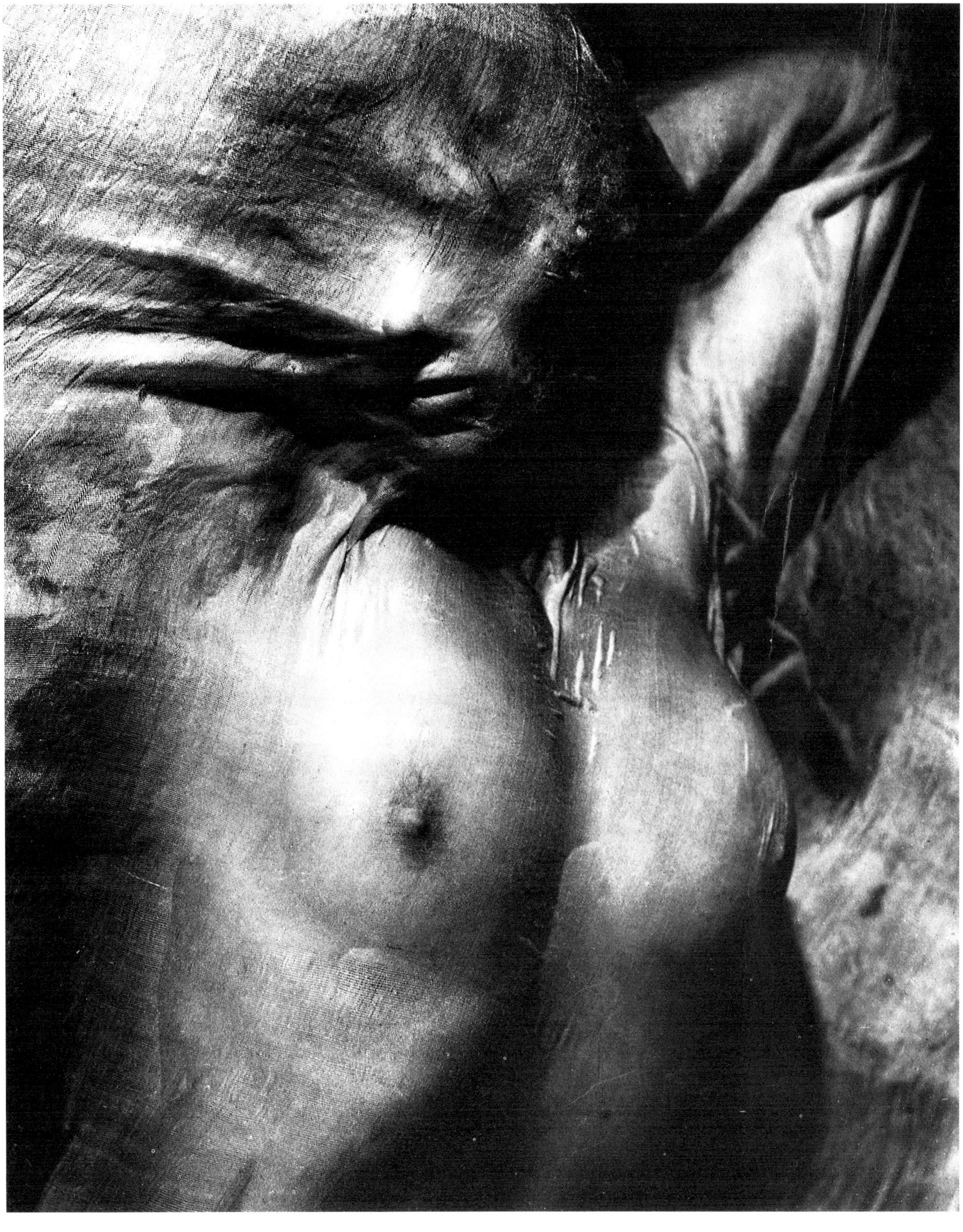

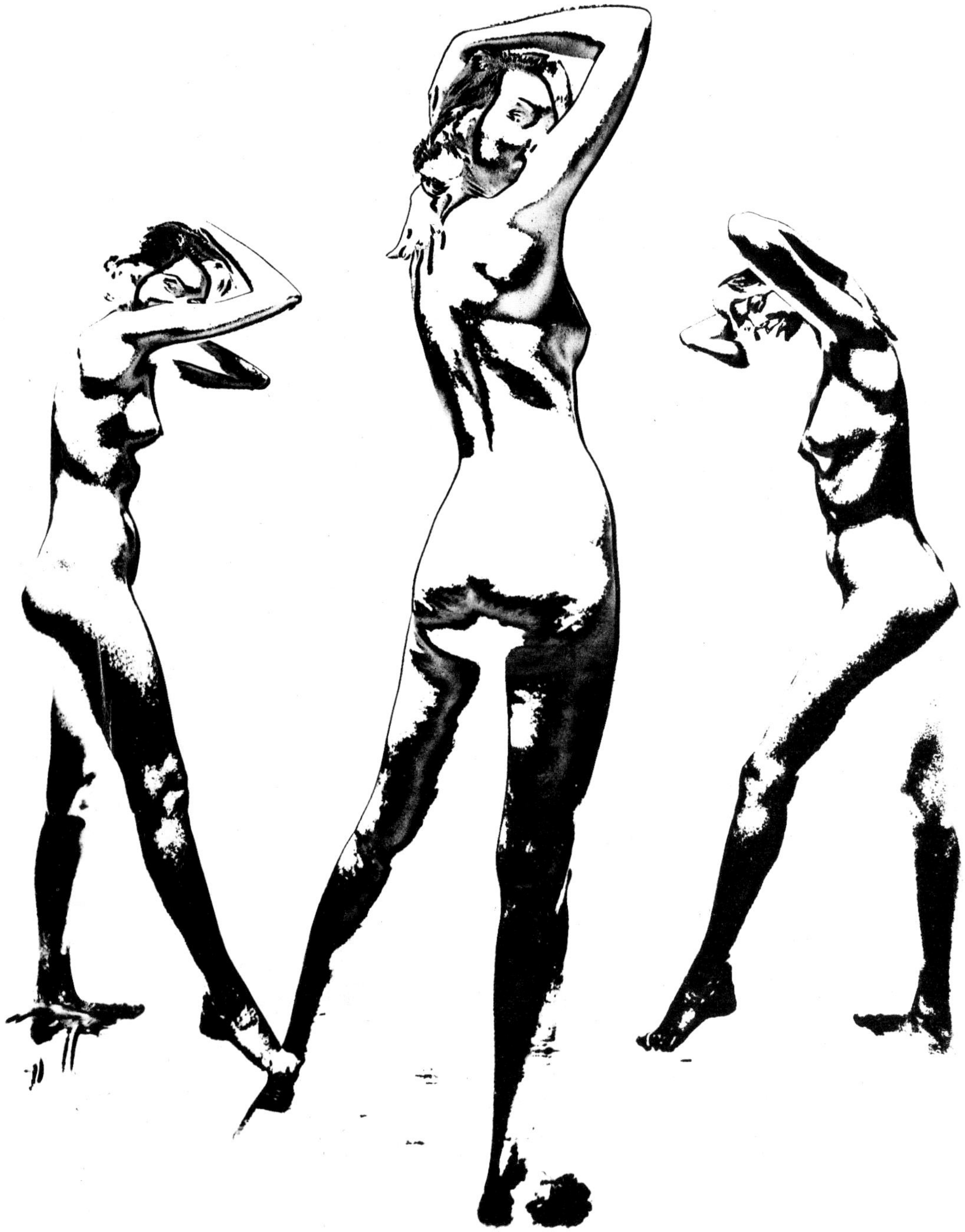

PLATE LX (Above)
ERWIN BLUMENFELD
Solarized Nude 1954
Photographers Gallery, London

PLATE LXI (Right)
ERWIN BLUMENFELD
Untitled 1937
Private Collection

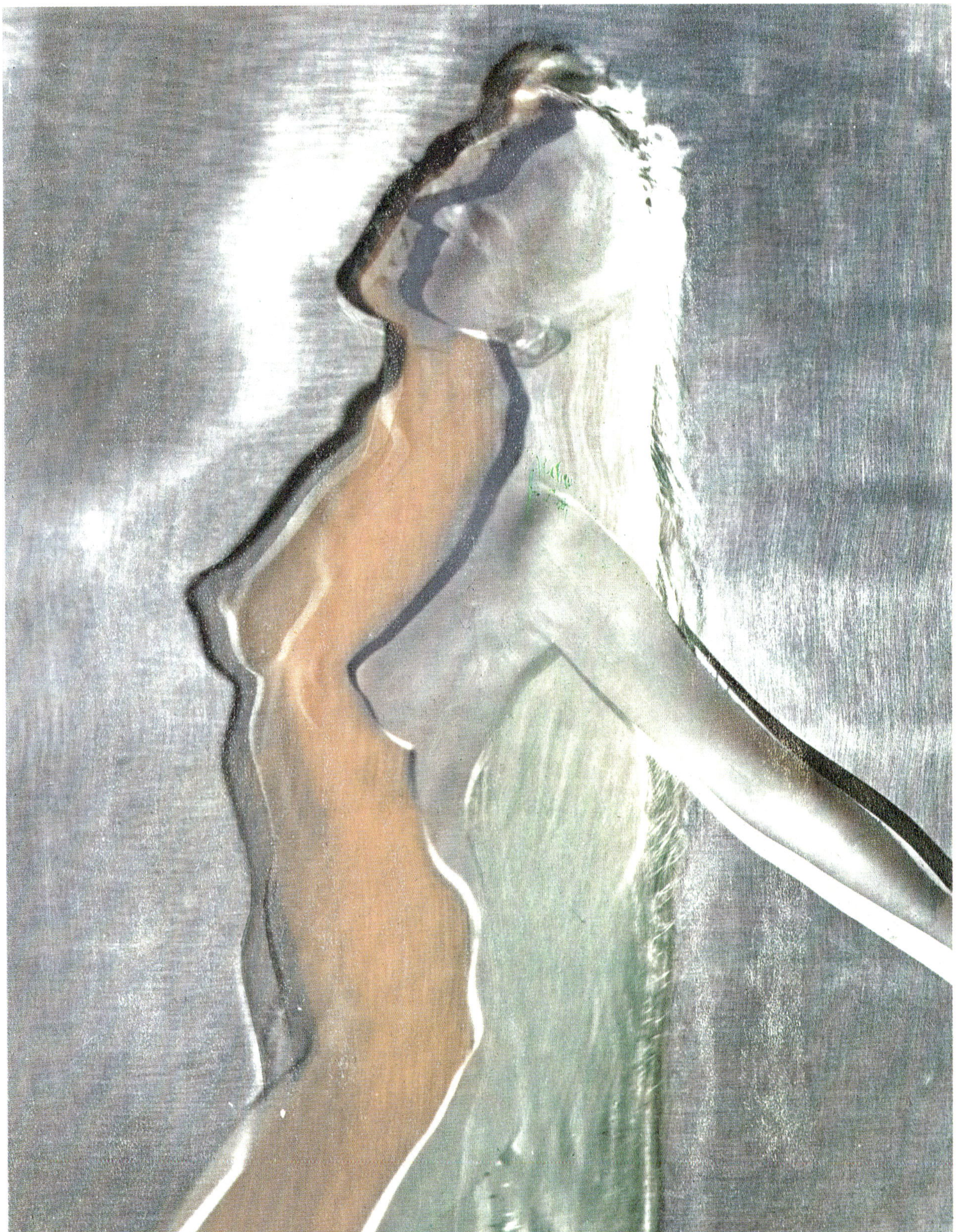

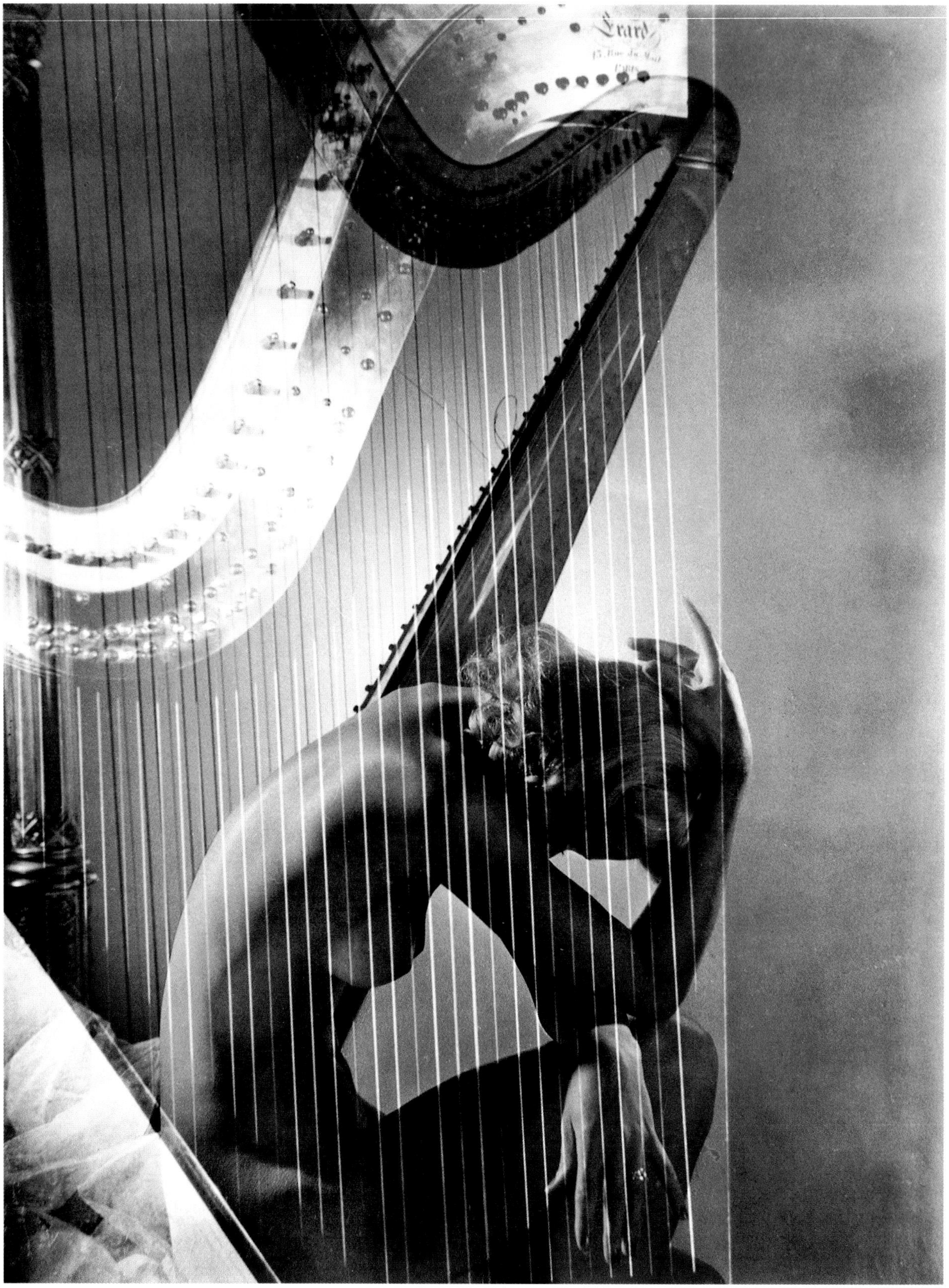

PLATE LXII
HORST P. HORST
Lisa Fonssagrives,
New York 1938
Hamiltons Gallery,
London

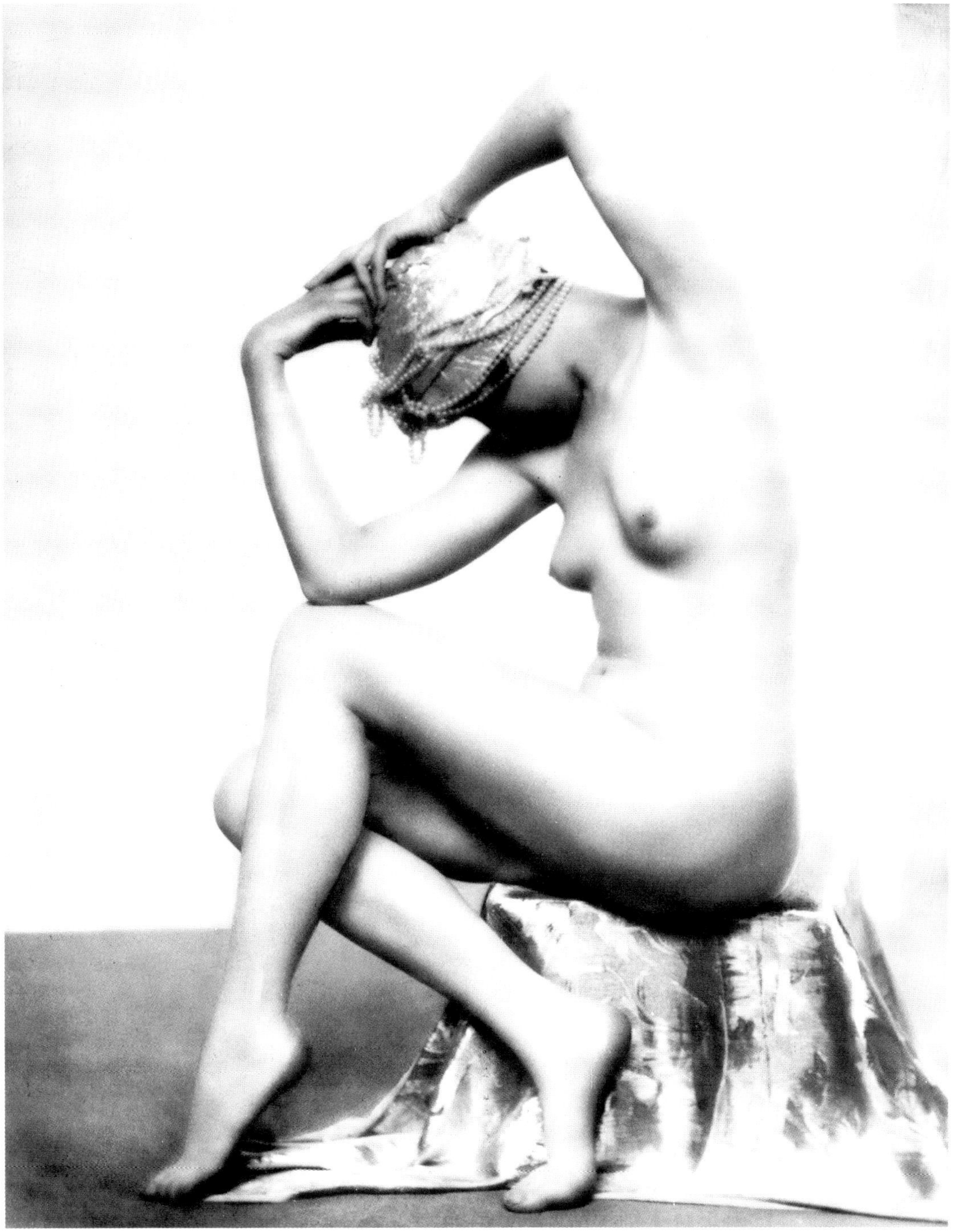

PLATE LXIII
DOROTHY WILDING
Untitled c.1930
Sotheby's, London

Dorothy Wilding's business making society portraits in London prospered to such an extent that she was able to open a New York studio in 1937. She continued to enjoy great success right up to 1970. Though sometimes criticized for being over-retouched, her work was always highly professional and, away from the constraints imposed by clients, sometimes quite imaginative.

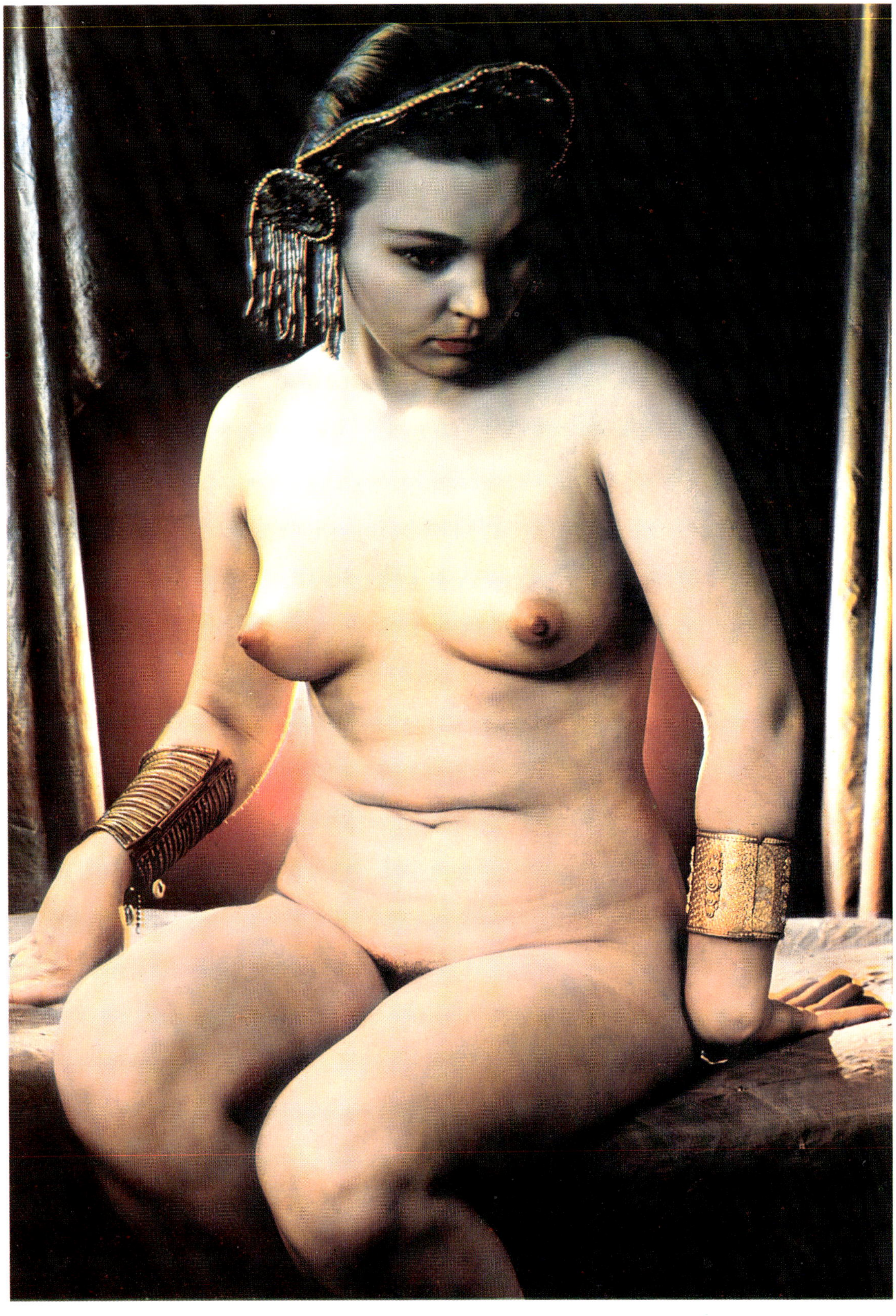

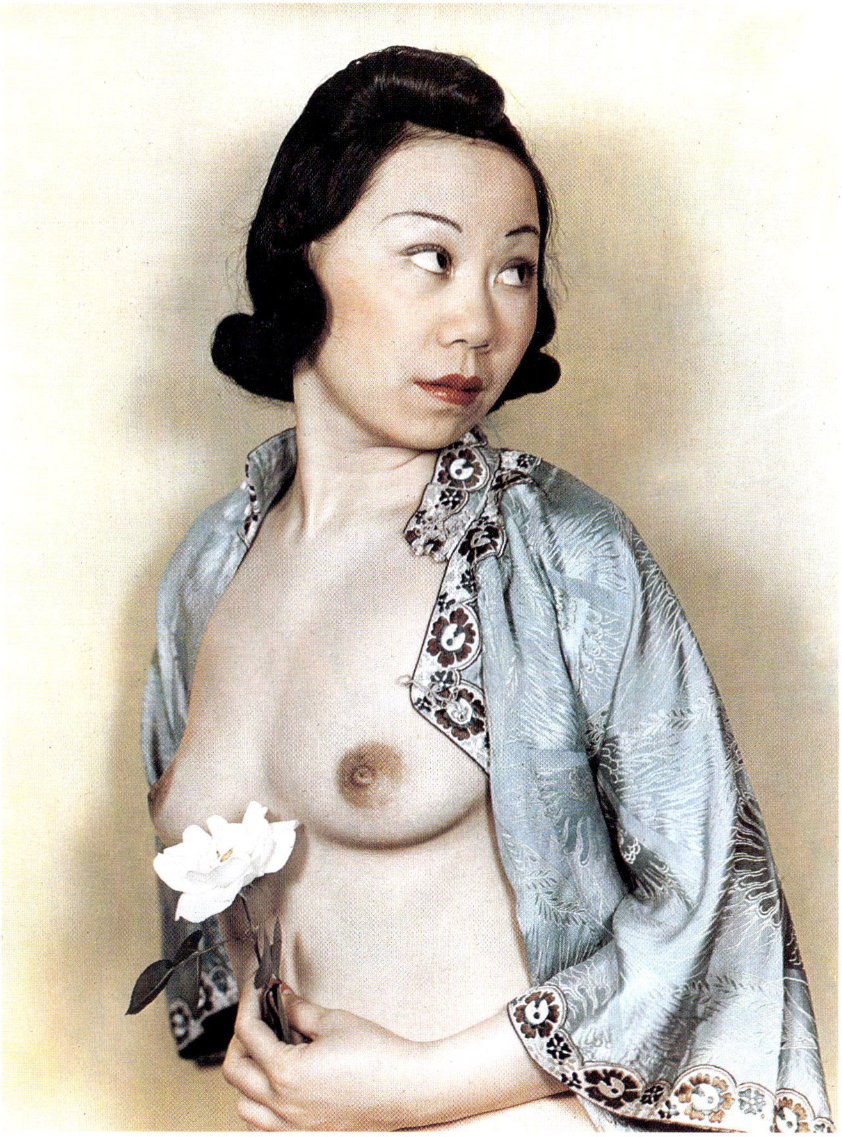

PLATE LXV (Above)
PAUL OUTERBRIDGE
Chinese Girl 1938
CARBRO COLOUR PRINT
Robert Miller Gallery, New York

Outerbridge's pioneering use of the carbro colour process ensured prints of great permanency as well as subtle colour rendition, perfectly suited to enhancing the slightly disturbing quality of these deceptively simple compositions.

PLATE LXIV (Left)
PAUL OUTERBRIDGE
Untitled c.1935
CARBRO COLOUR PRINT
Robert Miller Gallery, New York

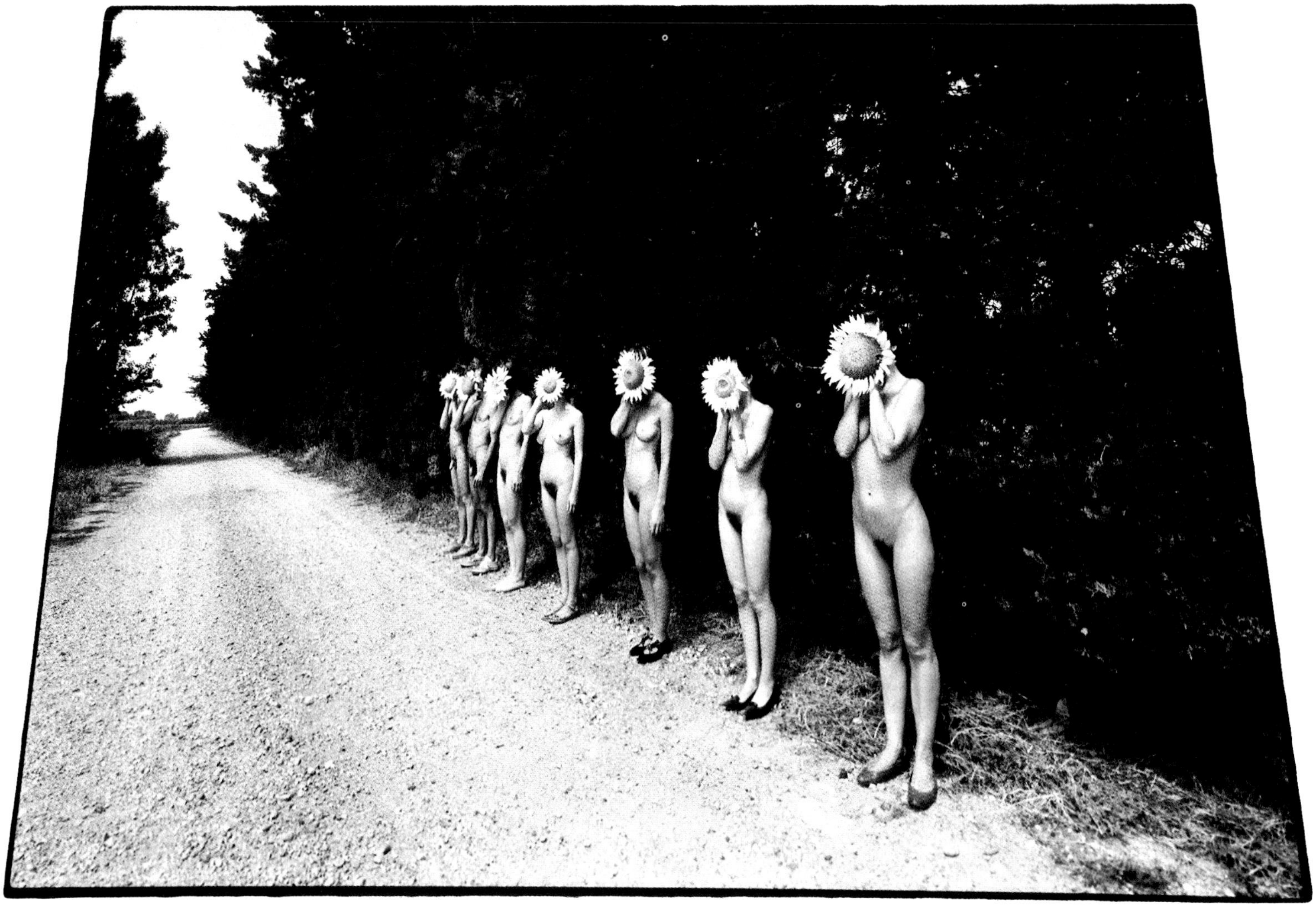

PLATE LXVI (Above)
EIKOH HOSOE
Sunflower Children. Arizona 1983
Courtesy the photographer

PLATE LXVII (Right)
EIKOH HOSOE
A Holy Maiden. Salzburg 1979
Courtesy the photographer

This picture seems to contain a tongue-in-cheek reference to the work of Von Gloeden, an unexpected but amusing allusion.

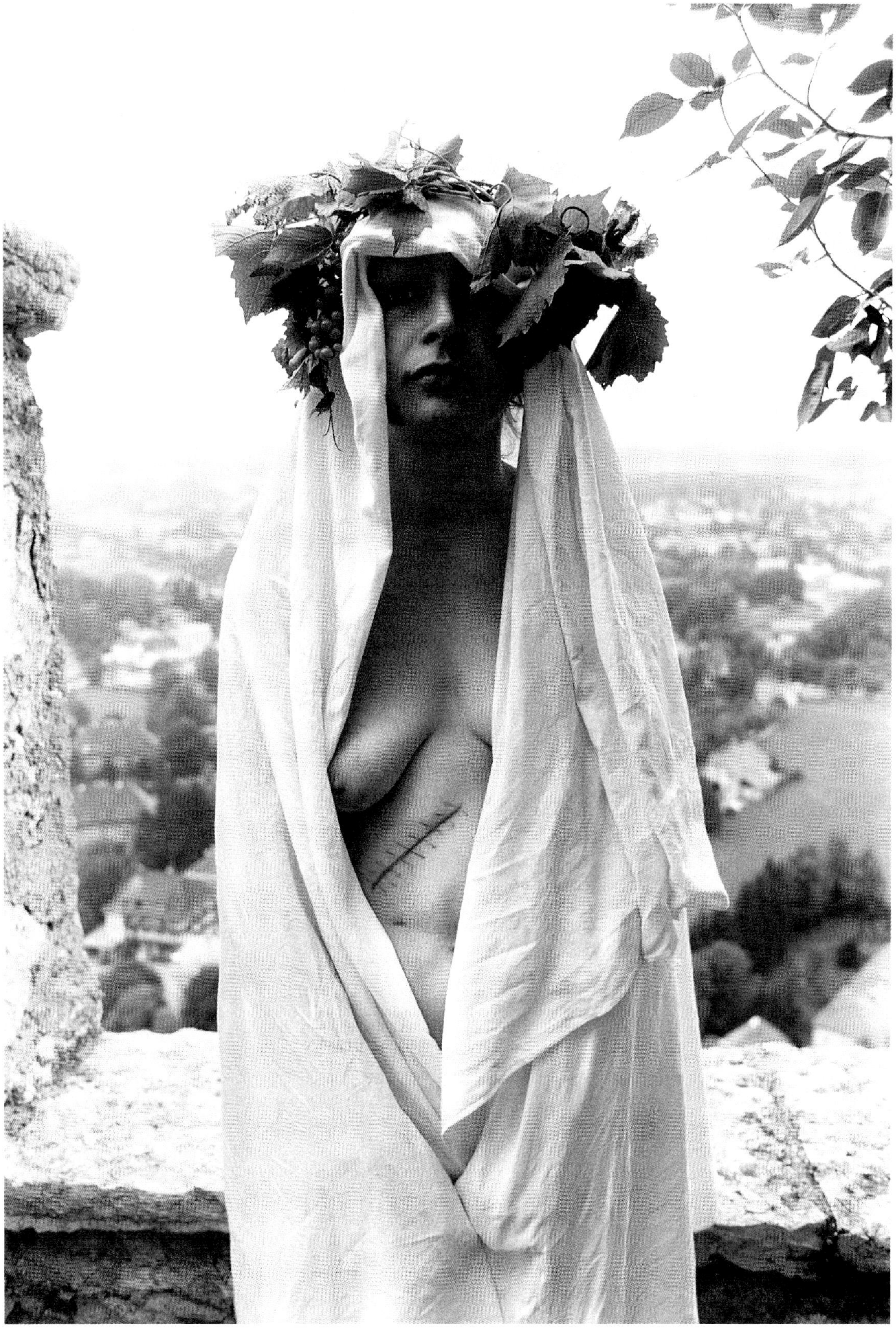

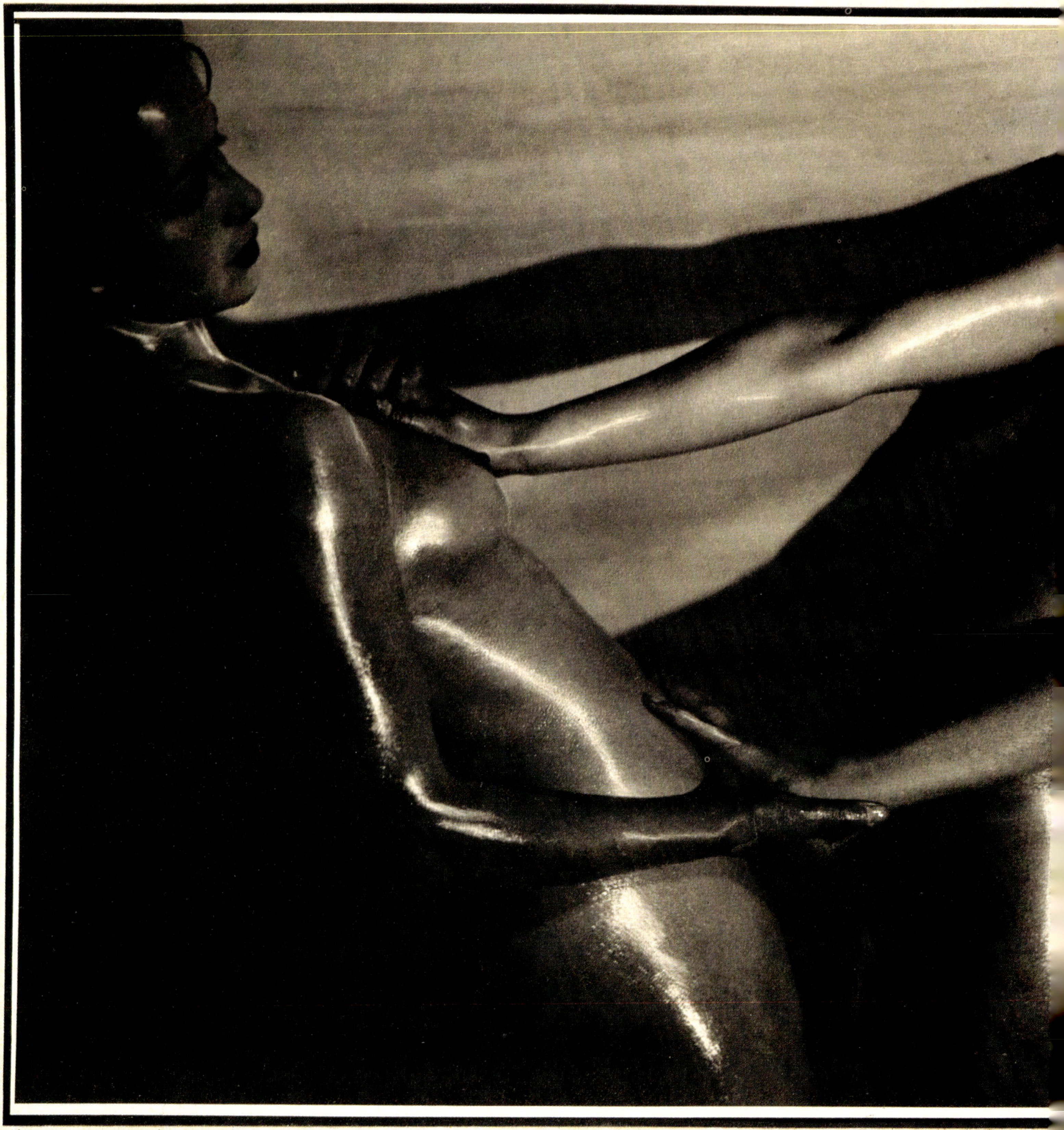

with love from Maurice
June 1945

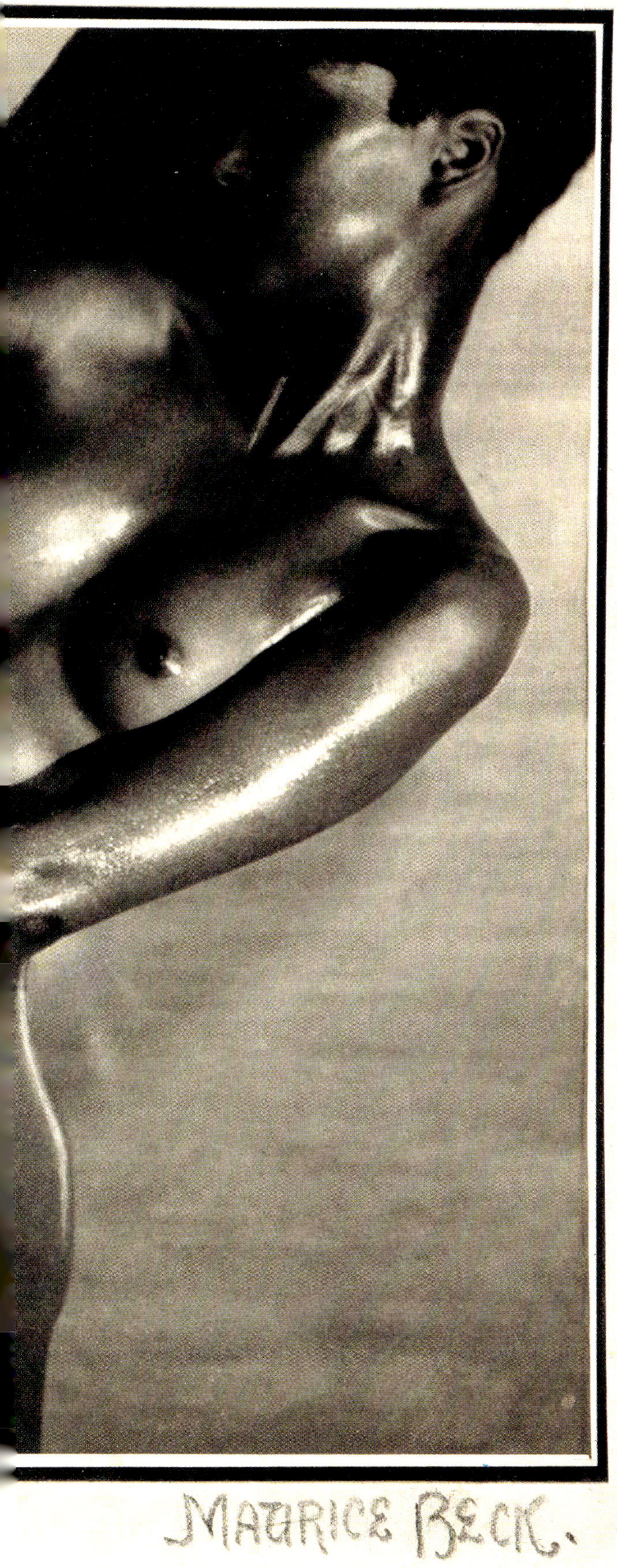

PLATE LXVIII

MAURICE BECK

Girls Wrestling c.1927 (Published in *The Graphic*, 1928)

Private Collection

In his loose partnership with Helen MacGregor, Maurice Beck was chief photographer for British *Vogue* in the 1920s. According to Cecil Beaton "they both admired the young women who resembled young boys and the young men who looked like girls. It was a 'trademark' that young sitters should be covered with oil in order to acquire a high polish before being photographed in the nude."

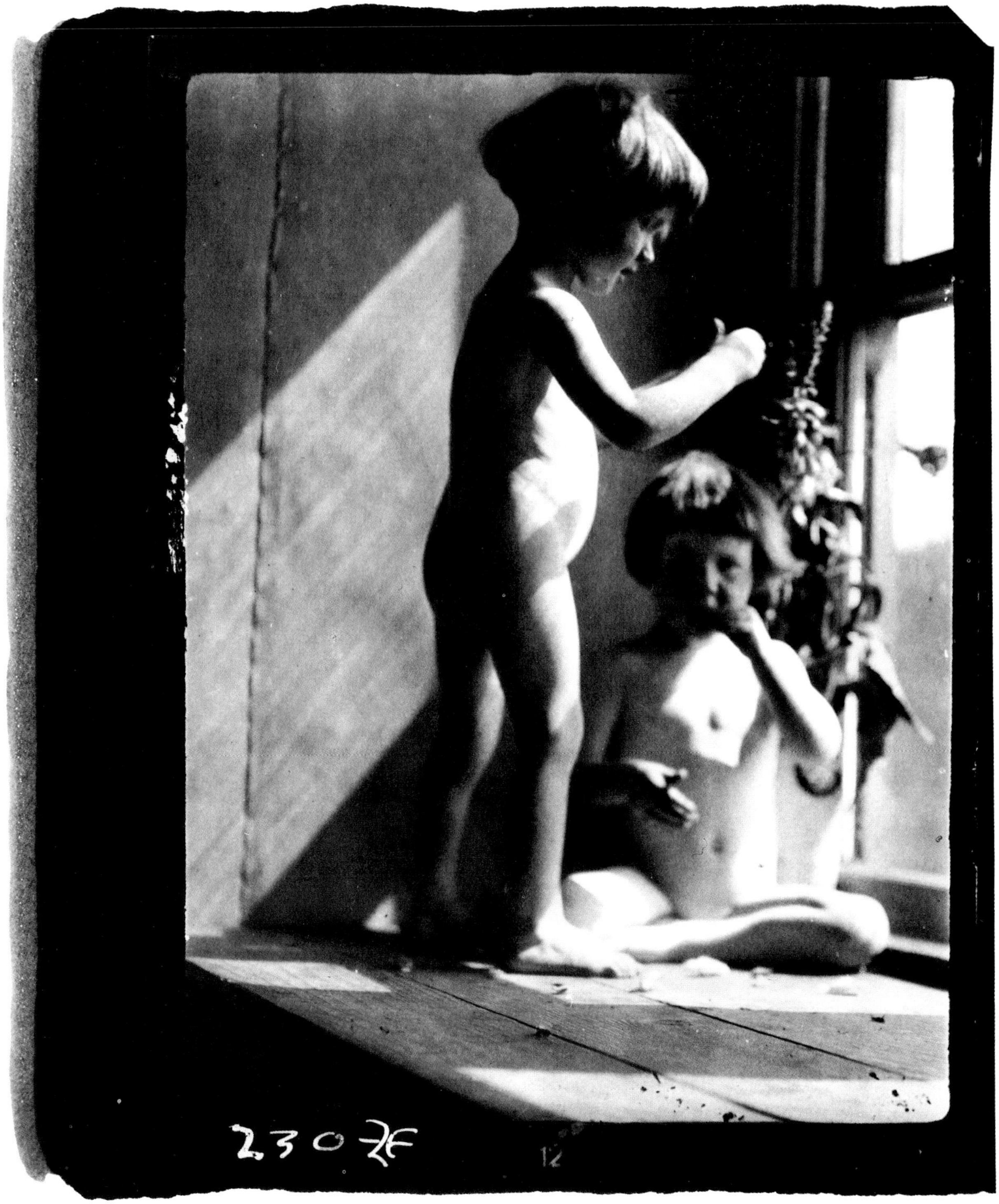

PLATE LXIX
IMOGEN CUNNINGHAM
Twins in the Window 1919
PLATINUM PRINT
Photographers Gallery, London

In 1932, Imogen Cunningham was a founder member of f/64, a group dedicated to the veracity of the sharply defined, purist image, but she soon reverted to the intimate kind of portraiture seen in these much earlier pictures.

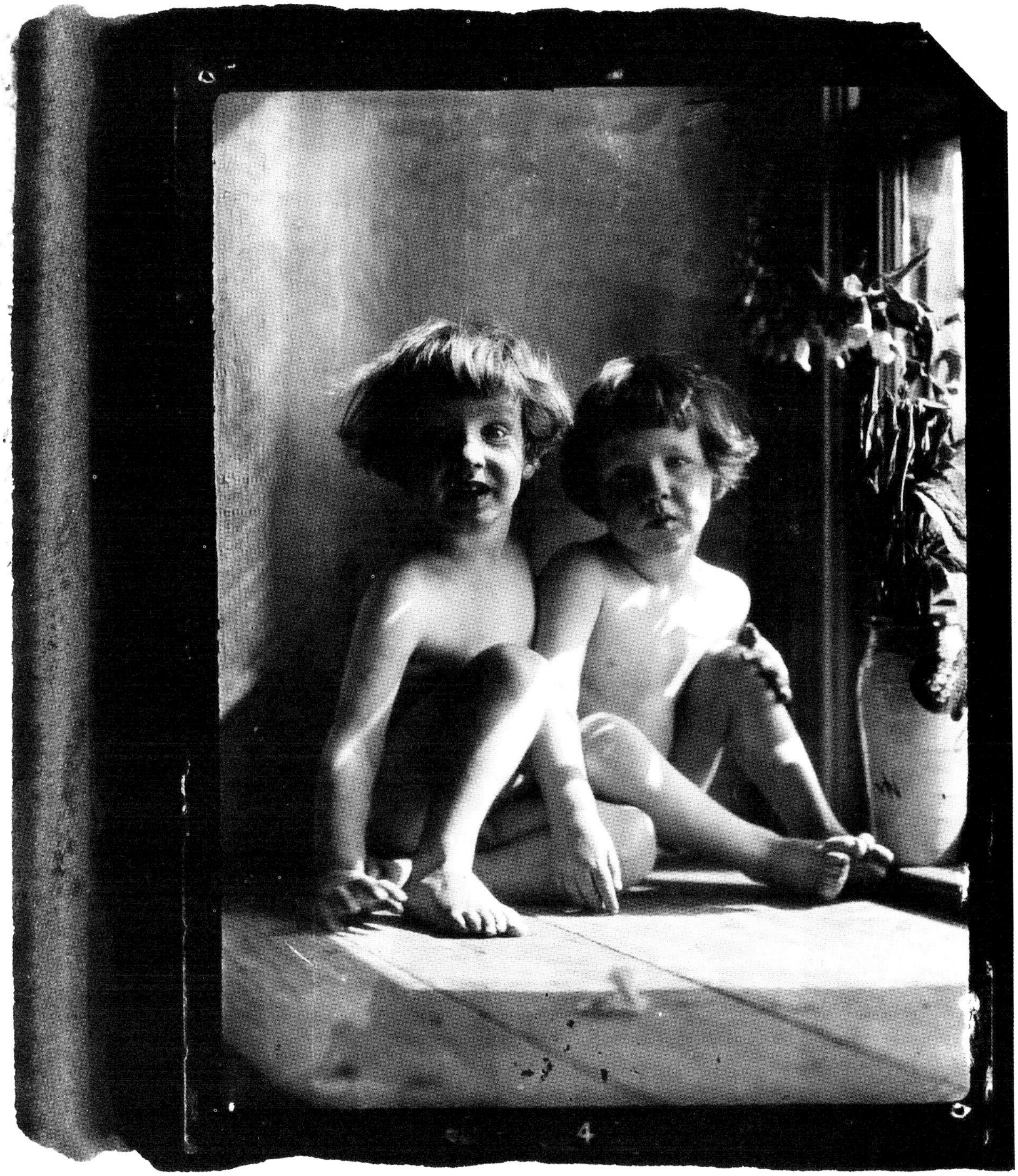

PLATE LXX
IMOGEN CUNNINGHAM
Twins Sitting 1919
PLATINUM PRINT
Photographers Gallery, London

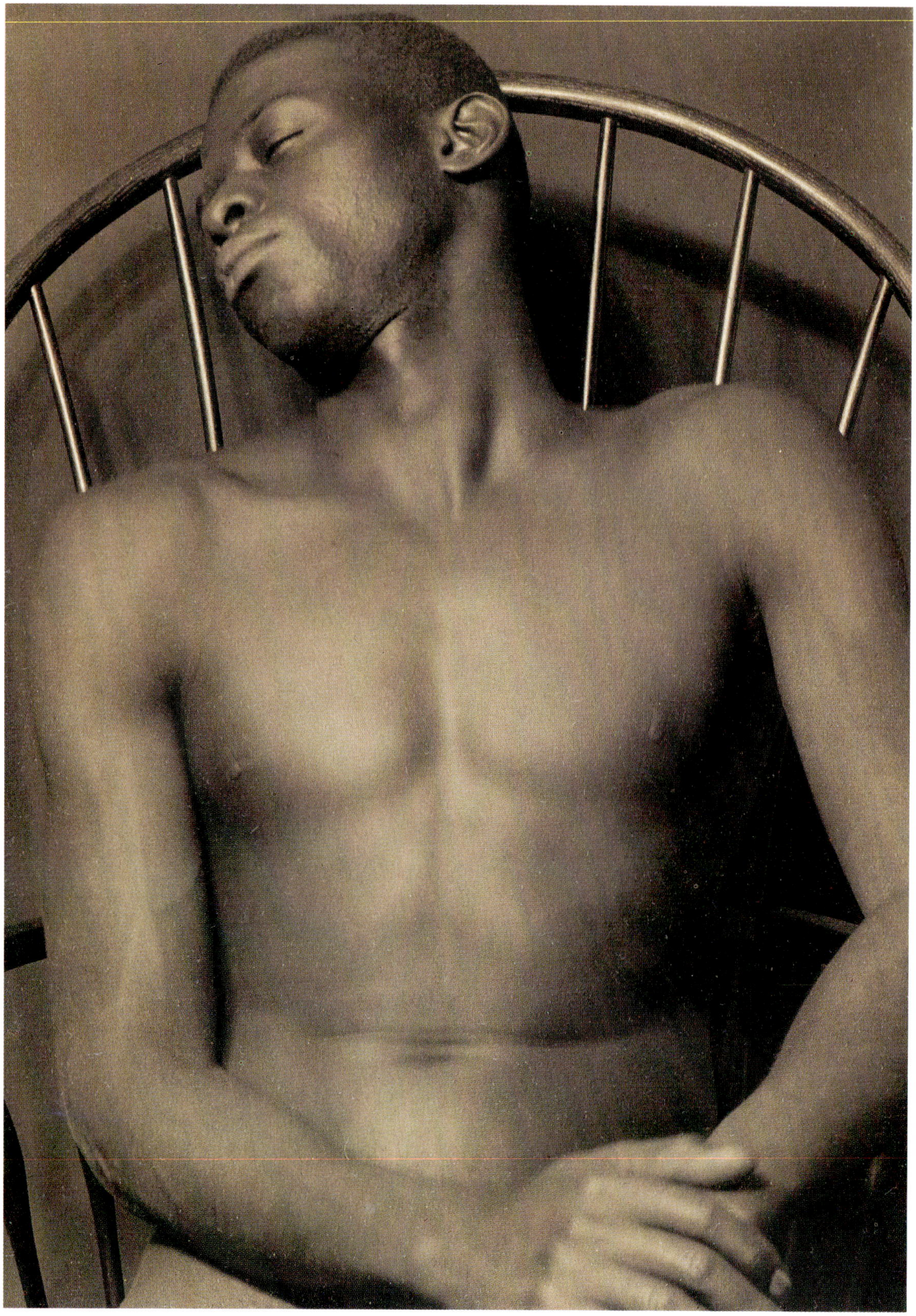

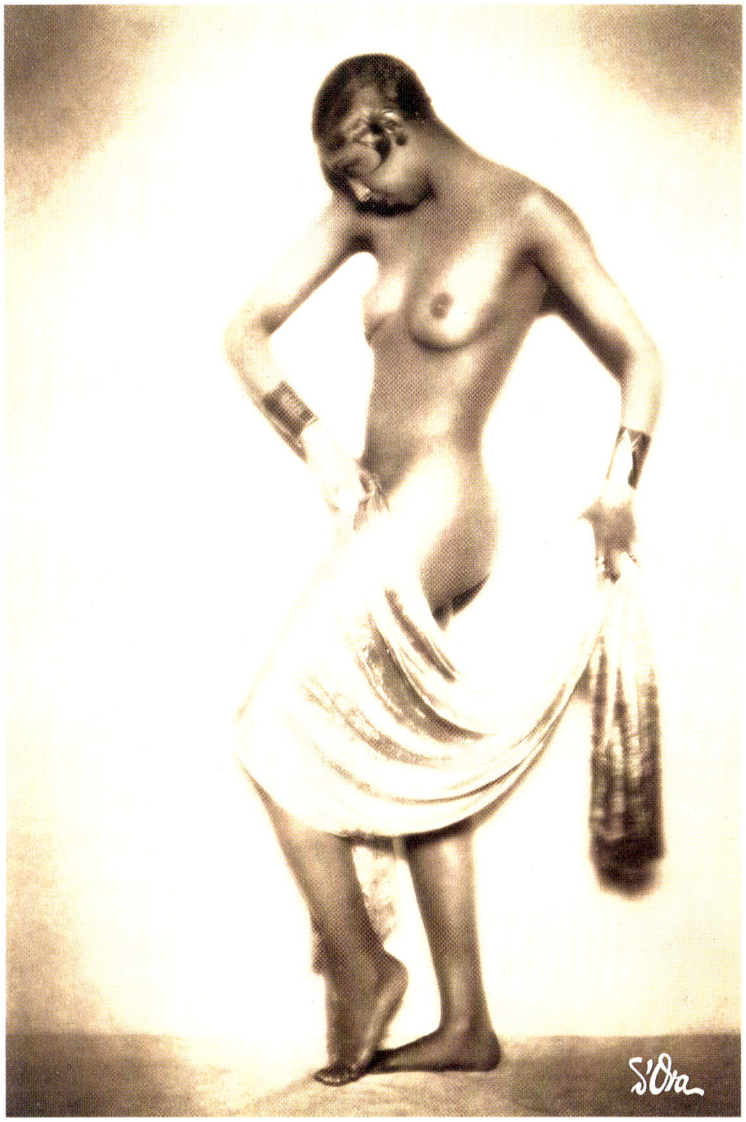

PLATE LXXII (Above)
MADAME D'ORA
Josephine Baker. Paris 1926
Private Collection

Madame d'Ora was the name adopted by a Viennese society and fashion photographer, Dora Kallmus, when she moved to Paris in 1907 and set up a studio in partnership with Arthur Benda. By the 1920s her work had become, as this photograph underlines, distinctly "moderne" in style.

PLATE LXXI (Left)
PAUL OUTERBRIDGE
Ethiopian Form 1923
PLATINUM PRINT
Robert Miller Gallery, New York

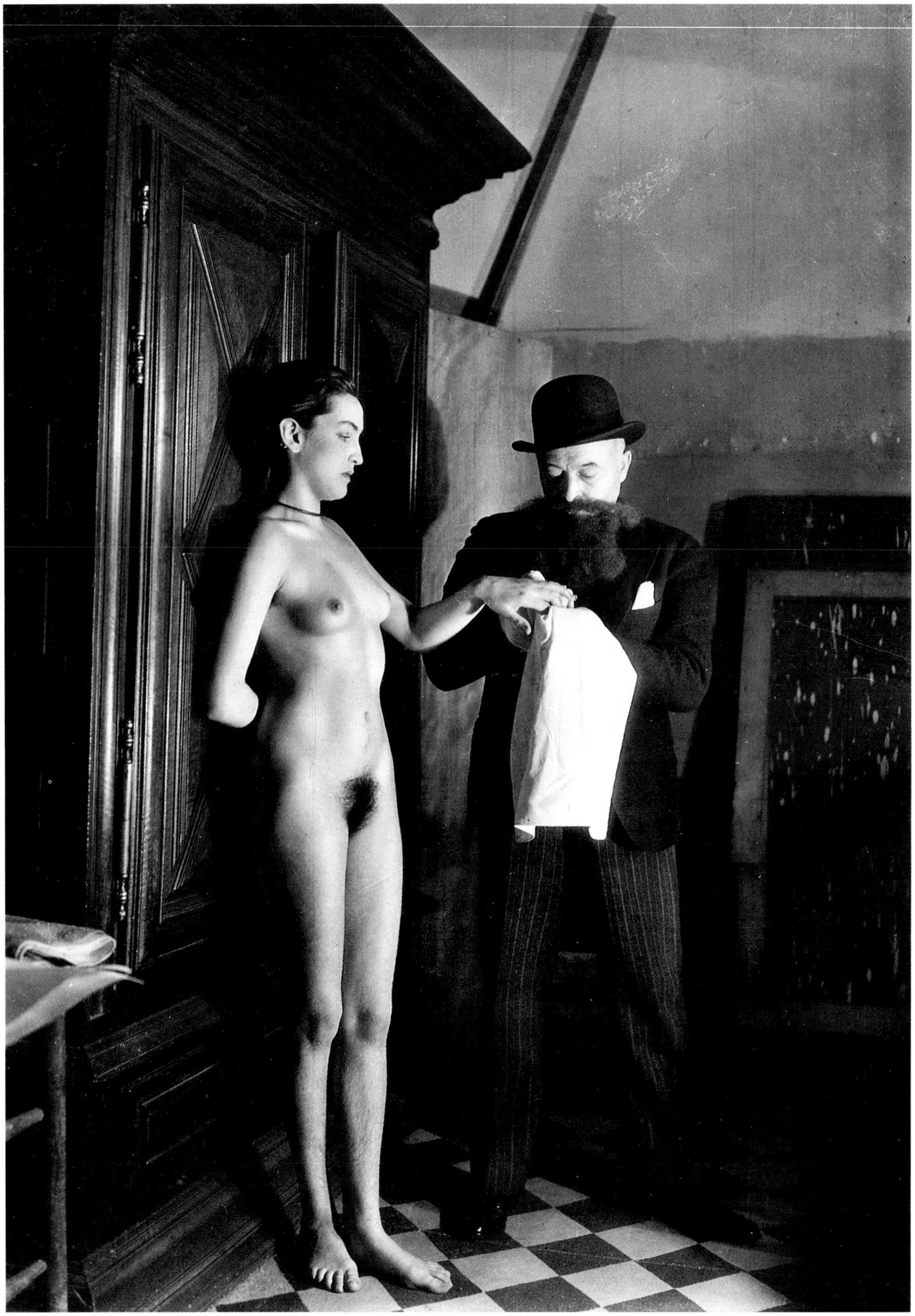

PLATE LXXIII
MAN RAY
Meret Oppenheim and Louis Marcoussis 1933
Lucien Treillard, Paris

The Surrealist Meret Oppenheim was introduced to Man Ray by Giacometti. Man Ray described her as "one of the most uninhibited women I ever met." This photograph was one of a series made in the studio of Louis Marcoussis, a Cubist painter who wore the rather unconvincing false beard to disguise his identity. It was still "a bit too scabrous for the deluxe art magazine for which it was intended" (*Minotaure*), and an alternative version of Meret alone was eventually published.

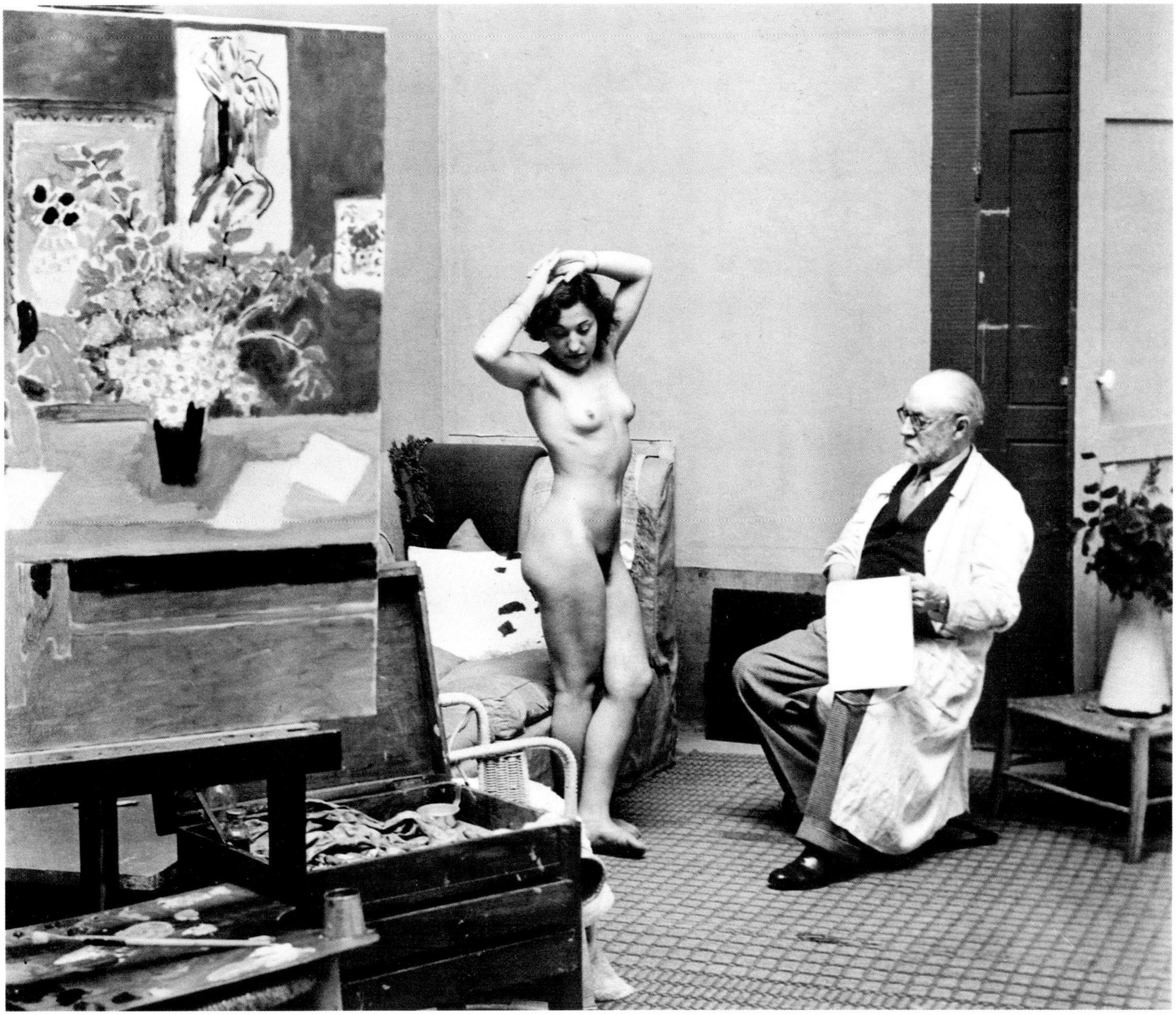

PLATE LXXIV
BRASSAI
Matisse with his model 1939
Victoria & Albert Museum, London

Though he used snapshot techniques, Brassai was never concerned with movement or with psychological nuance. He wanted his subjects motionless, self-composed, his and their concentration combining to reveal a broader truth.

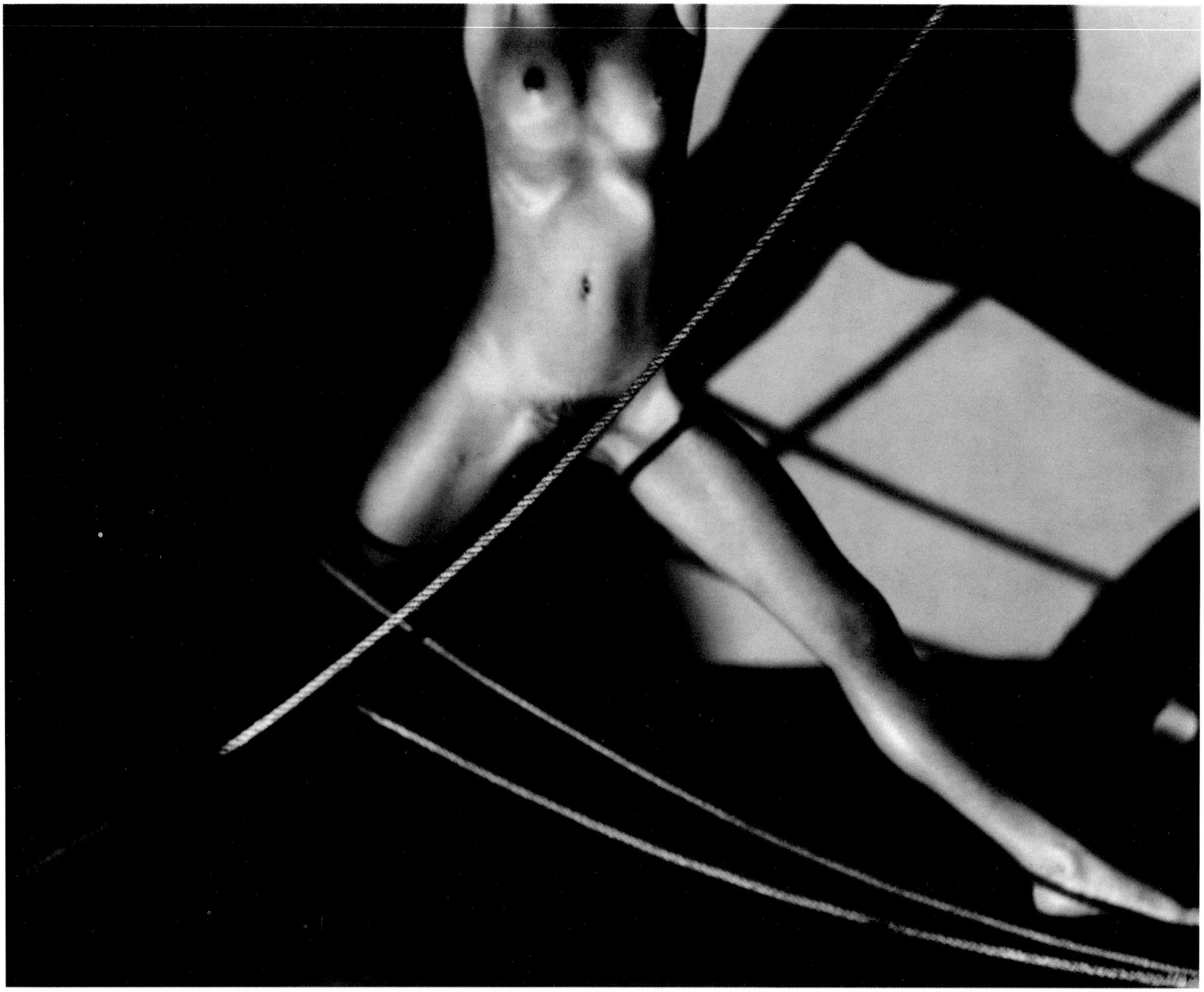

PLATE LXXV (Above)
FRANTISEK DRTIKOL
(Nudes with Ropes) 1929
Robert Miller Gallery, New York

Drtikol studied photography in Munich and his earliest nudes were strongly influenced by the German Photo-Secessionists. There was a major change in the direction of his work after his marriage in 1925 to a dancer, Ervina Kopferova, who became his favourite model. Her dance-like poses dominated his photographs thereafter, adding movement and dynamism to his Cubist forms and dramatic shadows.

PLATE LXXVI (Right)
FRANTISEK DRTIKOL
Composition (Peaceful Slope) 1929
Robert Miller Gallery, New York

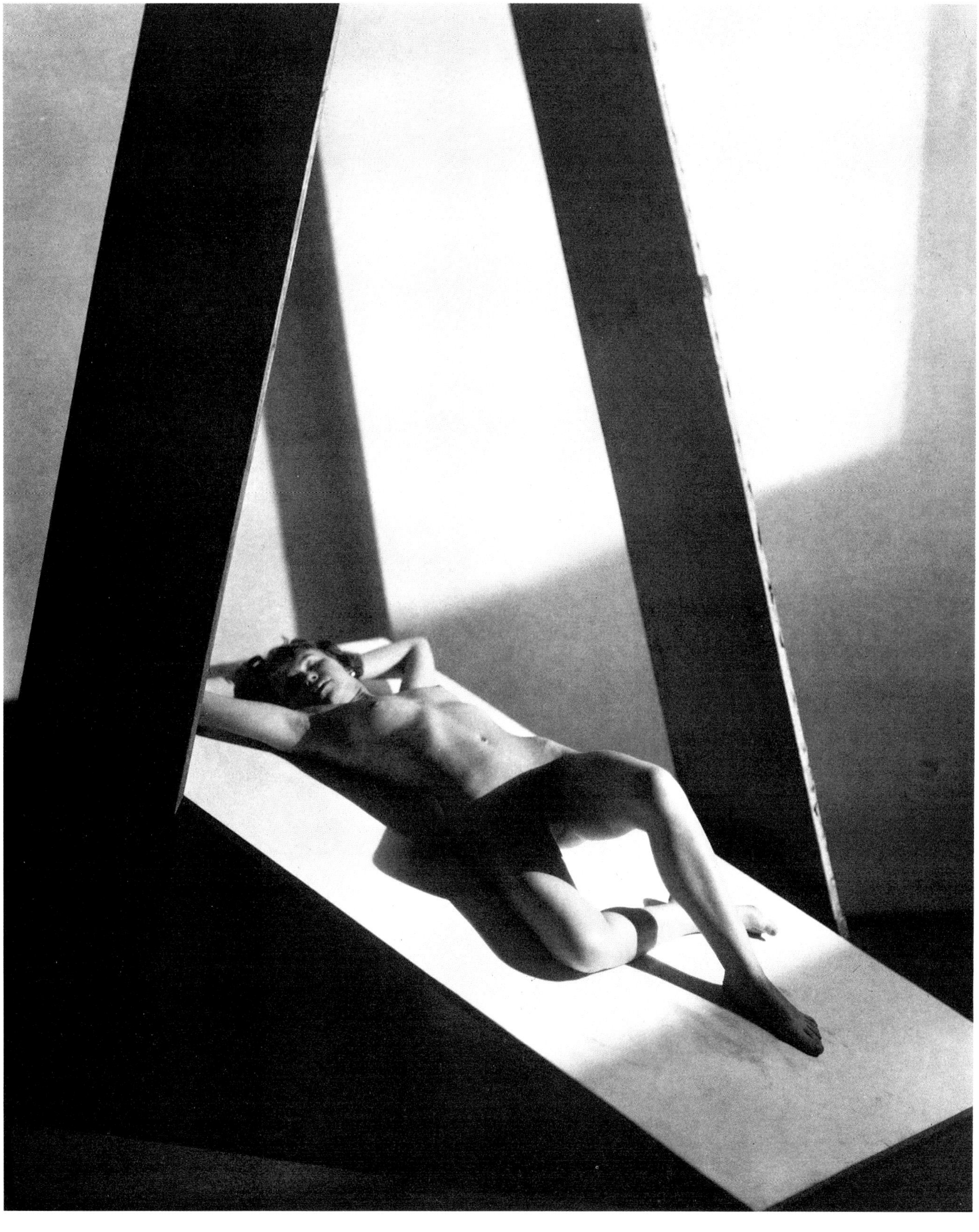

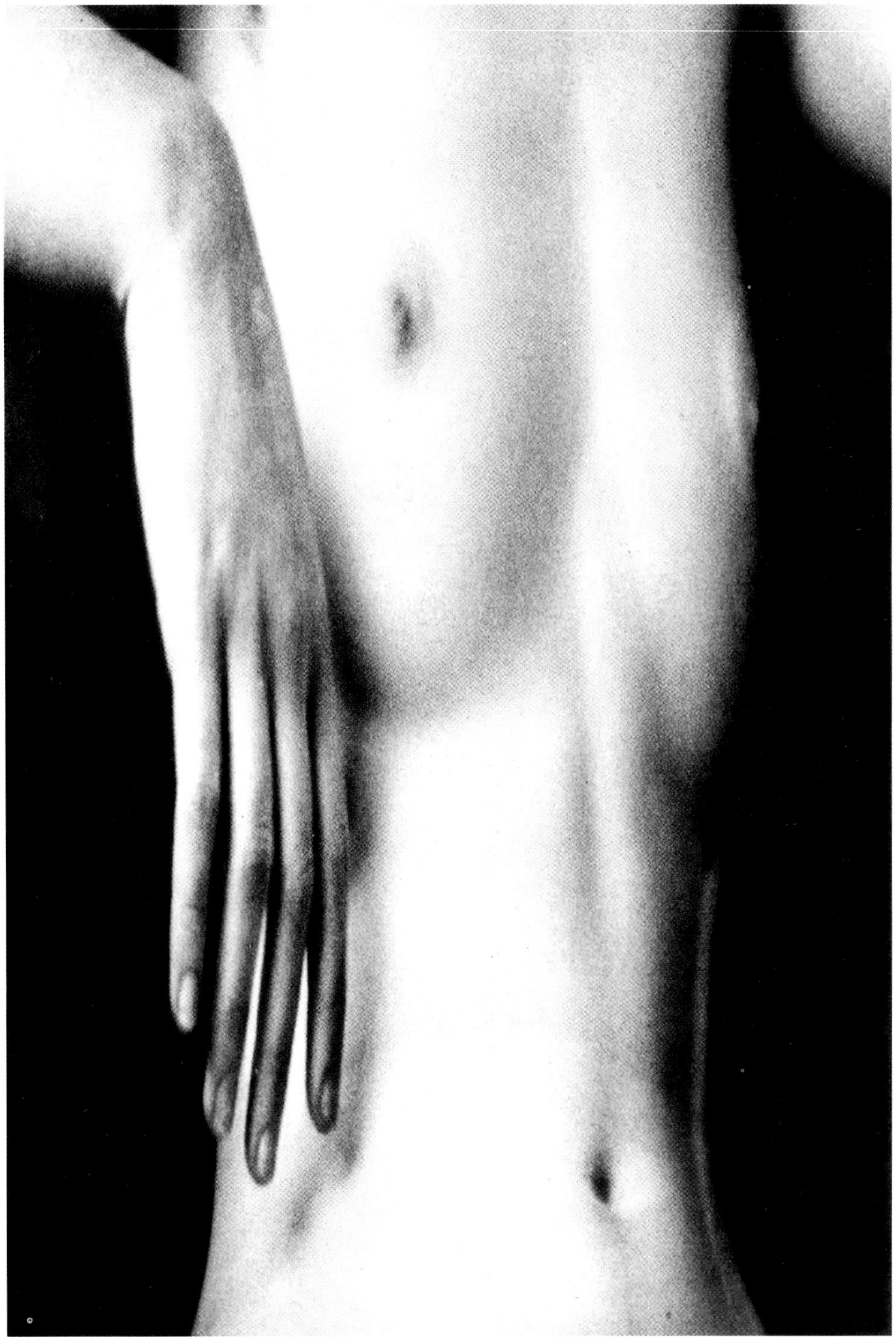

PLATE LXXVII
ANDRE KERTESZ
Distortion no. 6 1933
Victoria & Albert Museum, London

Kertész made an extensive series of nudes reflected in a distorting mirror in Paris in 1933, responding to the influence of the Surrealists, with whom he was acquainted.

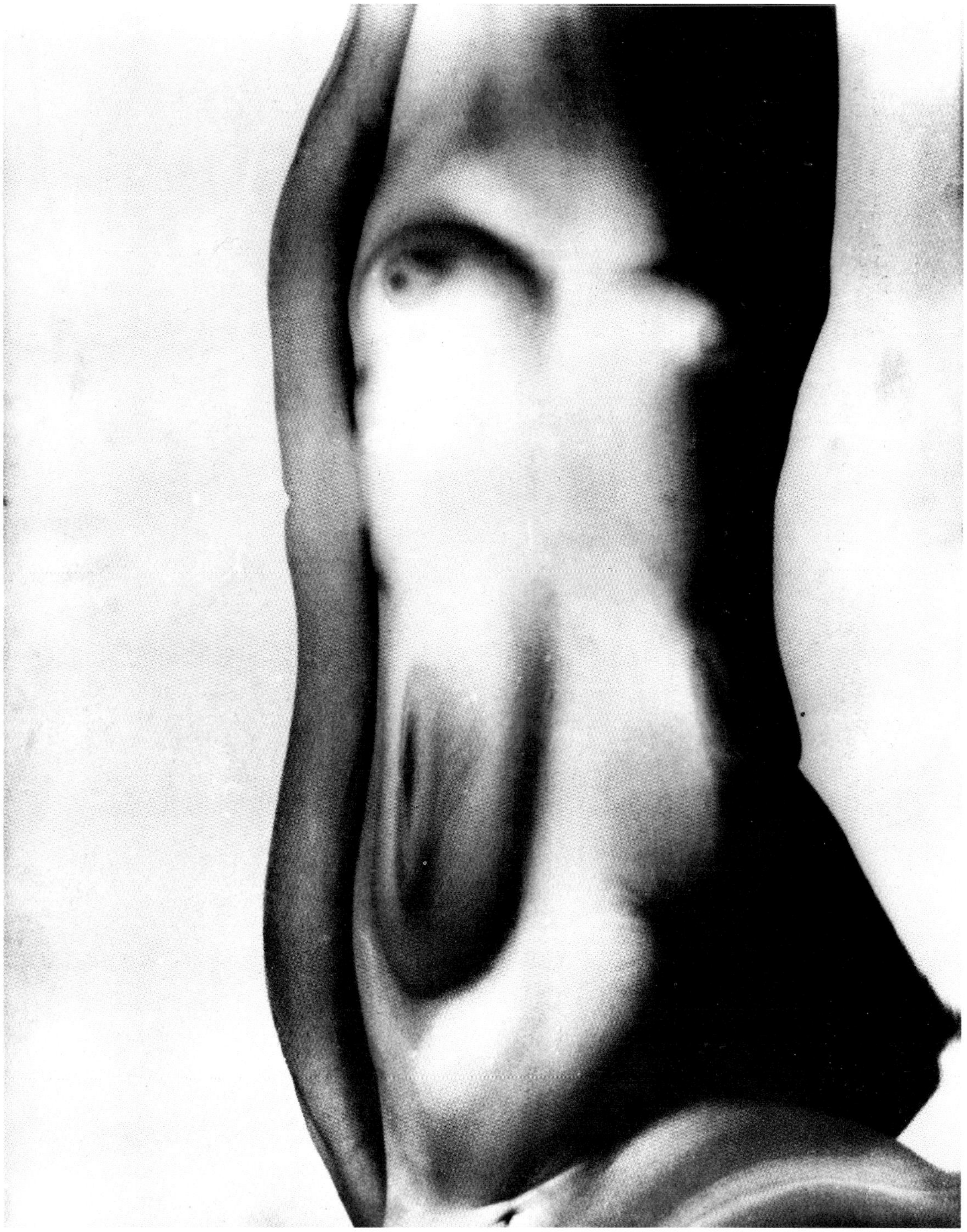

PLATE LXXVIII
ERWIN BLUMENFELD
Distorted Nude 1946
Photographers Gallery, London

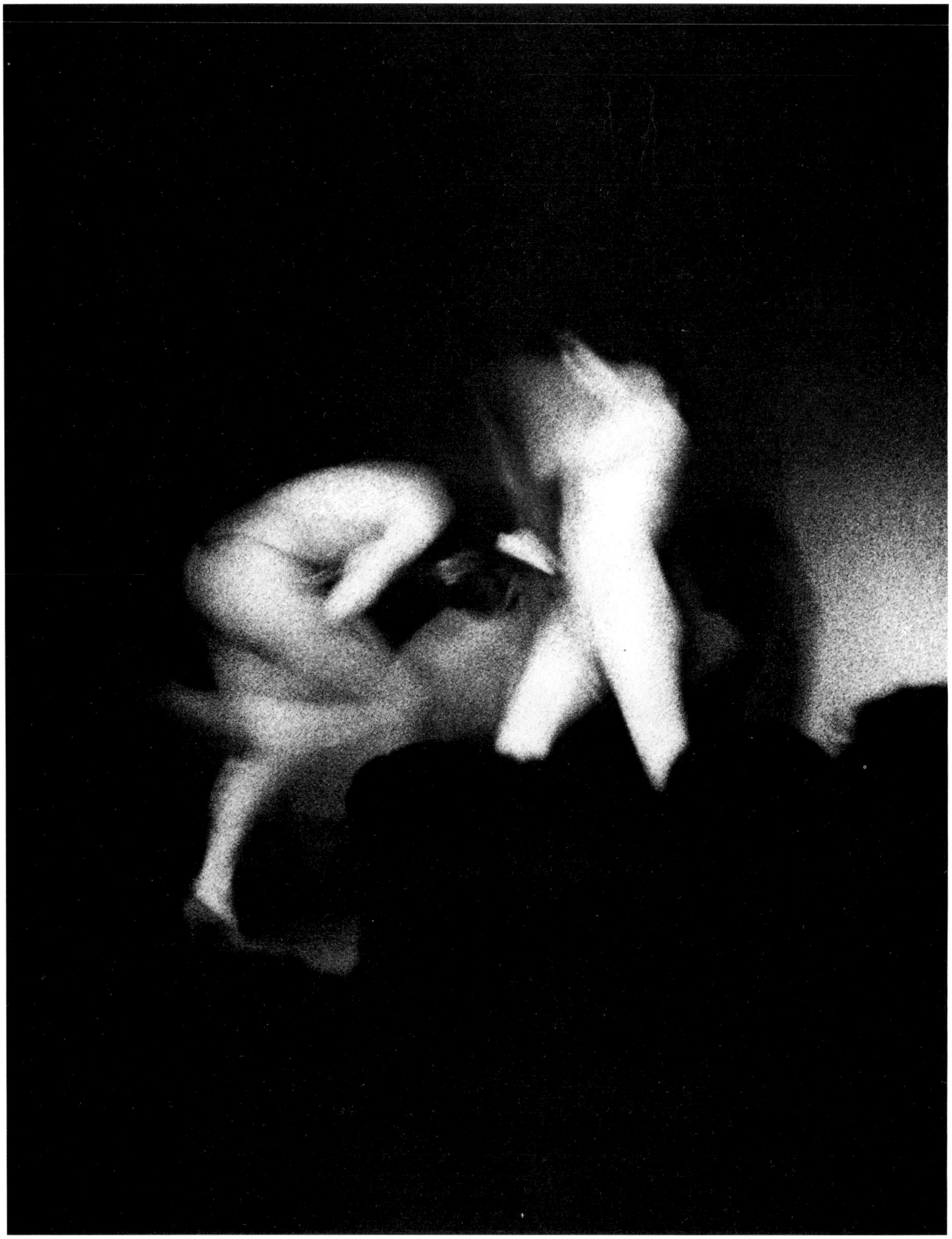

PLATE LXXIX
THURSTON HOPKINS
Bullfight – English Style:
Soho Club, London 1959
*Photographers Gallery,
London*

Thurston Hopkins was a fine photojournalist, particularly associated with the British magazine *Picture Post* in the 1950s. Reporting on a dimly-lit Soho club imposed technical restrictions which Hopkins turned to full advantage. Shooting in available light, he has produced an image full of movement that captures the seedy glamour.

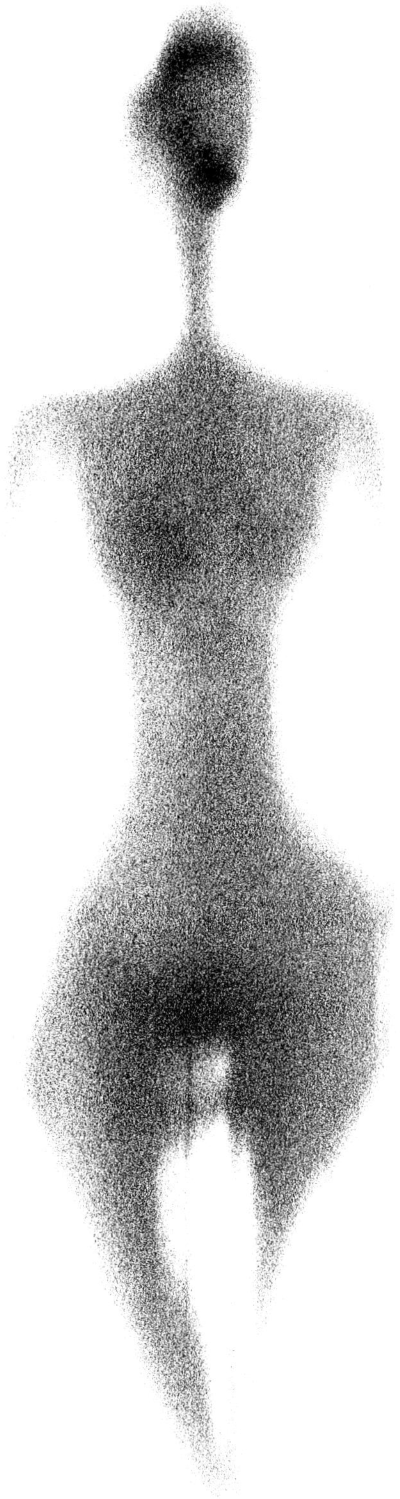

PLATE LXXX
PAUL HIMMEL
Untitled c.1960
Courtesy the photographer

Paul Himmel's photographs in the 1950s concentrated on graphic effects and movement, cleverly using harsh grain. Towards the end of his career as a professional photographer he was making a series of nudes where the forms became increasingly abstract.

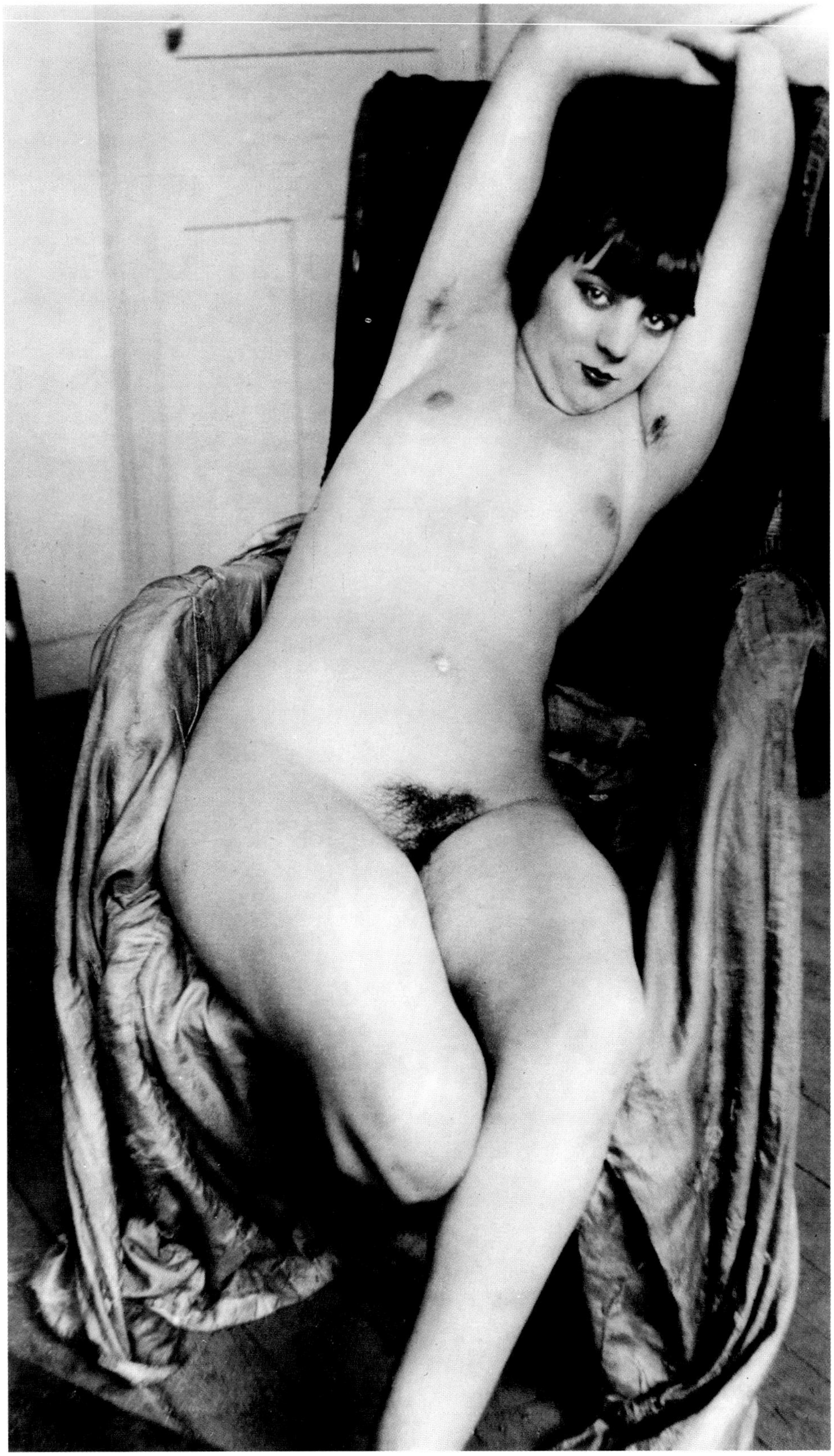

PLATE LXXXI
MAN RAY
Kiki de Montparnasse 1922
Lucien Treillard, Paris
© ADAGP 1987

Man Ray lived with Kiki for six years. They had fallen in love on the second occasion Kiki came to pose for him, as he said in his autobiography: "No pictures were taken that day; we stayed in bed all afternoon." This photograph, which is unusually straightforward for Man Ray, was one of his earliest shots of Kiki.

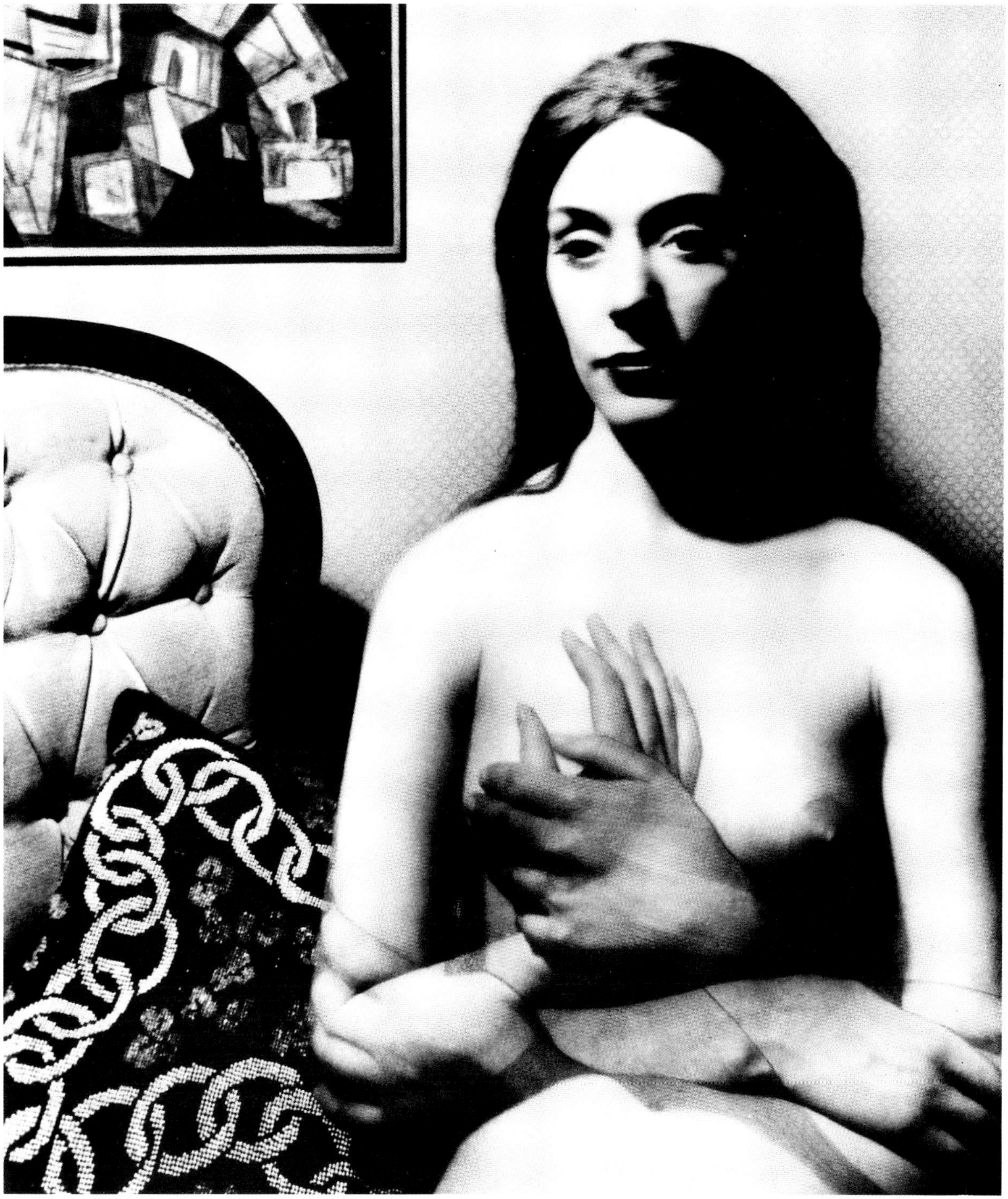

PLATE LXXXII
BILL BRANDT
Campden Hill, London 1956
Victoria & Albert Museum, London

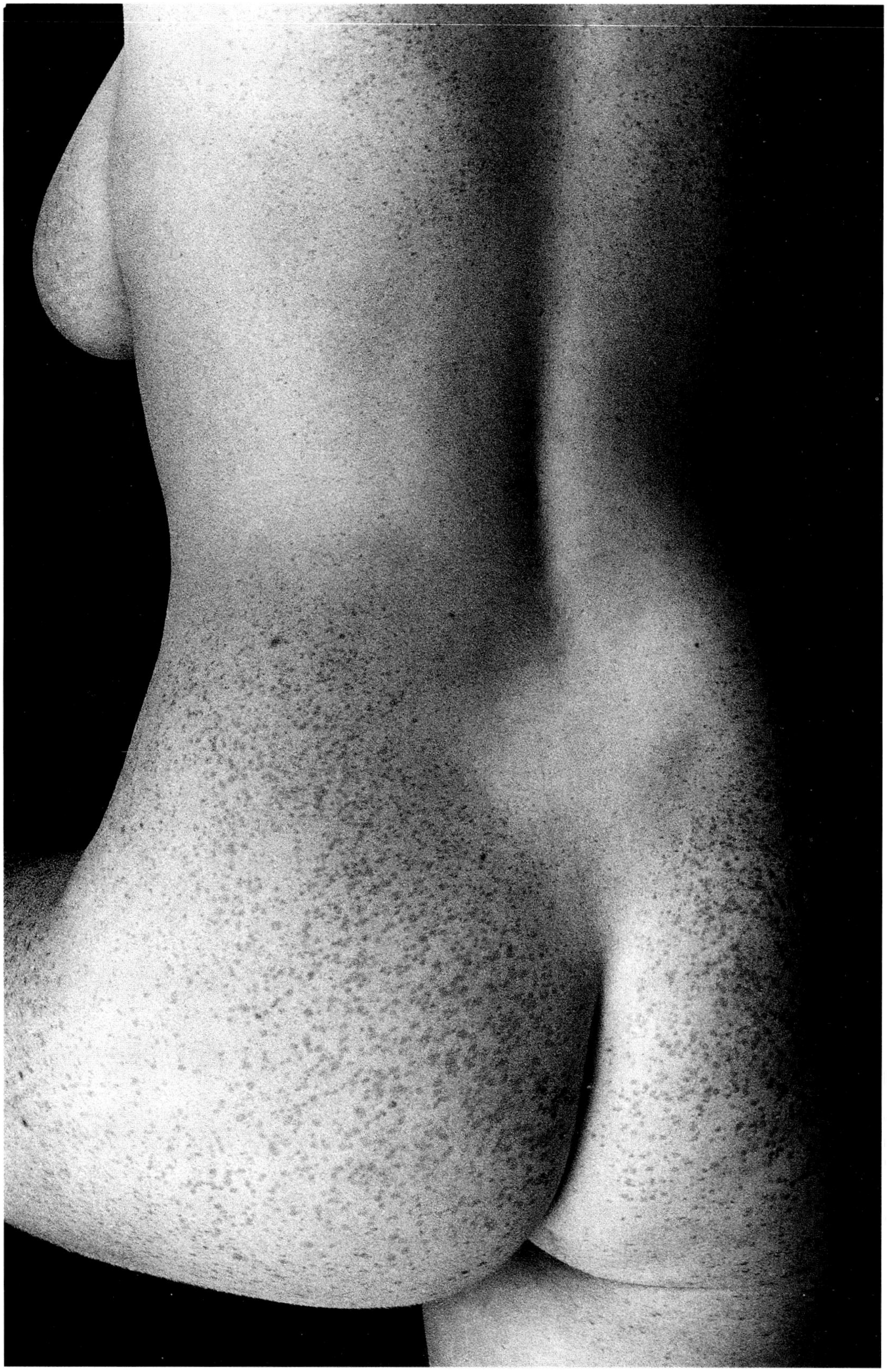

PLATE LXXXIII (Left)
RALPH GIBSON
Untitled 1984
Courtesy the photographer

PLATE LXXXIV (Right)
BILL BRANDT
London 1954
Noya Brandt

Bill Brandt's book, *Perspective of Nudes*, from which this photograph is taken, is an intriguing and inventive exercise in form and space, which combines abstract and spiritual values. It also reflects Brandt's prevailing obsessions with the mystery and sensuality of woman. In 1948, when he embarked on these nude studies, Brandt spoke of the need for the photographer to retain "the receptiveness of the child who looks at the world for the first time." This "simple pleasure of seeing" was clearly something he held to throughout his exploration of the theme.

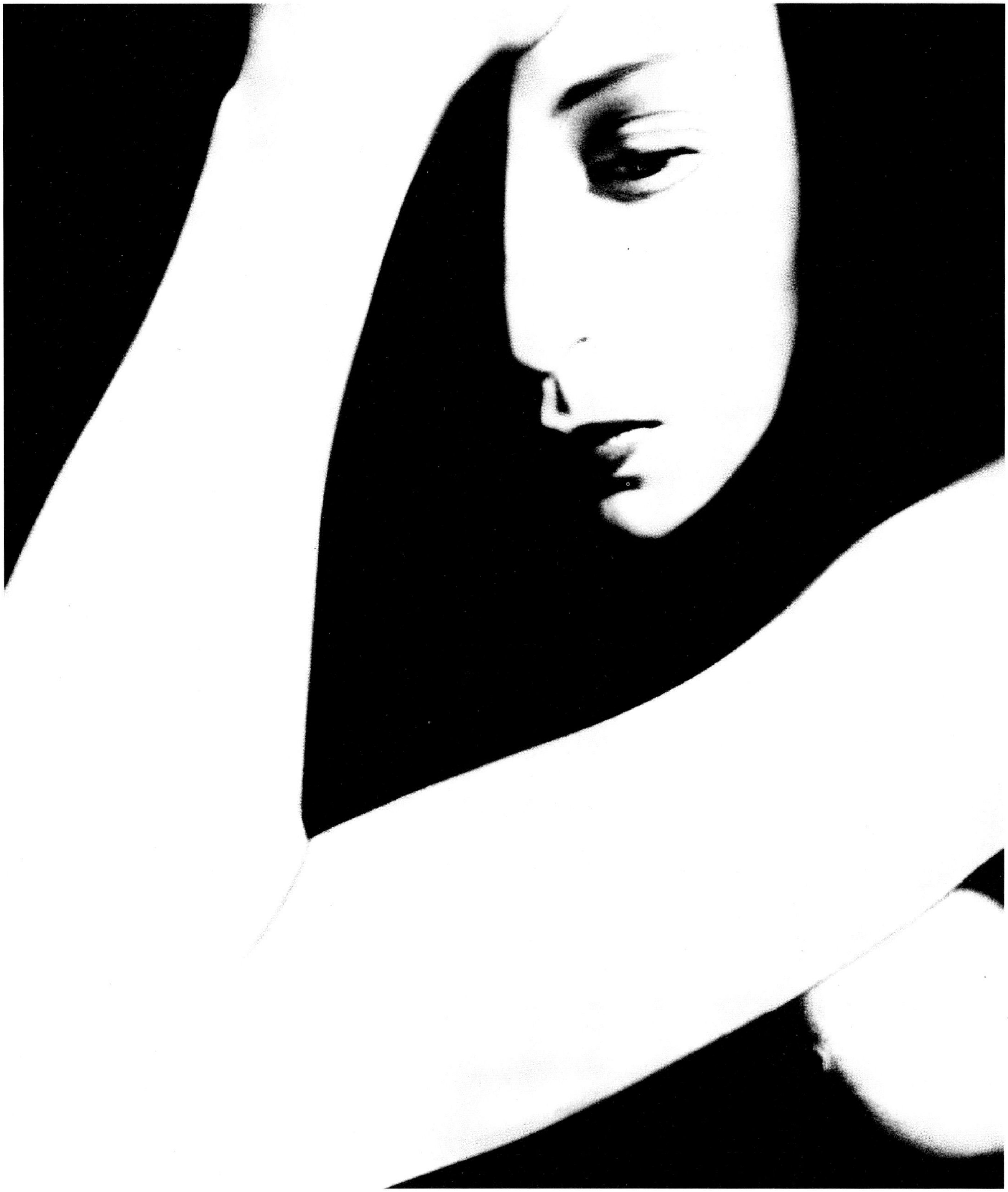

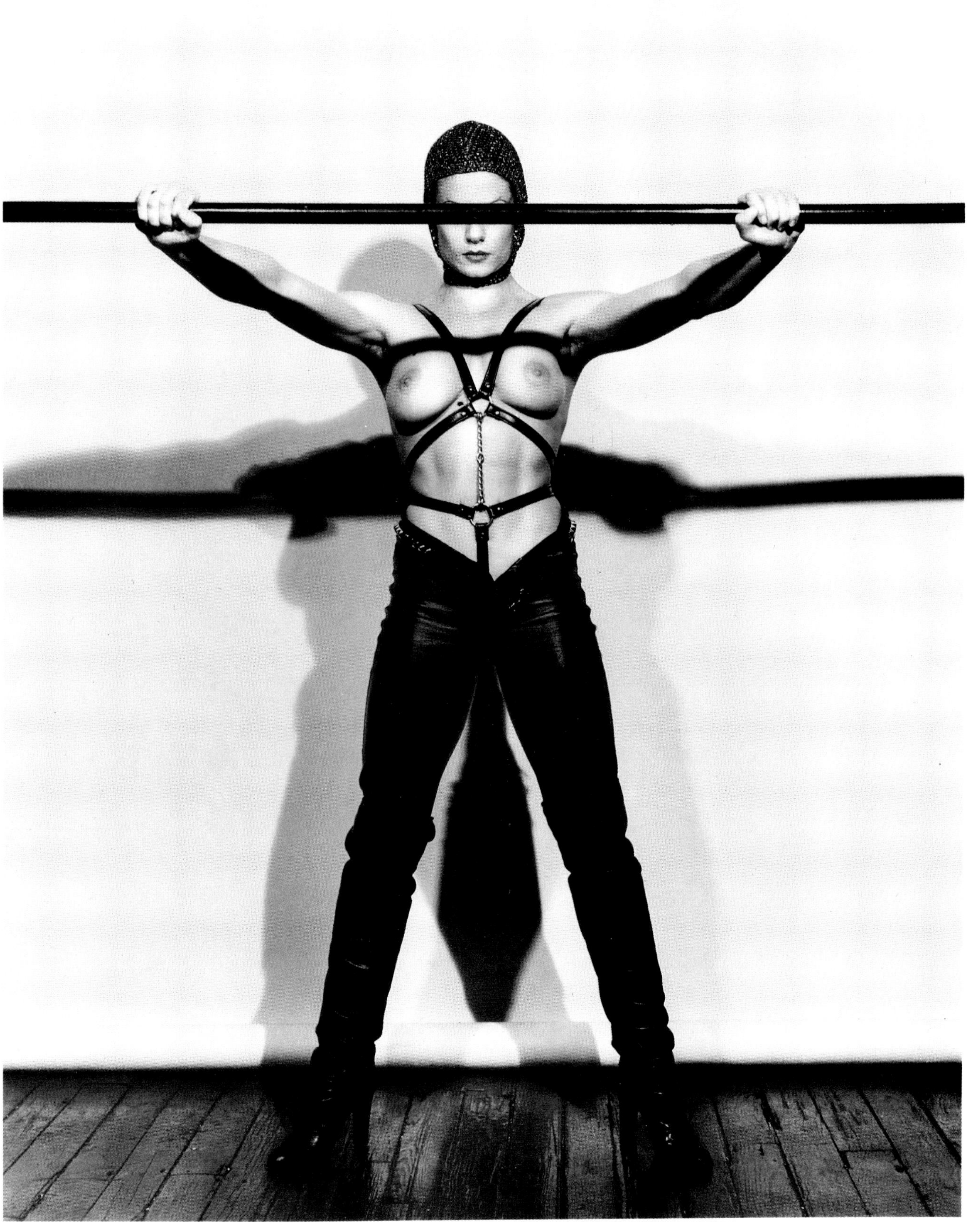

EROTICISM AND GLAMOUR

D

PLATE LXXXV

ROBERT MAPPLETHORPE

Lisa Lyon

Private Collection

Mapplethorpe's chief preoccupation in his photography has been the human body. A distinguished portraitist and still-life photographer, it is the latter discipline which is most often brought to bear on his nudes, which are at their best when conceived as cool, sharp, formally constructed arrangements.

question of the use of the bandaged body for purposes other than those of surgery. Therefore the possibility existed of utilizing bandages as elements of visual interest." Bravo, not given to analyzing his photographs, admitted a relationship with Surrealism in this photograph and others in the series: "The doctor arrived. He bandaged the woman and I took the photograph. I worked very suddenly and very rapidly, obeying a sense of surrealistic automatism." It should be added that *"La Buena Fama Durmiendo"* was made at the request of André Breton for the title page of a catalogue of a Surrealist exhibition he was organising in Mexico City.

Now the doyen of Mexican photographers, Bravo continues to include nudes among his wide-ranging interests. *"Fruta Prohibida"* (PLATE CVIII), made in 1977, was the first of a series of nudes photographed in his garden. He described the creation of this image: "At the moment she was disrobing, I asked her to pause. It is the moment she is making herself nude. Then, upon looking at the contact sheets I encountered this picture with the breast, as it is seen with the branches of the plant. It could have been the idea of a fruit. That immediately relates to the classic idea of forbidden fruit."

The nude never figured prominently in CECIL BEATON's visual vocabulary, possibly because the male nude, which reflected his sexual preference, was not openly publishable until his later years. Perhaps there was another reason, for Beaton recorded in his diary for 1924: "It's only the people who know me well now that think, or know, I'm unphysical." The nude of the Myers twins (PLATE LXXXVIII), dating from about 1967, thus qualifies as a rare Beaton image and has never been reproduced previously. In a sense it was Bailey's first selection for this book, since the original has been in his own collection for many years.

Beaton's only comparable published nude is his photograph of a black youth taken in Morocco in 1958, heroically posed with a flowing white drape covering the genitals. This contrast between masculine physique and effeminate drapery is a device taken even further in a recent photograph by HERB RITTS (PLATE CIV). Ritts, like Beaton, is a highly successful fashion photographer and his male nudes are unusual in retaining something of the fashion photographer's approach. Bailey liked this picture because of its 1930s Aryan youth character, taken to an extreme of decadent self-indulgence.

The most famous exponent of the male nude with overtly homosexual overtones was Baron Wilhelm von Gloeden, a Prussian noble who moved to Sicily, ostensibly for health reasons. Here, from his villa at Taormina, he photographed the youths of the village acting out Homeric tableaux. In fact, only his carefully draped figures were known at the time to a wider public, and it was not until the 1960s that the nudes themselves began finding their way into the salerooms and a broader audience. Von Gloeden's cousin, Wilhelm von Plüschow, also specialized in neoclassical nudes, and there were other practitioners working in a similar style in Europe. Bailey finds the fusion of classical props and naturalistic style in these pictures – and the far from noble youths – rendering the results ultimately kitsch. The one example he has chosen from this "school" was made by an Italian follower of Von Gloeden, VINCENZO GALDI (which is at least intriguingly androgynous) (PLATE LXXXVII).

Homoerotic pin-up magazines have been with us since the 1920s and few of the images in these or the girlie versions are of any interest to Bailey. He did, however, make an exception in the case of the extraordinary male nude by BRUCE OF LOS ANGELES (PLATE CIII). What Bruce Bellas did, with conspicuous success, in the late 1950s and early 1960s, was to graft the female pin-up approach on to the male nude. The photographic skills required by pin-up magazines were pretty minimal, but Bellas brought to his pictures unlooked-for talents in both composition and use of natural lighting. He worked mostly in black and white, but the image chosen by Bailey shows Bellas' intelligent use of colour. It is both an early example of an R-type print (made direct from a transparency) and immediately post-dates the lifting of legal restrictions on the inclusion of genitalia in photographs in the United States.

ROBERT MAPPLETHORPE is the most celebrated photographer of the male nude working today. He has also photographed flowers, fashion and interiors and makes incisive and revealing portraits. But perhaps his most unexpected body of work was the one hundred and nine photographs of the champion female body builder, *Lady Lisa Lyon*, published in 1983 (PLATE LXXXV). A strange vehicle for the fantasies of both photographer and model. Bruce Chatwin in his introduction to the series wrote: "Their glorification of the body is an act of will, a defiance of nihilism and abstraction, a story of the Modern Movement in reverse." Sam Wagstaff astutely pointed to a new tongue-in-cheek character in Mapplethorpe's work which *Lady Lisa Lyon* heralded, "some nonsense for a change." Mapplethorpe, whom he calls "the shy pornographer," is seen to be taking himself less seriously and, considering the ambitious variety of images in the project, with great success.

The kind of female "glamour" shot found in calendars or in tabloid newspapers is anathema to Bailey. His first attempt at shooting a calendar series, a few years ago, was not a great commercial success because he insisted on trying to get away from the usual concept of the glamour photograph. The closest thing in this collection to a glamour photograph is probably the work of JOHN RAWLINGS (PLATES XCIII and XCIV). Bailey first heard of Rawlings when he was learning the business of fashion photography as assistant to John

French: "John always thought Rawlings was the cat's whiskers." French's approach to fashion photography had much in common with Rawlings, a gentle touch with the emphasis on quiet elegance rather than drama and a predilection for natural daylight. Not only was Rawlings a very successful photographer for *Vogue* in the 1940s and 1950s, he was also highly regarded for a type of glamour photography which flourished then but hardly exists now. As a genre, it fell somewhere in between fashion and nude photography; a typical 1950s vehicle for such photographs was *Charm Photography*, a long-forgotten journal which was nevertheless a forum for the work of some of the most distinguished commercial photographers of the period.

Rawlings produced two books devoted to the nude, *100 Studies of the Figure* in 1951 and *The Photographer and His Model* in 1966. *100 Studies* was much the better of the two books, partly because of the model for all the pictures, the very beautiful Evelyn Frey, and also due to the much tighter continuity of Rawlings' photography. The two images Bailey has selected from this series were both ultimately rejected by Rawlings from inclusion in his book; this is probably because they would have violated Rawlings' extremely circumspect criteria for inclusion, which studiously side-stepped anything controversial.

Of JACQUES-HENRI LARTIGUE, Bailey once said: "It's impossible to place Lartigue in any photographic school. His unique quality must be that he has never taken a photograph for anyone but himself." To those who knew him, it seemed that Lartigue, who took his first photographs at the age of seven in 1901, would go on forever. At ninety, he was still sprightly and full of enthusiasm, but sadly he died in 1986. Bailey had been friendly with Jacques and his wife Florette since 1970. His feelings about Lartigue's photography were summed up when he wrote in 1984 of their most recent meeting: "in Paris earlier this year, at the studio I was using for fashion advertising photography. There was the usual gaggle of beautiful girls and Lartigue was snapping away. My fashion pictures were a success, they were published and instantly forgotten. Lartigue's snaps came out and will probably be around forever, because only he can turn a snap into a work of art."

Strictly speaking, few of Lartigue's photographs qualify as nudes, but it only required a slight flexibility in the rules for Bailey to nominate Jacques' beautiful photograph of his young wife Florette, taken in Paris in 1944 (PLATE I).

HELMUT NEWTON is probably the most widely respected photographer of nudes over the last decade. Before the publication in 1976 of *White Women*, his first book of erotic photographs, he had been working as a fashion photographer for more than twenty years and the restrictions imposed on him at *Vogue* and other magazines considerably influenced the development of his style. Bailey points out: "For Helmut, *Vogue* acted as a sort of Hayes Office. He was always trying to bend their rules about what was permitted in a fashion photograph. The forbidden fruit is in any case always more erotic: if it's available it's not so interesting."

Helmut Newton was born in 1920 in Berlin, where from 1936 to 1938 he assisted Yva, a well-known portrait, fashion and nude photographer. Forced to flee Nazi persecution, Newton emigrated to Australia. It was as if his natural development in Germany had been artifically cut short: later in his career his photographs would often evoke a return to his spiritual homeland. In his book, *World Without Men*, he recalled a return visit to Berlin in 1979 for the recently revived German edition of *Vogue*. Instead of staying in one of the grand hotels ". . . I felt it was more appropriate to put up in a real Berlin pension, like the one immortalized by Christopher Isherwood. The Pension

Dorian is very special: during the [illegible] period it was a famous brothel, the most elegant in town. He picked it for the party [illegible] bigwigs.

At first there was no question that Newton would push *Vogue* towards nudity, but even in the 1960s he was finding ways to circumvent the rules by introducing erotic elements into his fashion pictures. In 1971, [illegible] then at the top of his profession, he suffered a heart attack. This forced him to reconsider his future and he decided that he would only accept commissions which would allow him the freedom to develop his own ideas. The world in which he operates is one of luxury, wealth and power, a world of artifice which he prefers. His photographs since the 1970s have been widely criticized as sexist, anti-feminist and [illegible] white counter offensive against the new feminist consciousness [illegible]. His world, it is claimed, is "... represented with the cold distance of [illegible] automaton, an extension of the technology which [illegible] becomes an object." More recently Newton has [illegible] backdrops for his erotic photographs in [illegible] approach, isolating his models against plain studio [illegible] PLATES [illegible] and [illegible] were from Newton's [illegible]. When giant enlargements of these were exhibited [illegible], a feminist group attacked the [illegible] with green paint. The special object of their anger was [illegible] with its connotations of bondage.

Today, [illegible] regards Newton's work as pornographic [illegible] that he is in fact exploiting his models [illegible] and his photographs depict only adult, [illegible] women who show neither weakness nor doubt [illegible] his personal obsessions out into the public domain, in a social climate which he was partly responsible for creating. Newton is always concerned with making his nudes look beautiful. He says, "I've seen nudes that are not beautiful and at times they may be valid photographs, but they are not the kind of thing I want to do." And about his models he wrote: "I want a woman who has personality, who is the real thing. She may have a less than perfect body because a perfect form is not interesting by itself. In fact, it is a turn-off. To me, imperfections are much more attractive."

Newton credits the sympathetic editors of French *Vogue* for allowing his work to develop along the lines that it did in the 1960s and Paris continued to be the most fertile breeding ground for chic erotica. JEANLOUP SIEFF (PLATES LXXXVI, XCVII and XCVIII) was born and works in Paris. Since the late 1950s he has been highly regarded as a fashion photographer and is also esteemed for his nudes. There, any comparison with Newton ends, for Sieff, who Bailey also regards as "one of the really great photographers" is "so very French." Bailey is right, though the "Frenchness" that makes all Sieff's work so distinctive is a difficult quality to define. One of Bailey's selections (PLATE XCVIII) is a recent fashion shot Sieff made for *Amica* magazine. The commission was for a colour photograph and, when the magazine had what it wanted, Sieff shot an alternative version in black and white for his personal satisfaction. By way of underlining Bailey's admiration for this image, it might be noted that he chose the same photograph for inclusion in his fashion retrospective, *Shots of Style*, at the Victoria and Albert Museum in 1985. Sieff's nudes have been included in the many books and articles devoted to his work since 1962 and monographs devoted entirely to nudes were published in 1980 and in 1986, the year of his major retrospective at the Musée d'Art Moderne in Paris.

PETER LINDBERGH is one of the newer names in fashion photography and is also now based in Paris. With great stubbornness he insists on shooting nearly all his fashion series in his preferred medium of black and white: to succeed in this at a time when fashion magazines are almost entirely orientated towards colour is a considerable achievement. He has also held out for the kind of settings which he can shoot as a sequence to be organized as sequential spreads around which he has woven the threads of a storyline. The relatively few nudes he has shot tend to be singular situations which do not present an opportunity for introducing his interest in narrative, but, as Bailey's selections show (PLATES [illegible] and [illegible]), they retain the powerful and gritty glamour of his *Vogue* pictures.

Since Bailey's own commercial pursuits centred for so long on fashion photography it is not surprising that several of the photographers whose work he particularly admires are colleagues from the same field. South African born BARRY LATEGAN has been a friend since he moved to London in the 1960s. For nine years he was based in New York, latterly concentrating on television commercials as much as stills, but in 1987 Lategan made a welcome return to London. He brought with him two photographs from a series of nudes on which he has been working for three years. They had been specially requested by Bailey for inclusion in this collection and it is typical of Lategan's meticulous perfectionism that the prints arrived beautifully printed and mounted within an embossed presentation box. The works themselves do more than live up to expectations (PLATES [illegible] and [illegible]). Although he has built up a formidable reputation as a fashion, beauty and portrait photographer, few of Lategan's nudes have ever been published previously, and to many these perfectly realized pictures may come as a surprise. Apart from the tonal solidity of the printing, they do not at first sight bear a close relationship with Lategan's fashion photographs, though it will be clear that he has striven to portray the nude form in terms of beauty and elegance, characteristics with which all of his work is imbued.

When, as is Lategan's intention, this series is eventually published, it may well be hailed as his most original contribution to photography so far. The conspicuously dark tonality evident from this small preview is carried right through the series, building a quiet and contemplative atmosphere which is typical of their creator. Lategan first arrived in London at the height of 1960s zaniness, but even then his work for *Vogue* stood apart from the general trend, painstakingly conceived and carried out, and seen with a cool, slightly detached but still incisive eye.

Having decided it would be invidious to include his own work in the fashion photography retrospective he selected for the Victoria & Albert Museum, Bailey was criticized for the omission. Bowing to popular demand he has chosen four of his current favourites on this occasion, and patiently awaits criticism for the opposite reason! The four photographs (PLATES II, XCVI, CVII and CXXIV) are all relatively recent, and relate to those published in *Nudes 1981-1984*, a book which came as a shock to those who expected more in the vein of his hugely successful *Trouble and Strife*. Any pretension to glamour is banished: if Bailey was preoccupied with surface values in *Trouble and Strife*, here he is determinedly peeling away the surface to reveal more of himself. Most of the pictures are, like Lategan's, printed very dark, which, as Bailey explained, was because "I wanted these pictures to have mystery . . . You have to look at the image rather than just glance at the image: the darker the image, the more you look into it." The image of the girl on the car (PLATE CVII) also has mystery, but of a different, less crepuscular kind. Bailey likes it "because of its filmic quality" and the feeling of arrested action and grainy.

indistinct appearance does indeed suggest a blown-up still frame from a movie.

Bailey has been painting and drawing since childhood, in fact art was the only subject in which he excelled at school. Considering how prolific he is in both still photography and television commercials his continued prodigious output as a painter is extraordinary and may well come as a surprise to many people since his paintings are kept private and have never been publicly exhibited. On rare occasions he has incorporated painting with photographs; the portrait of his wife, Catherine, is an example of this mixing of media, and is reproduced here for the first time (PLATE XLVI).

While painting was Bailey's favourite scholarly pursuit, most of his spare time as a child was spent in the cinema, which he visited three times a week. His early dreams were ones of Hollywood and it is easy to understand his continuing admiration for the accomplishments of such great Hollywood stills photographers as Clarence Sinclair Bull and George Hurrell. He was eager to include in the book stills which typified the publicity stills approach, while realizing that Hayes Office rulings, first enforced in 1927, meant that such material was scarce.

Bailey eventually found three pictures of this kind which greatly appealed to him. The still from the film *Bright Lights* (PLATE LXXXIX), taken by an unidentified MGM studio photographer in 1925, is a faithful record of the opulent excesses of the set designer, the renowned illustrator and decorative designer Erté. Erté began his career in fashion, sketching for the Paris couturier Poiret and designing covers for *Harper's Bazaar*. He only worked briefly in Hollywood, mainly for director King Vidor, having previously gained considerable experience in realizing his theatrical fantasies as designer for the Folies Bergère in Paris.

PLATE LXXXVI
JEANLOUP SIEFF
Voilette, Paris 1985
Hamilton's Gallery, London

Sieff's best work has always been in black and white. The examples here (see also PLATES XCVII and XCVIII) clearly show his feeling for chiaroscuro and his love of dense blacks, which bring a graphic strength to the most delicate and elegant subject matter.

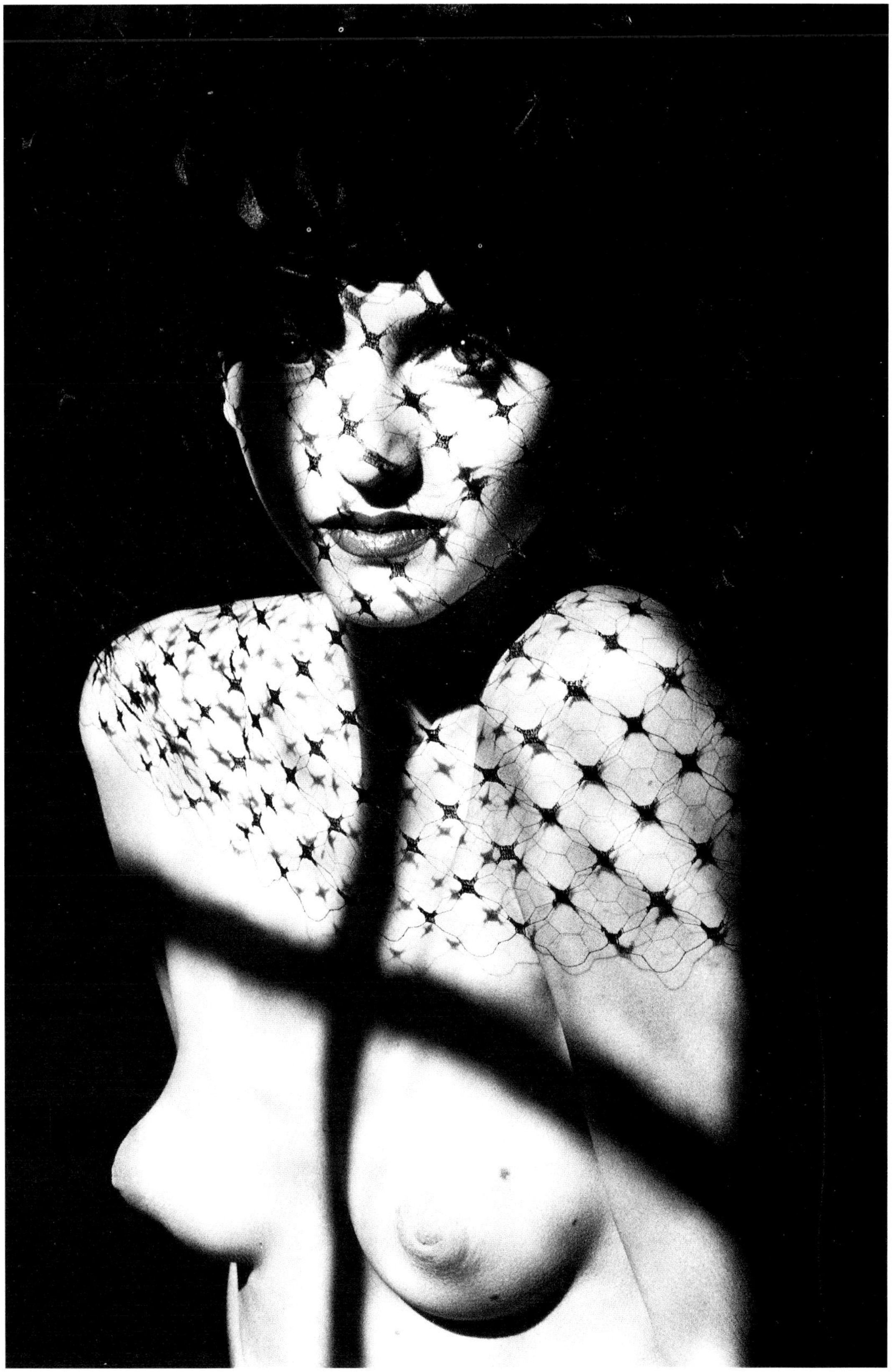

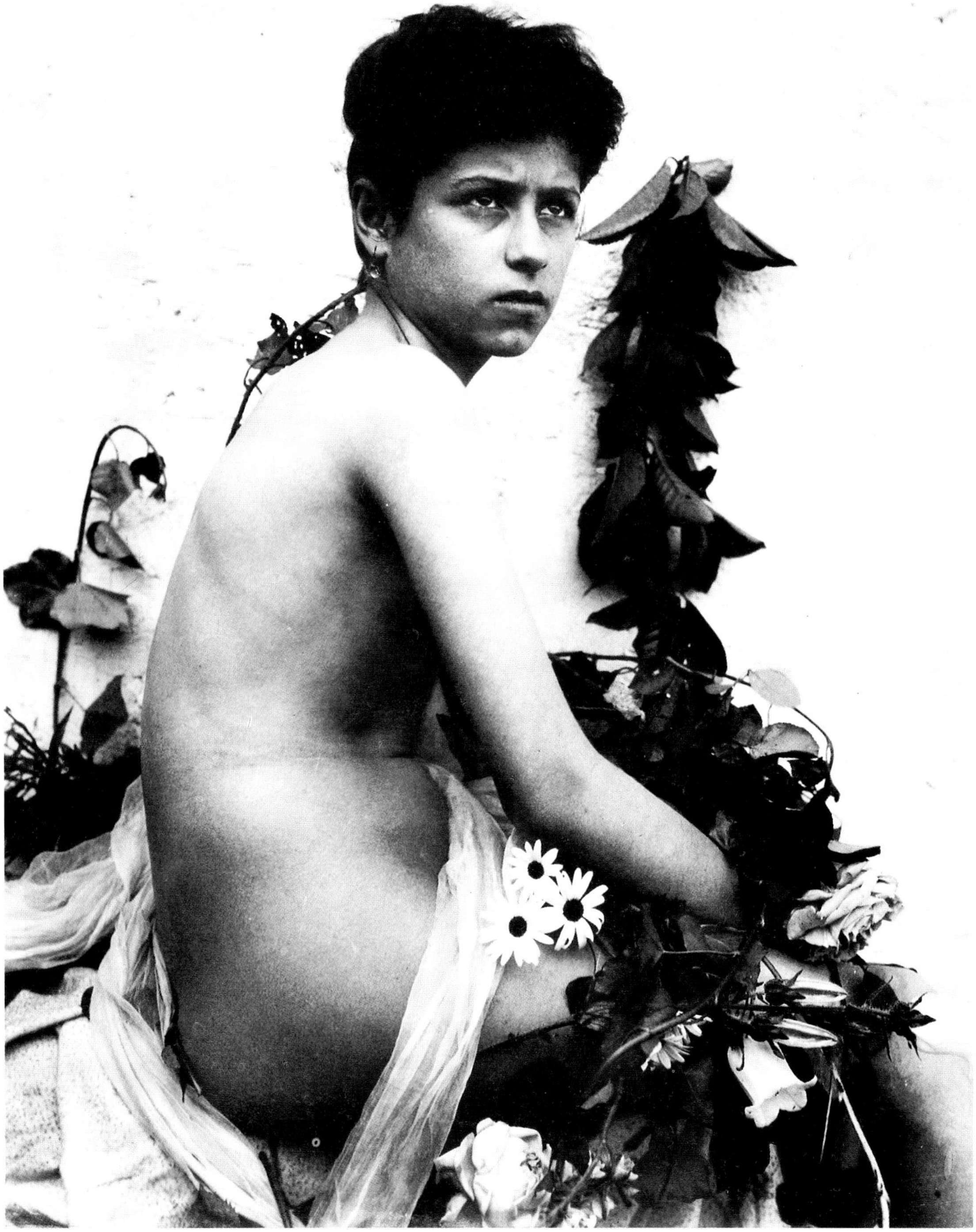

PLATE LXXXVII
VINCENZO GALDI
Untitled c.1905
Julian Hartnoll Collection

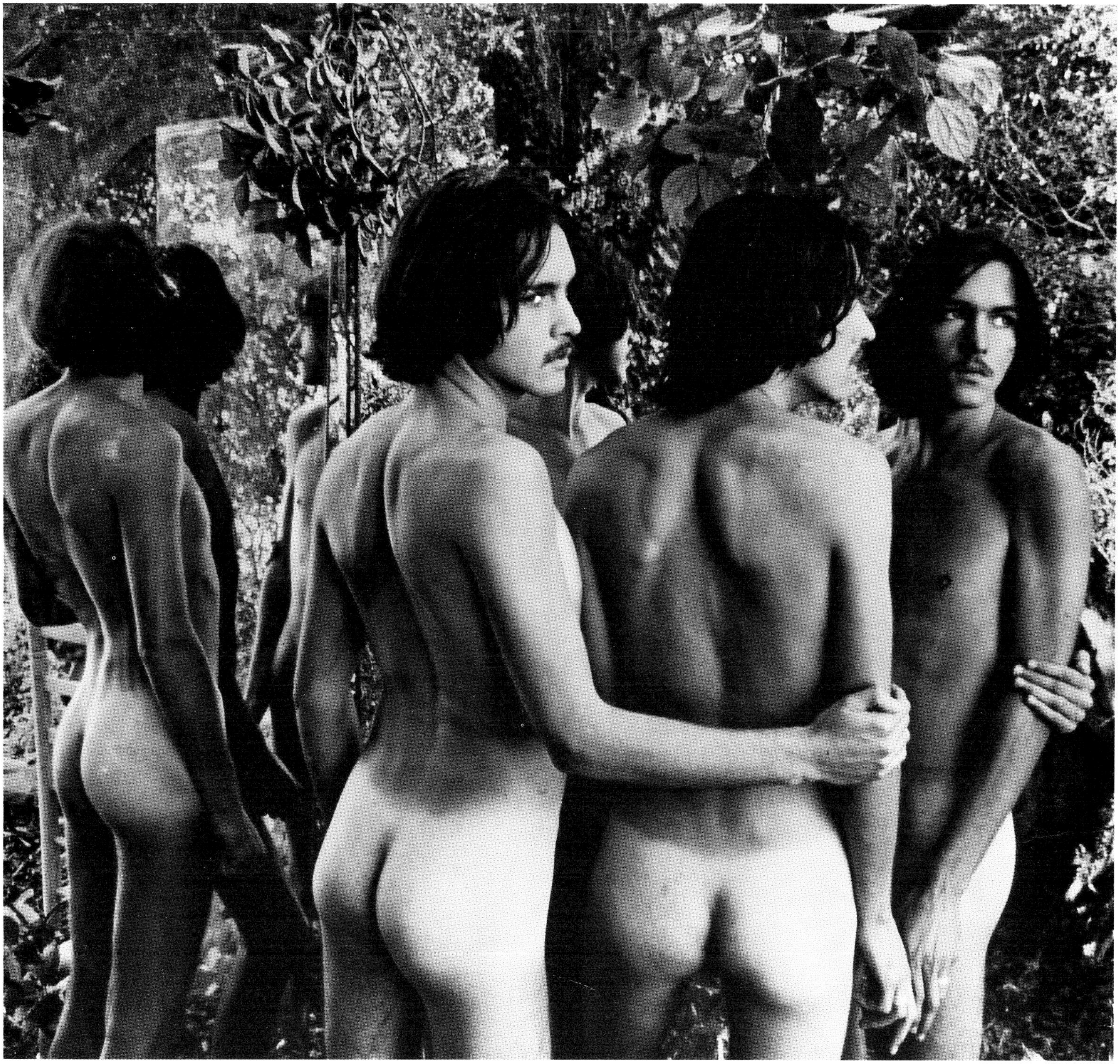

PLATE LXXXVIII
CECIL BEATON
Myers Twins c.1967
David Bailey Collection

In the 1960s, Beaton made portraits of many of the leading personalities in London, including (along with Bailey himself) Mick Jagger and David Hockney, as well as this unusual photograph of two fashionable young London photographic assistants.

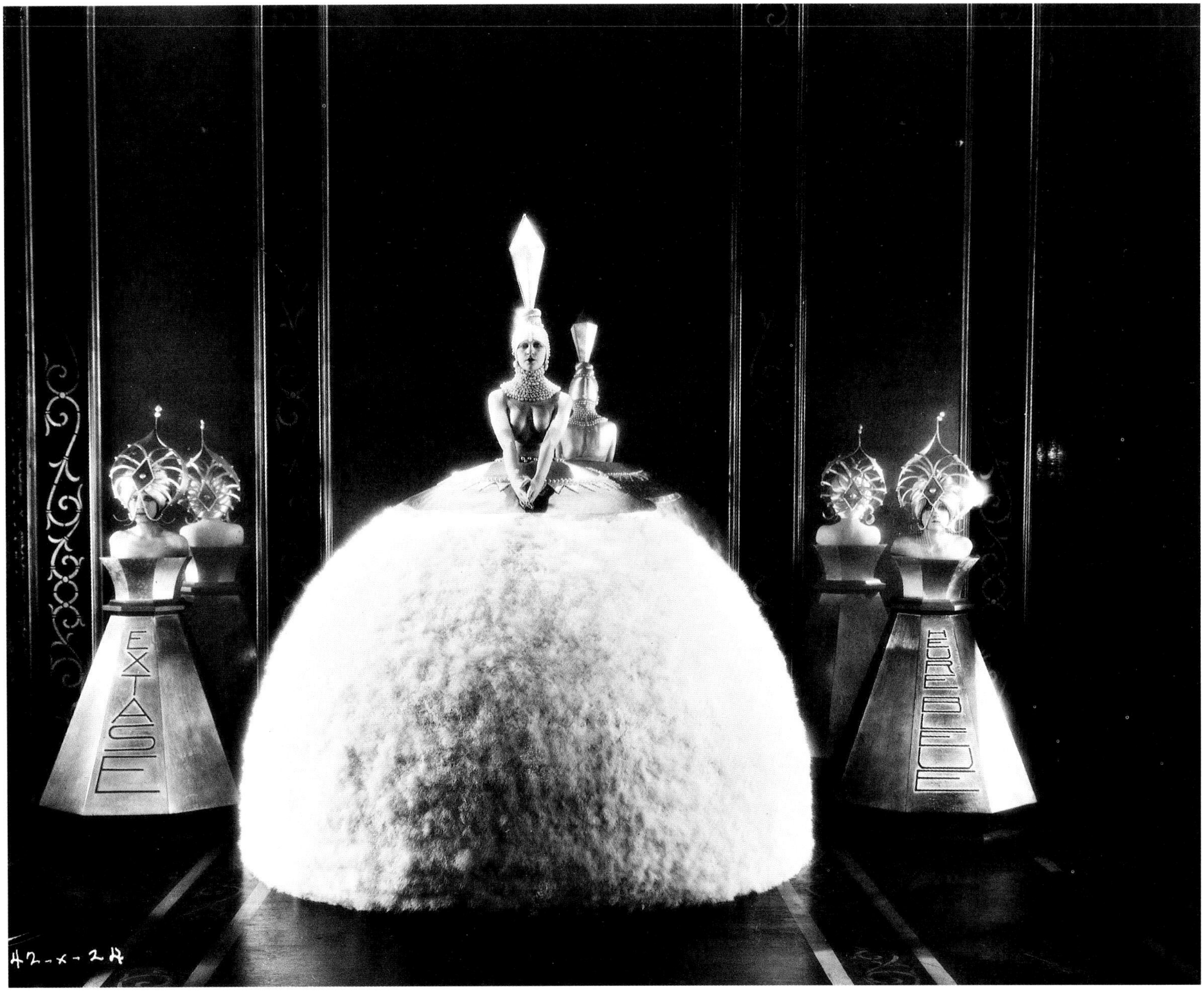

PLATE LXXXIX (Above)
MGM STUDIOS
Still from *Bright Lights* 1925
John Kobal Collection

PLATE XC (Right)
MURRAY KORMAN
Marion Martin c.1935
John Kobal Collection

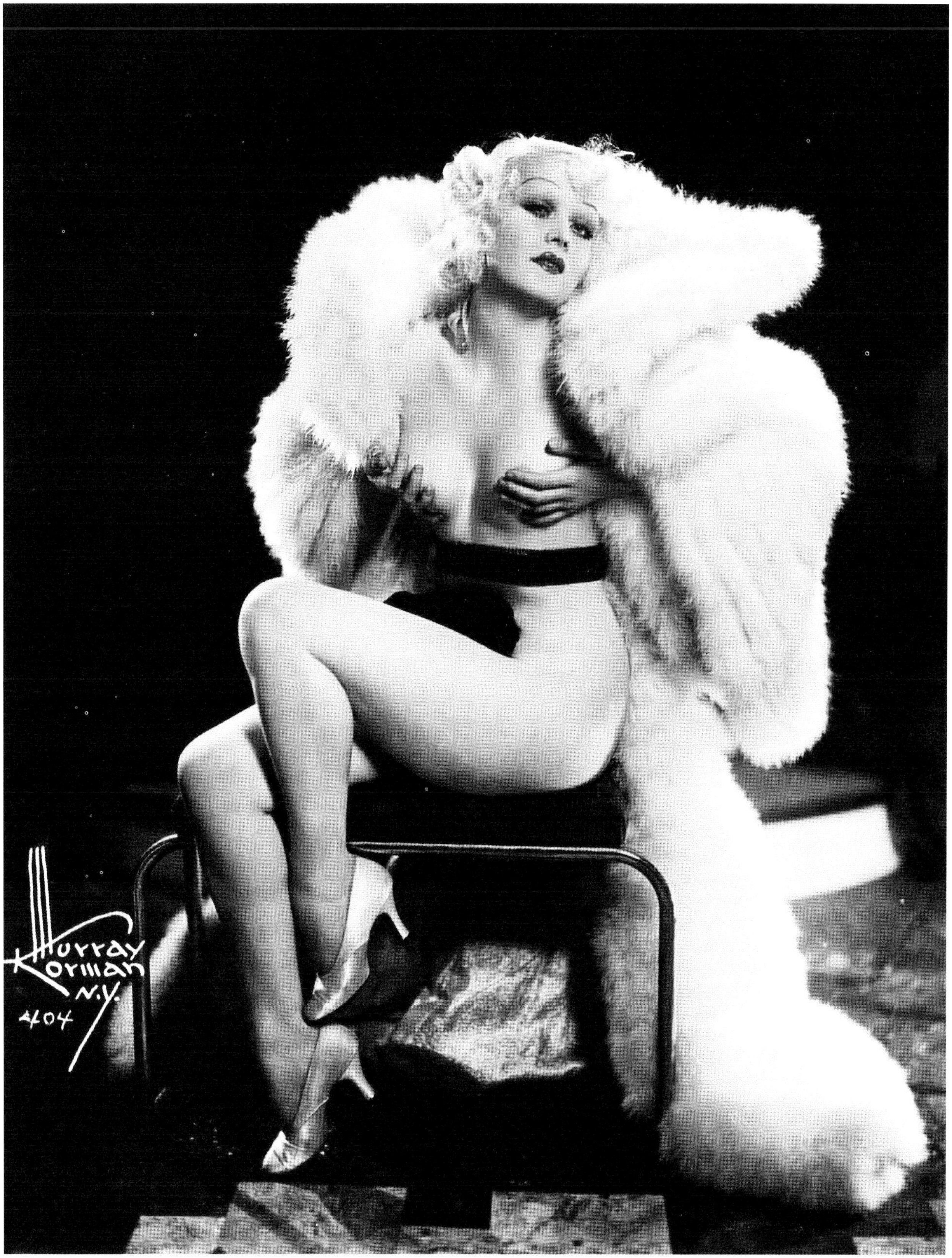
Murray
Korman
N.Y.
404

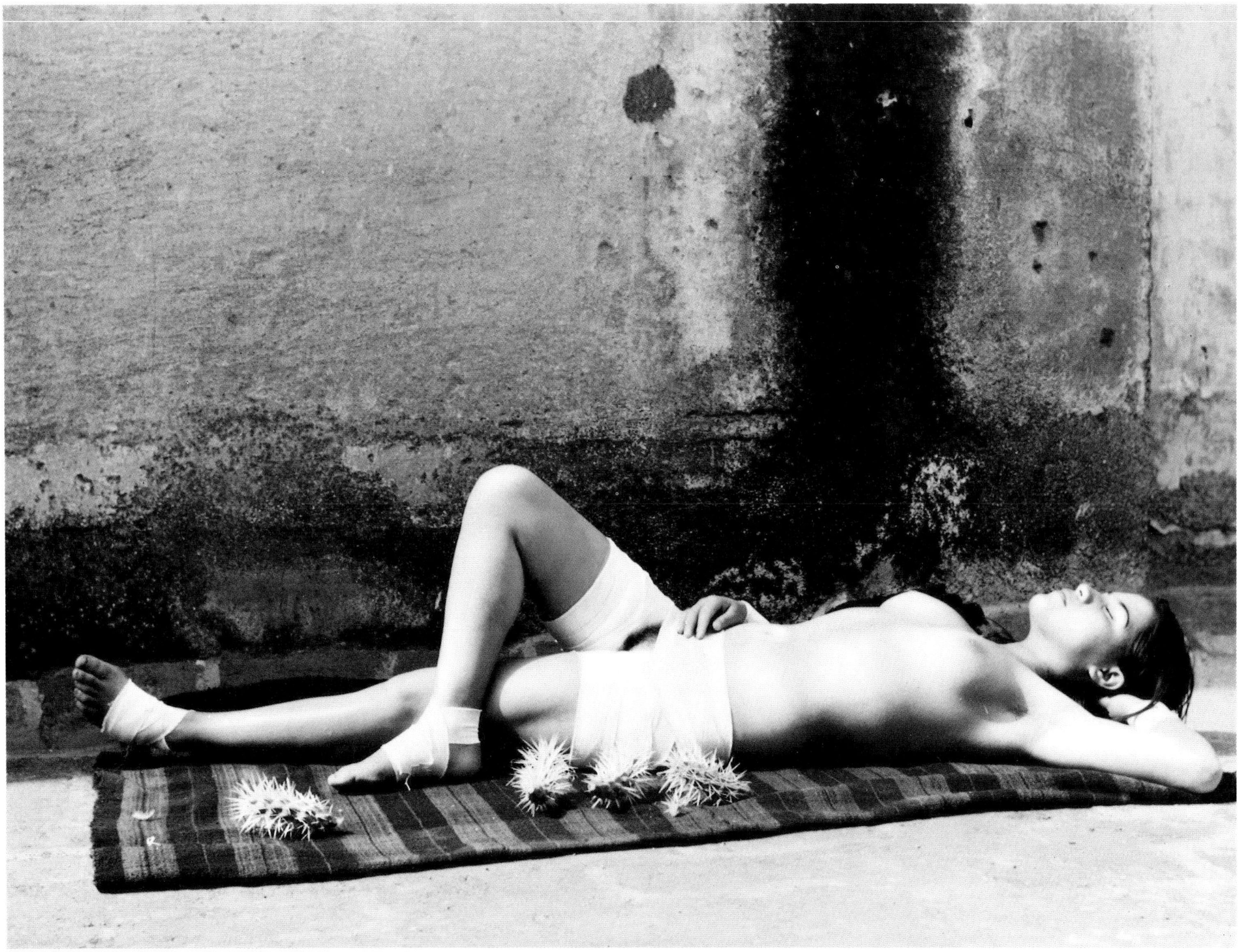

PLATE XCI
MANUEL ALVAREZ BRAVO
La Buena Fama Durmiendo 1938
Victoria & Albert Museum, London

Probably the best known of all Bravo's nudes, it was this image which haunted Bailey and provided a starting point for his own series of nudes, made between 1981 and 1984.

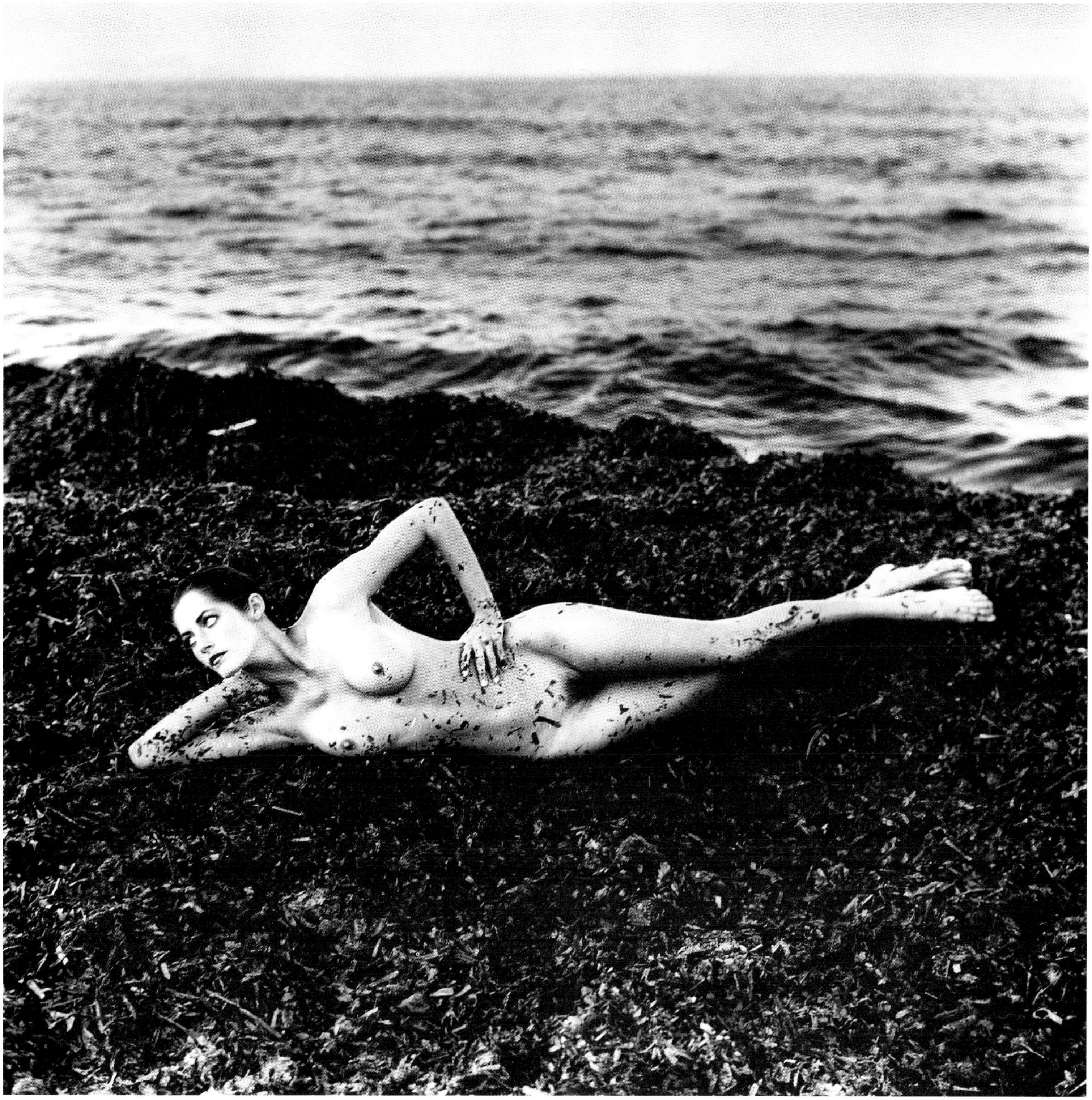

PLATE XCII
HELMUT NEWTON
Nude in Seaweed, Saint Tropez 1981
Courtesy the photographer

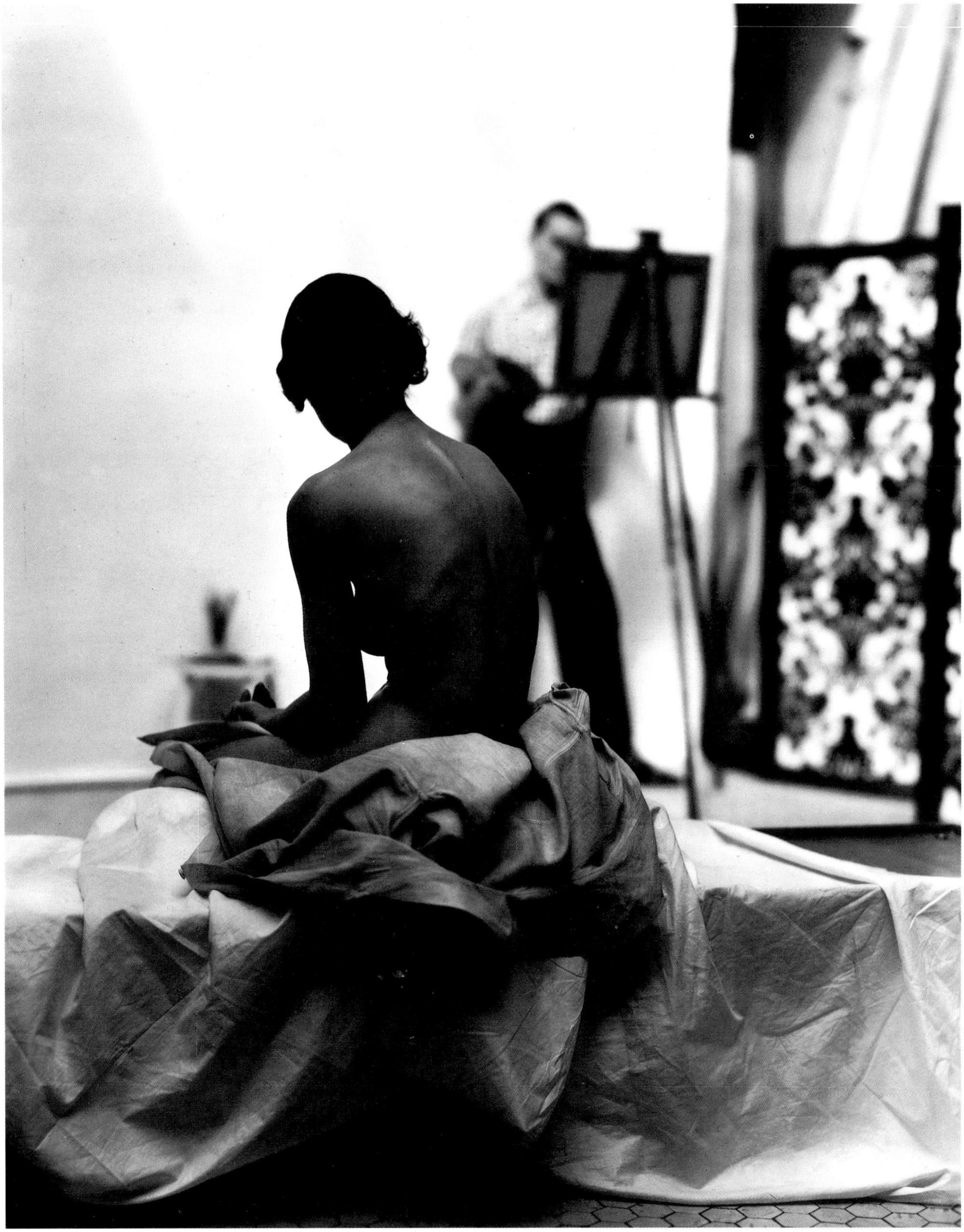

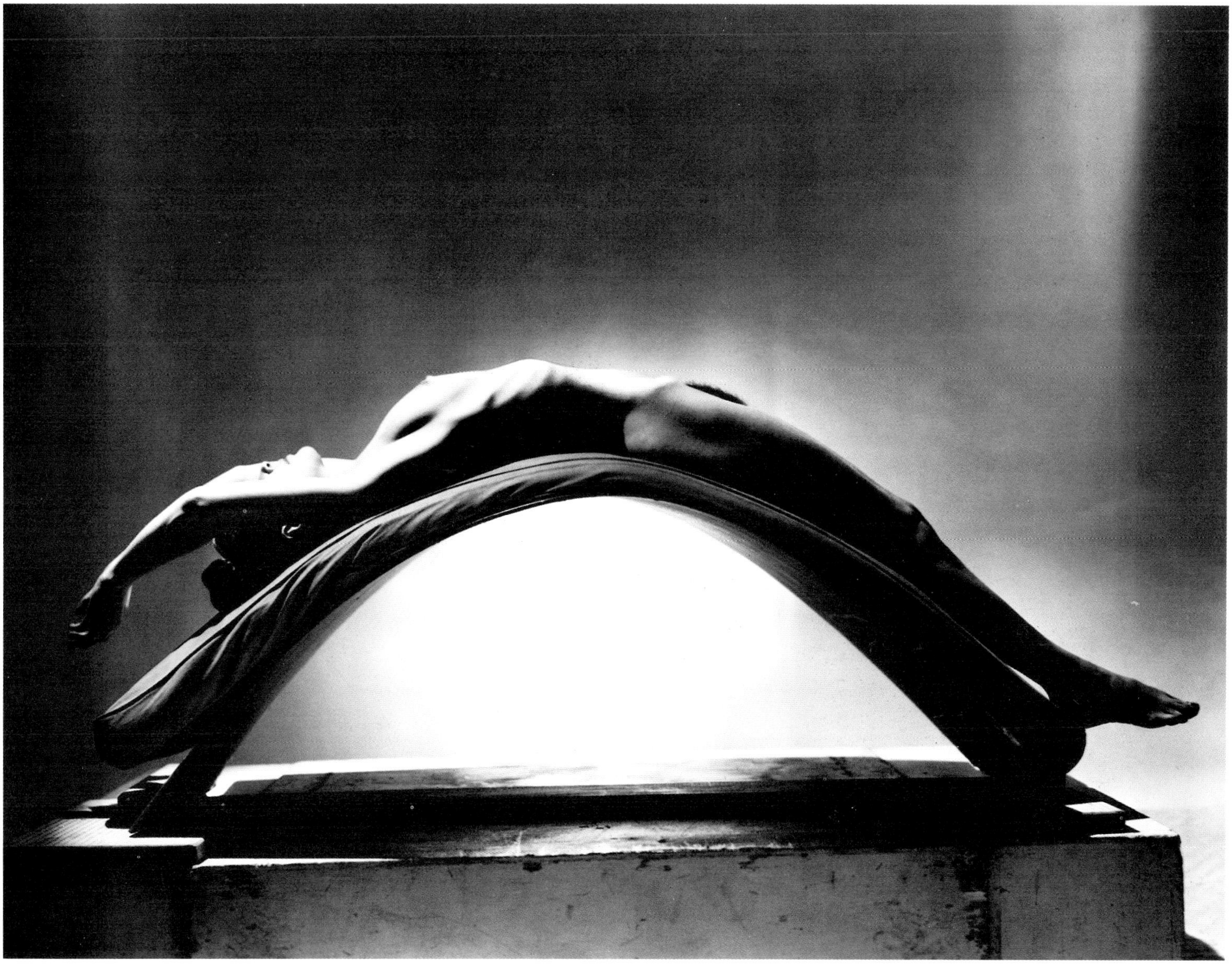

PLATE XCIV (Above)
JOHN RAWLINGS
Untitled c.1950
Fashion Institute of Technology, New York

At the time these pictures were made, Rawlings took nearly all of his photographs, including those for *Vogue*, in natural light. He believed this was of special value when taking nudes: "The model is not pinned down by spotlights but can move about freely." Occasionally, as in these examples, he would forego spontaneity in favour of more carefully composed studio shots.

PLATE XCIII (Left)
JOHN RAWLINGS
Untitled c.1950
Fashion Institute of Technology, New York

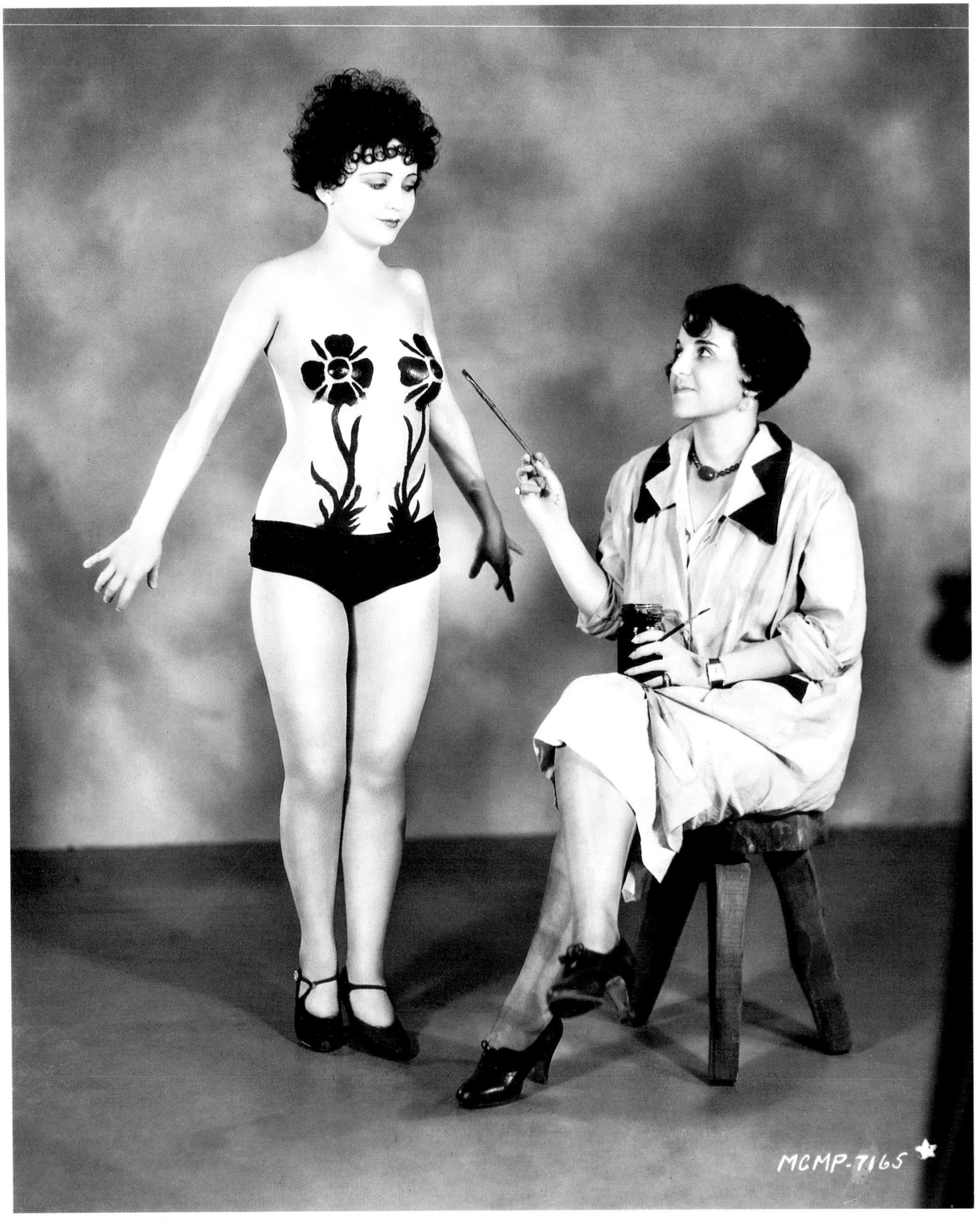
MCMP-7165

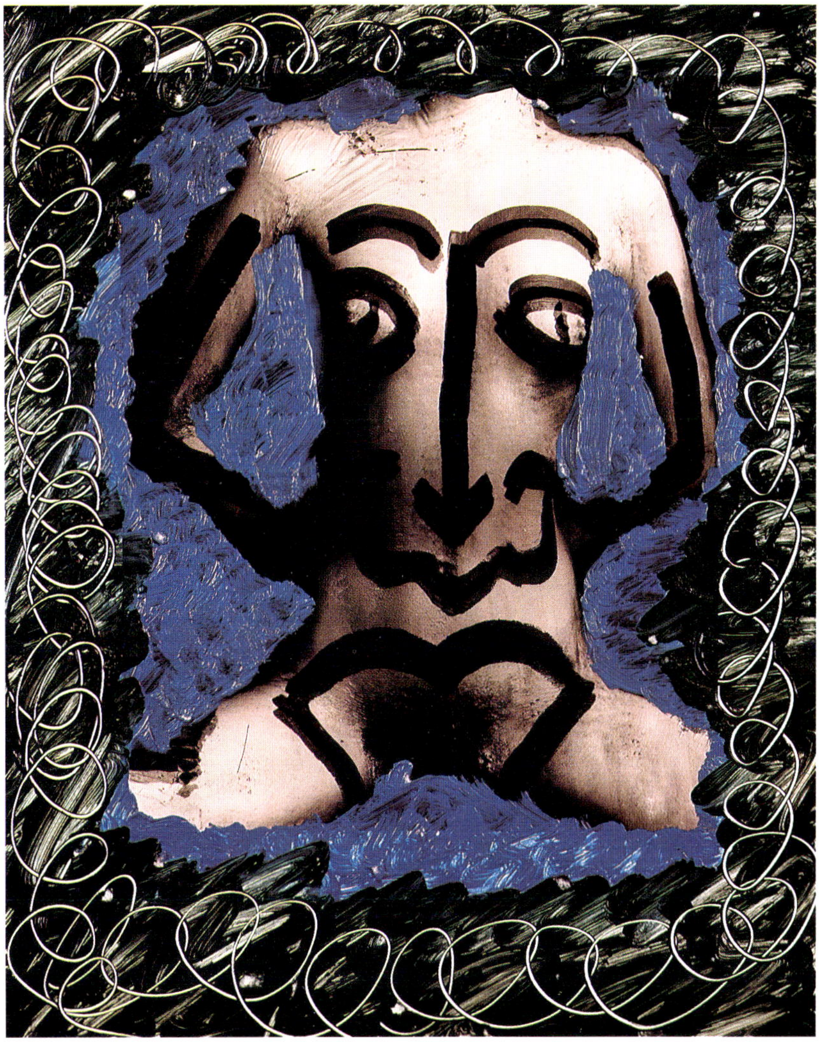

PLATE XCVI (Above)
DAVID BAILEY
Untitled 1983/86
OILS ON SILVER PRINT

Bailey's boldly painted additions to this photograph of his wife, Catherine, reflect his interest in tribal art, of which he has a large collection.

PLATE XCV (Left)
CLARENCE SINCLAIR BULL
Subject unidentified 1928
John Kobal Collection

The purpose of this intriguing picture is unknown. It is one of Bull's earliest works for MGM, but lacks the high gloss perfection which he achieved throughout his long career as one of Hollywood's leading photographers.

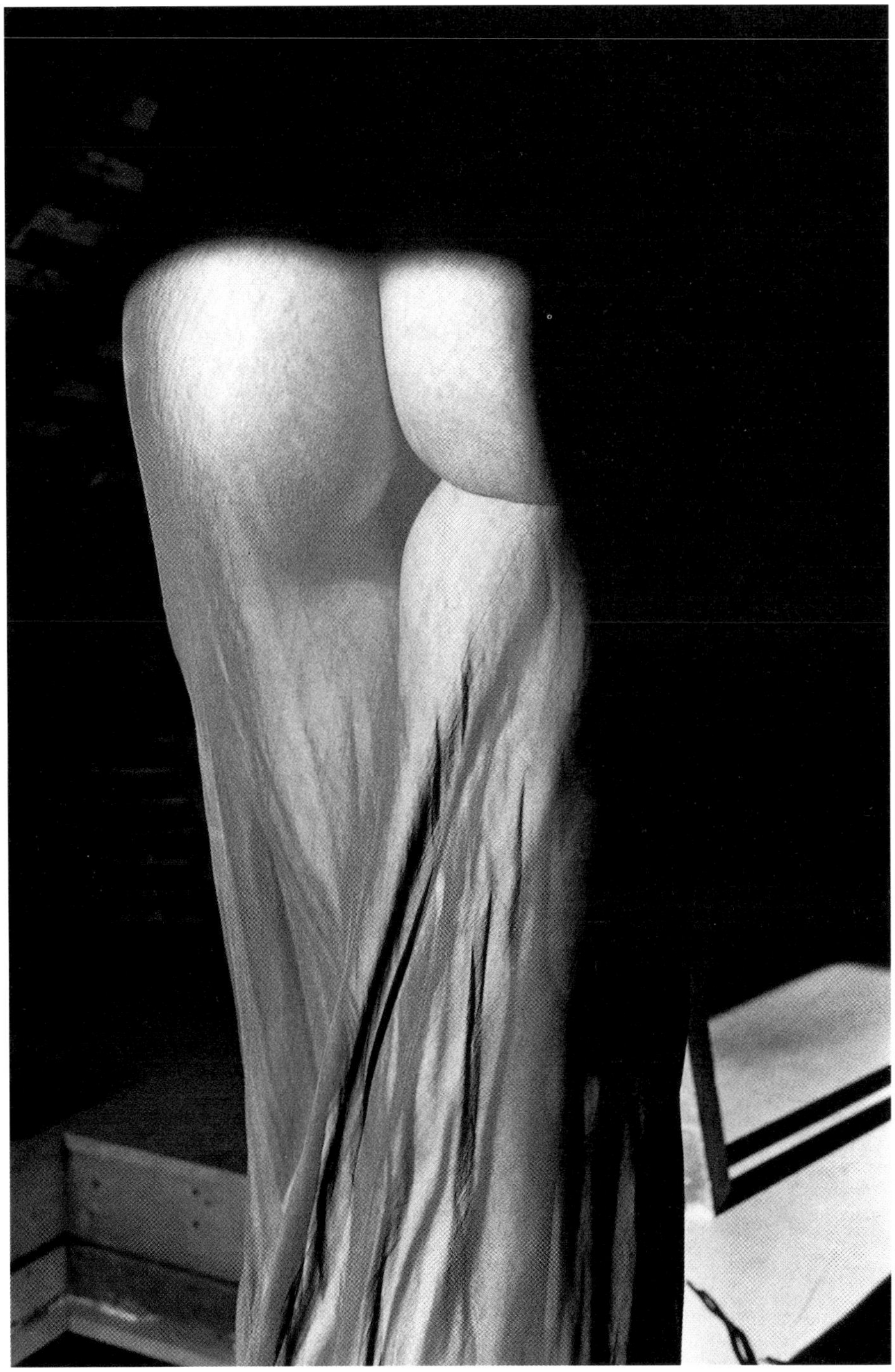

PLATE XCVII
JEANLOUP SIEFF
La Veuve Joyeuse, Paris 1985
Hamilton's Gallery, London

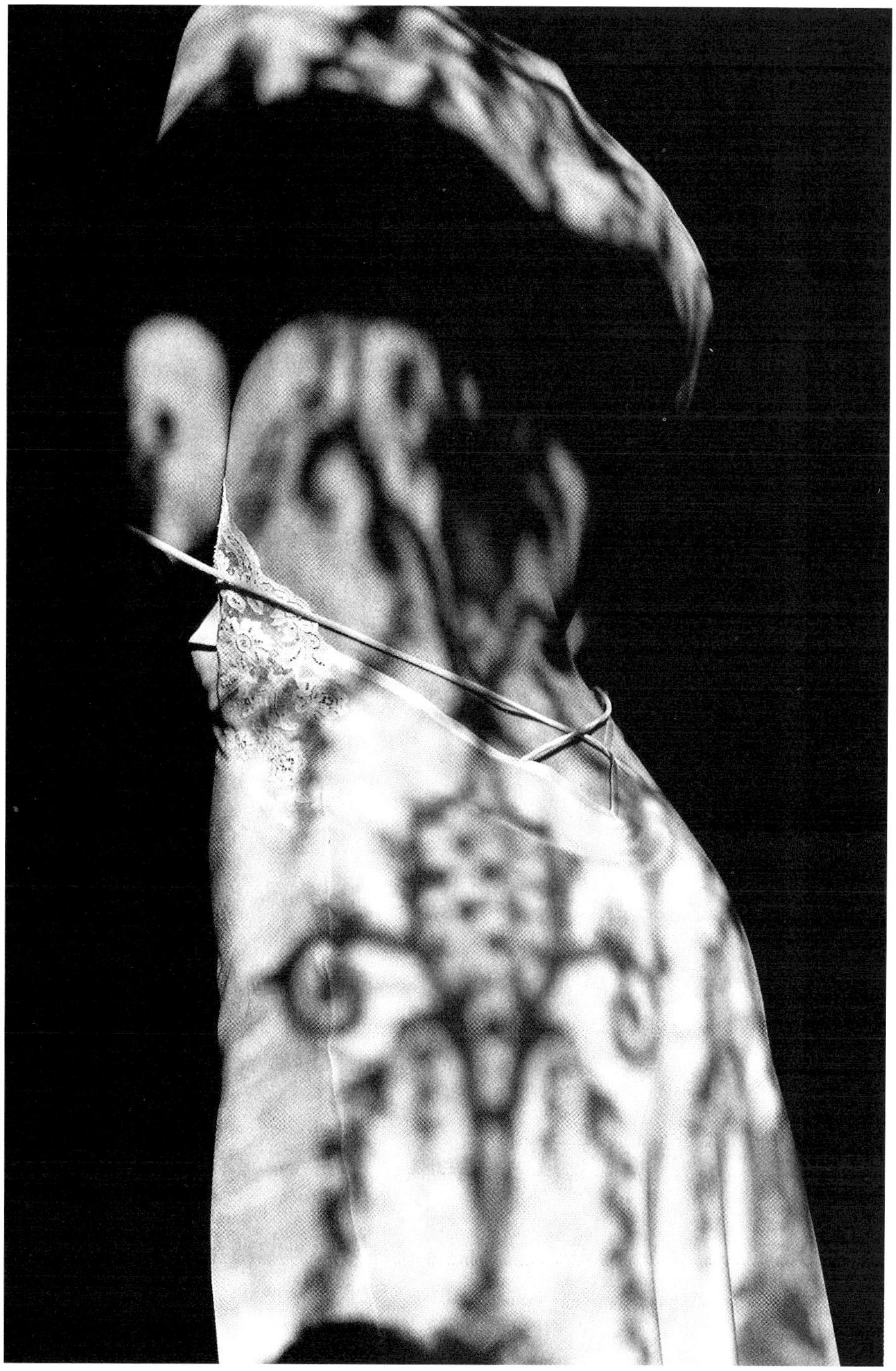

PLATE XCVIII
JEANLOUP SIEFF
Shadow and Light. Paris 1984
Hamilton's Gallery, London

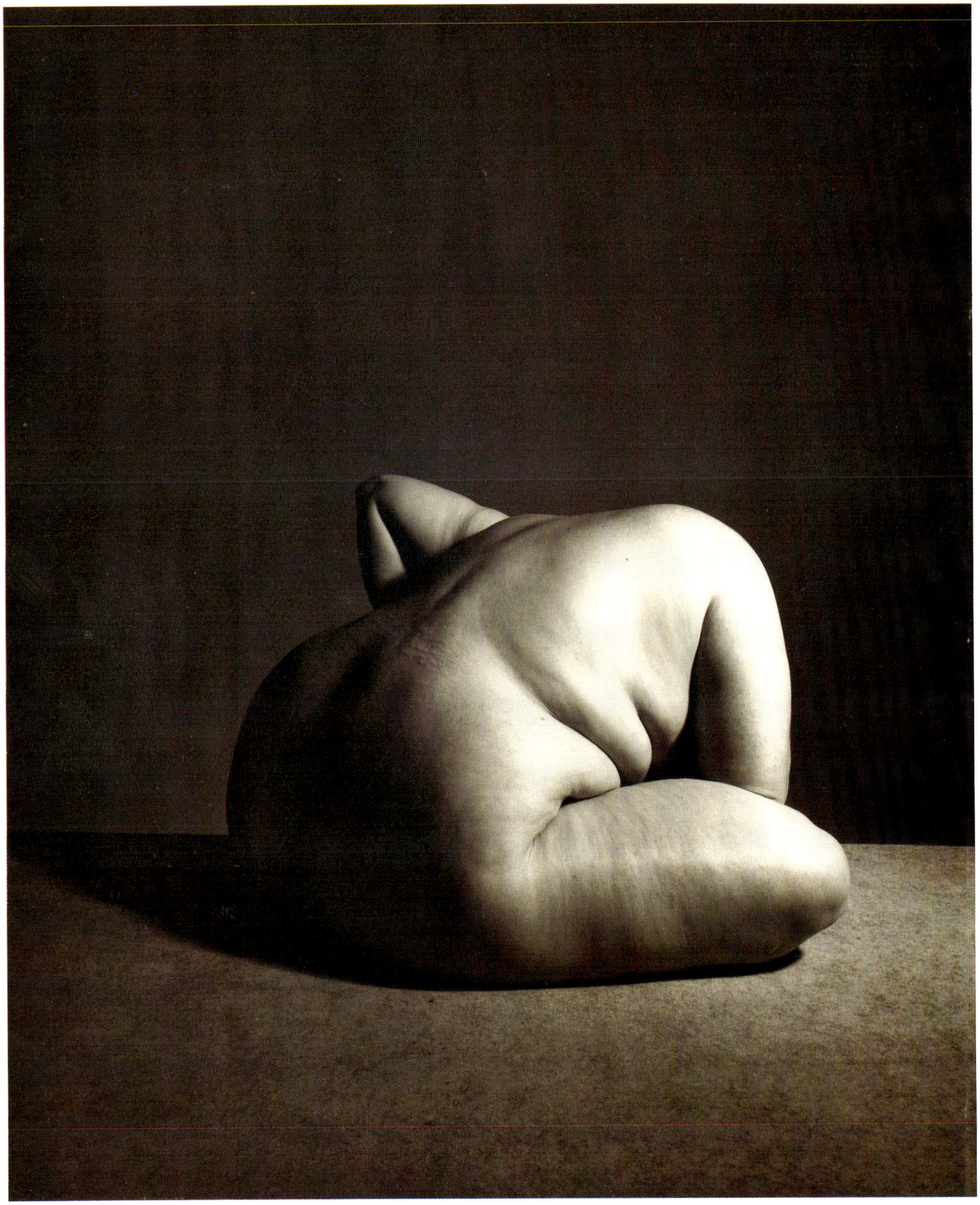

PLATE XCIX
BARRY LATEGAN
Jane 1985
David Bailey Collection

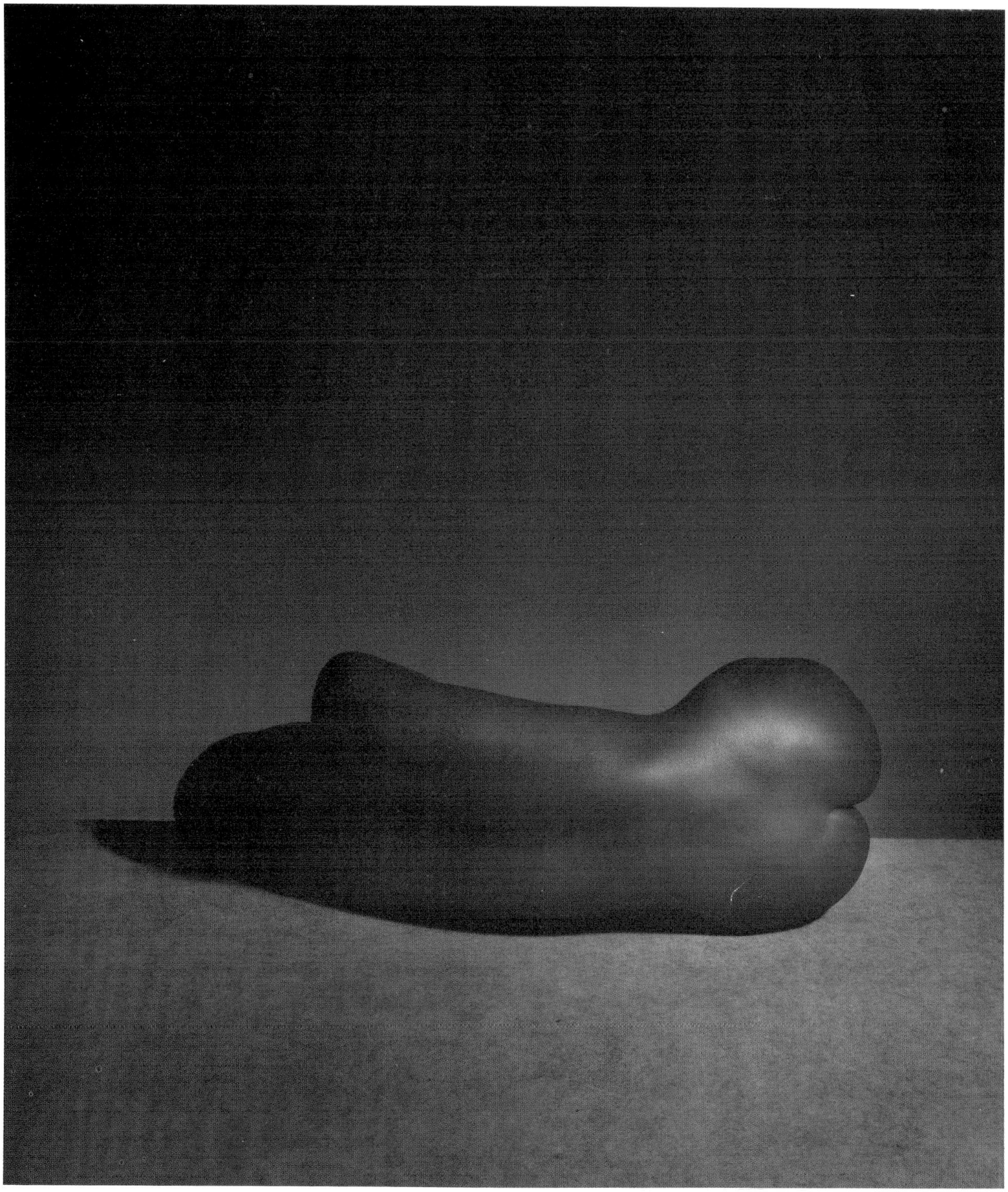

PLATE C
BARRY LATEGAN
Shelley 1985
David Bailey Collection

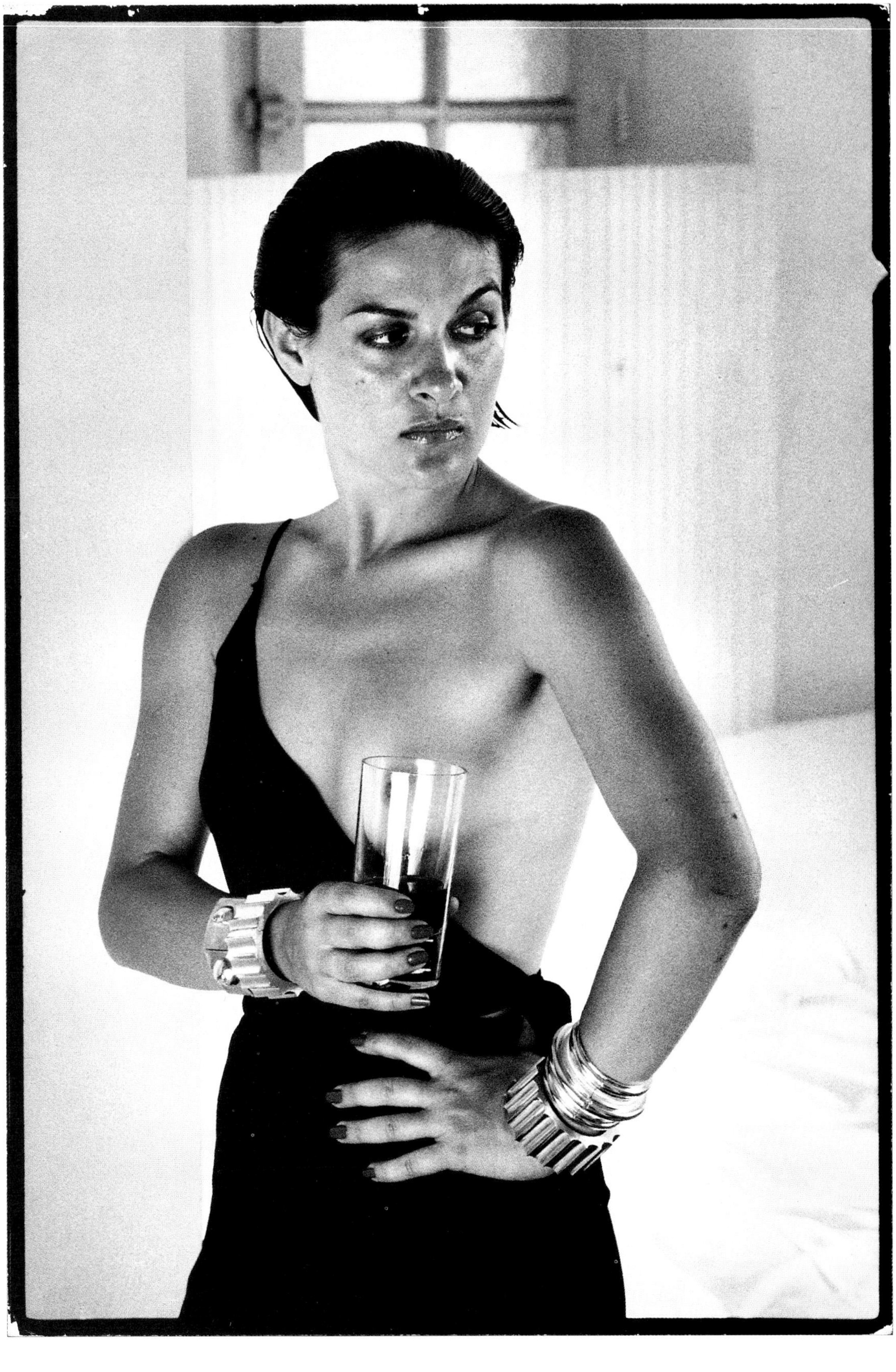

PLATE CI
HELMUT NEWTON
Paloma Picasso, Saint Tropez 1973
Courtesy the photographer

"The ideal nude," says Helmut Newton, "is erotic. It doesn't always happen, but it's the ideal. Getting an erotic feeling and retaining a highly aesthetic figure is a big problem." Comparing "Paloma Picasso" with the more recent "Tied up Torso" we see how Newton's work has progressed towards bolder, less graphically complex imagery.

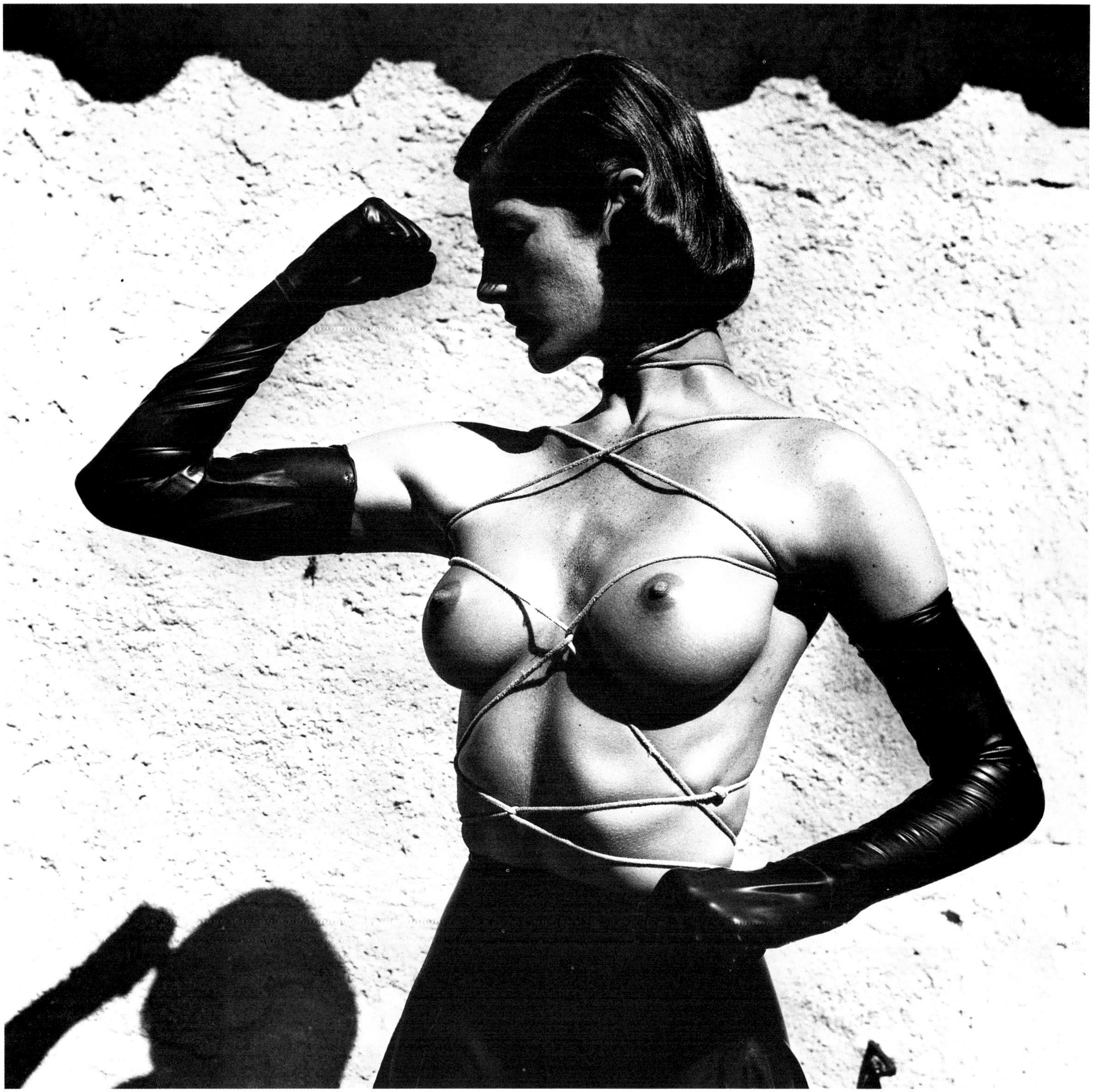

PLATE CII
HELMUT NEWTON
Tied up Torso. Ramatuelle 1980
Courtesy the photographer

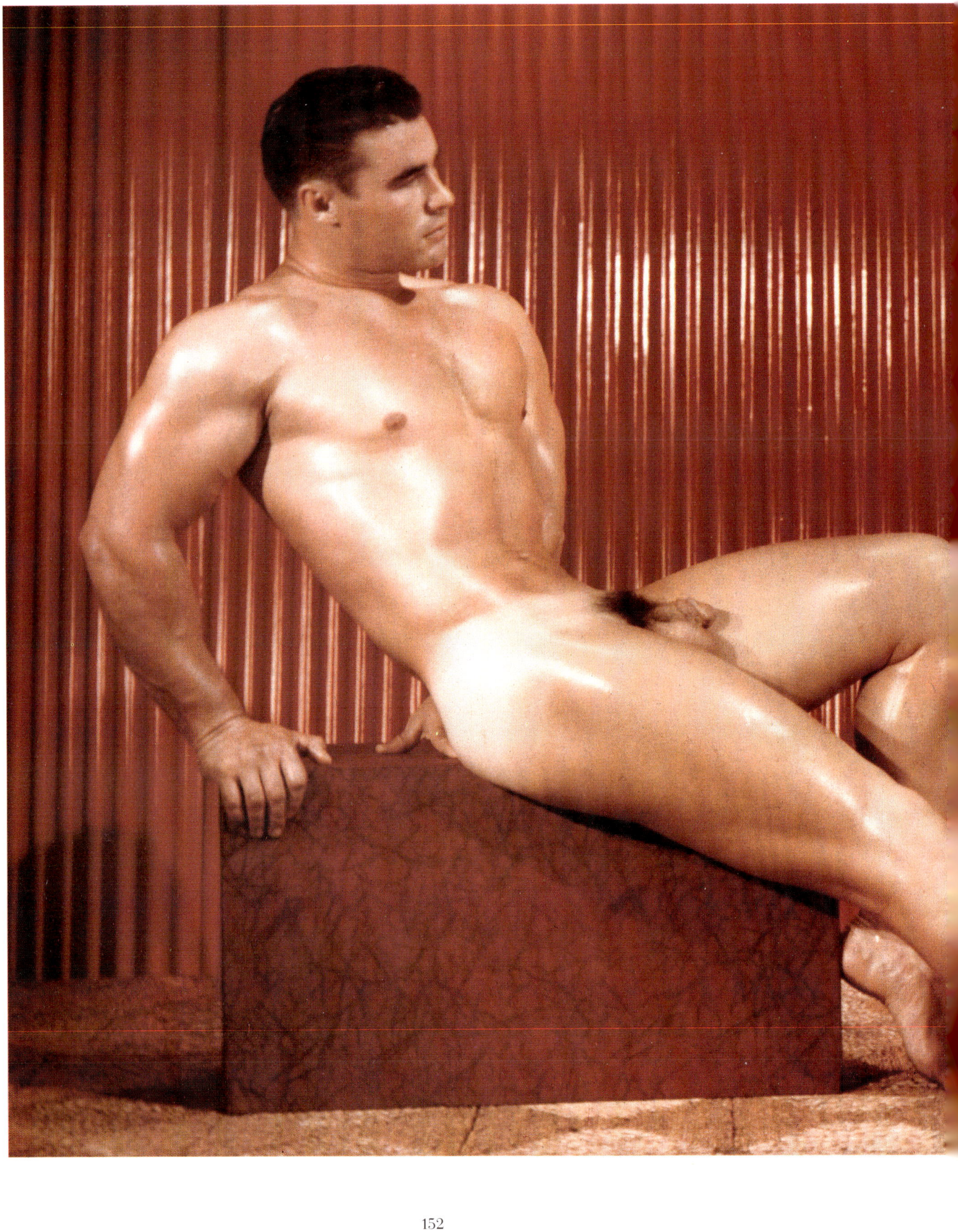

PLATE CIII
BRUCE (BELLAS) OF LOS ANGELES
Untitled 1962
R-TYPE COLOUR PRINT
Joseph Vasta, New York

Bruce Bellas' deliberate choice of dominant red in this photograph foreshadowed the interest in colour relationships which would be a prime concern of the New Colour photographers of the 1970s, such as William Eggleston and Joel Meyerowitz.

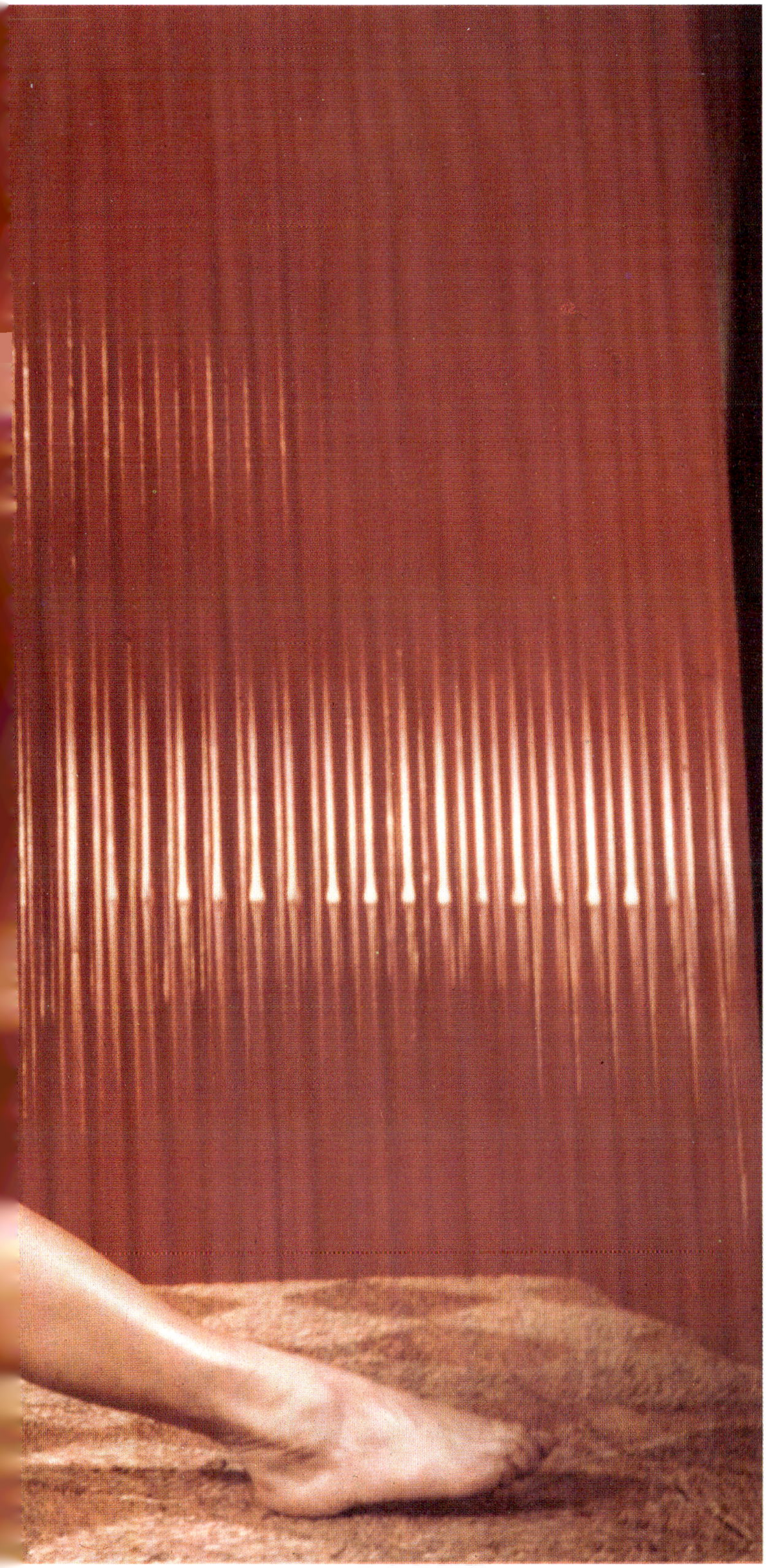

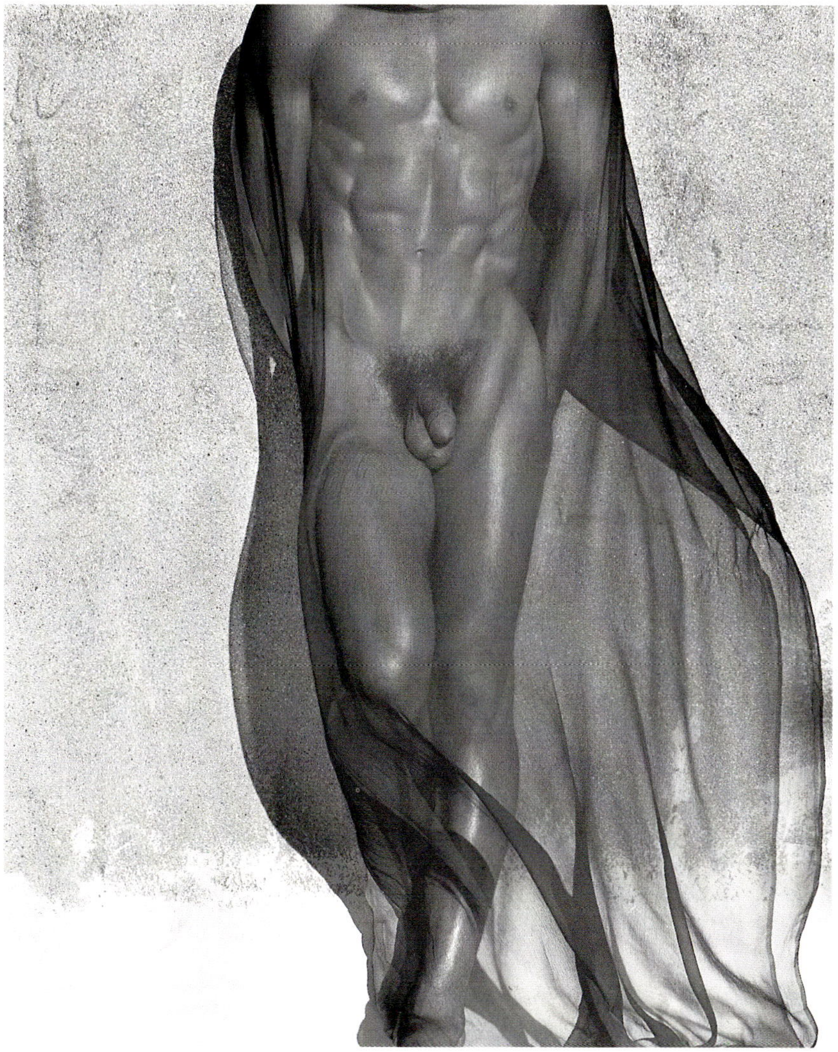

PLATE CIV
HERB RITTS
Veiled Nude 1985
Staley-Wise Gallery, New York

In a 1984 issue of the Italian fashion magazine *Lei*, Ritts draped female models in semi-transparent voile to illustrate a feature entitled "Goodbye to Androgyny." Its use with a male model adds an intriguing element of capriciousness.

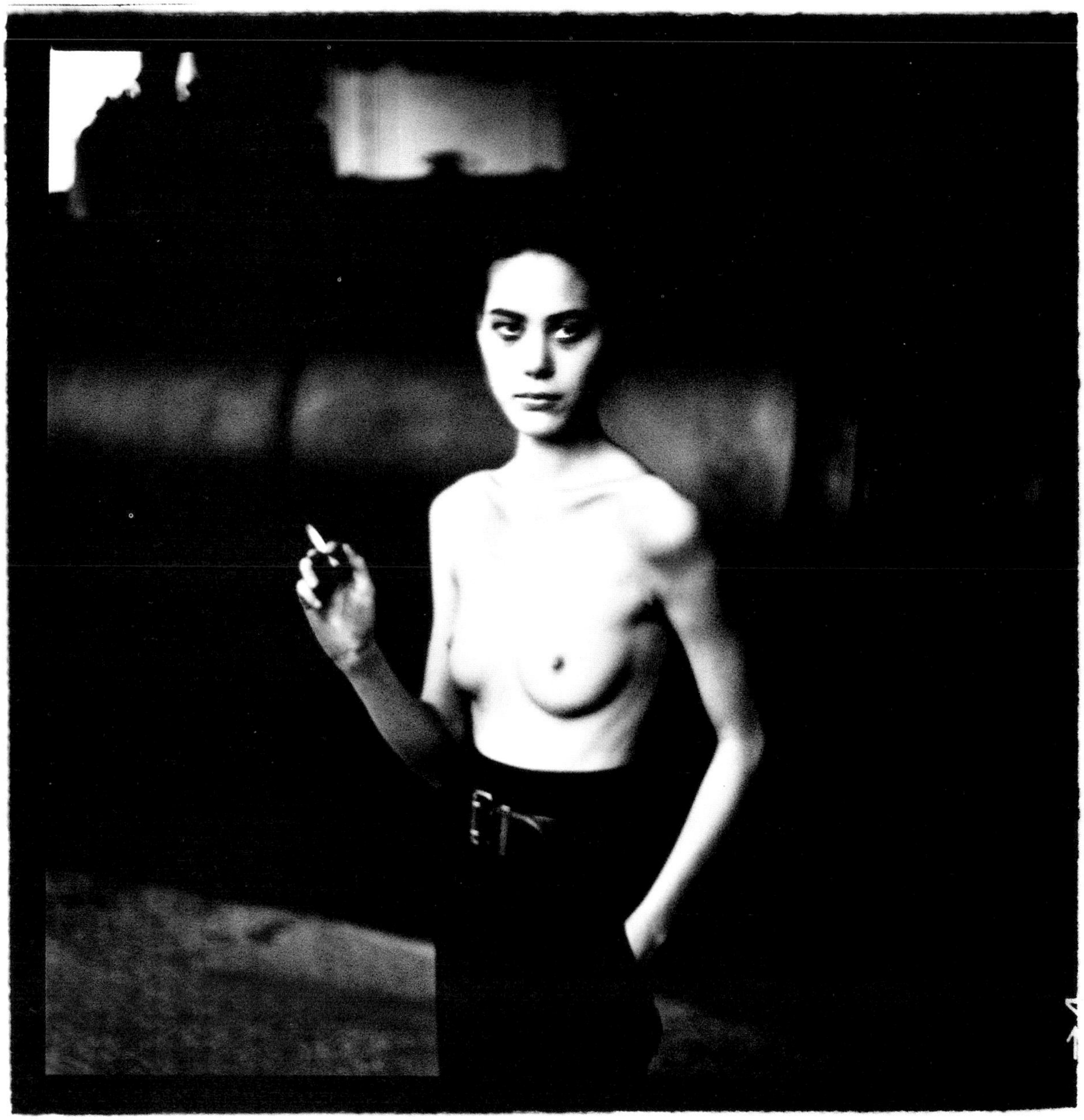

PLATE CV (Above)
PETER LINDBERGH
Ariane Koizumi, Dusseldorf 1985
Azzedine Alaia

Nudity, or semi-nudity, has become more widely accepted in fashion photography in recent years. This photograph was made in this form for the designer Azzedine Alaia, as part of a project to record his own designs.

PLATE CVI (Right)
PETER LINDBERGH
Marie Sophie, Paris 1987
Courtesy the photographer

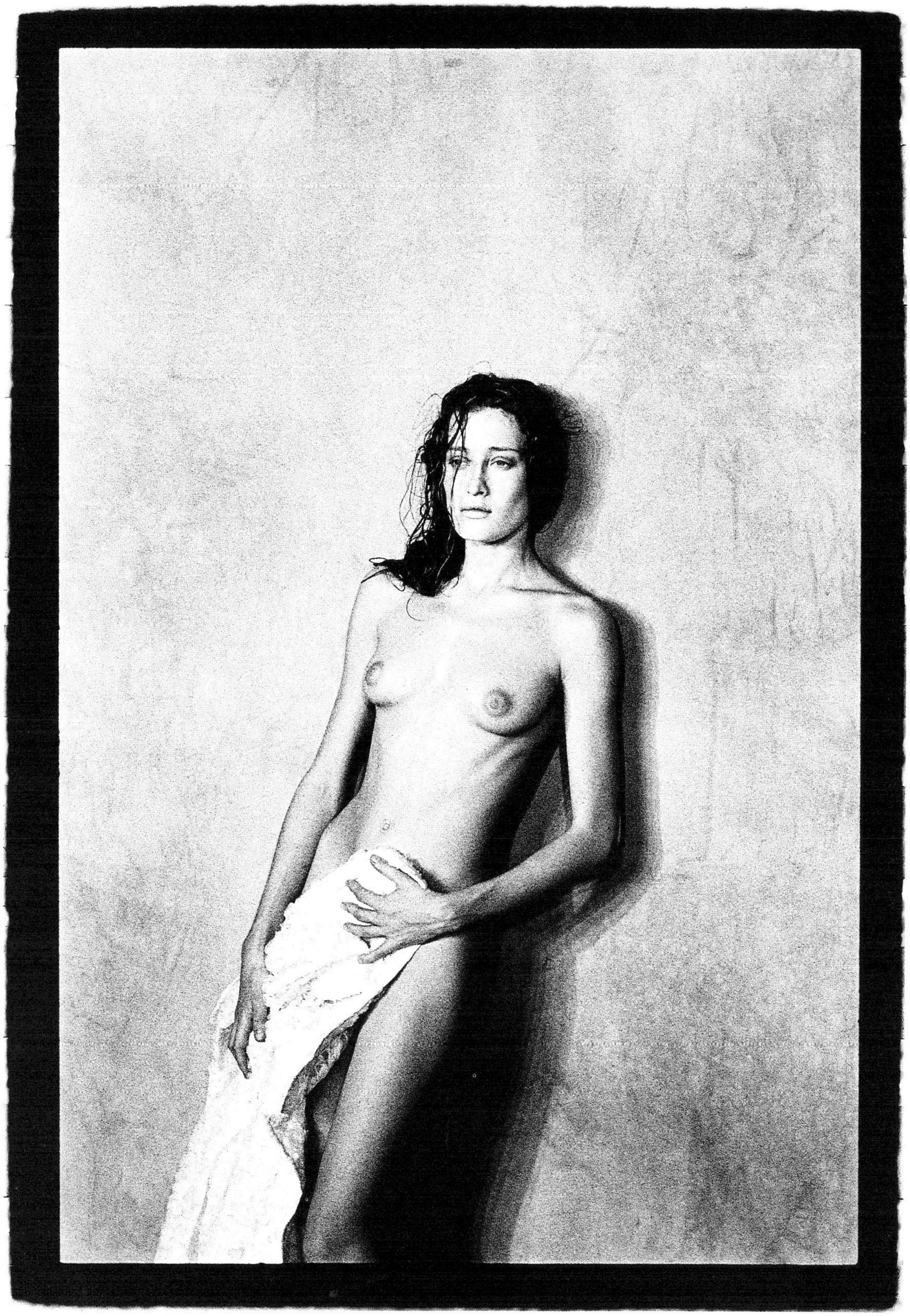

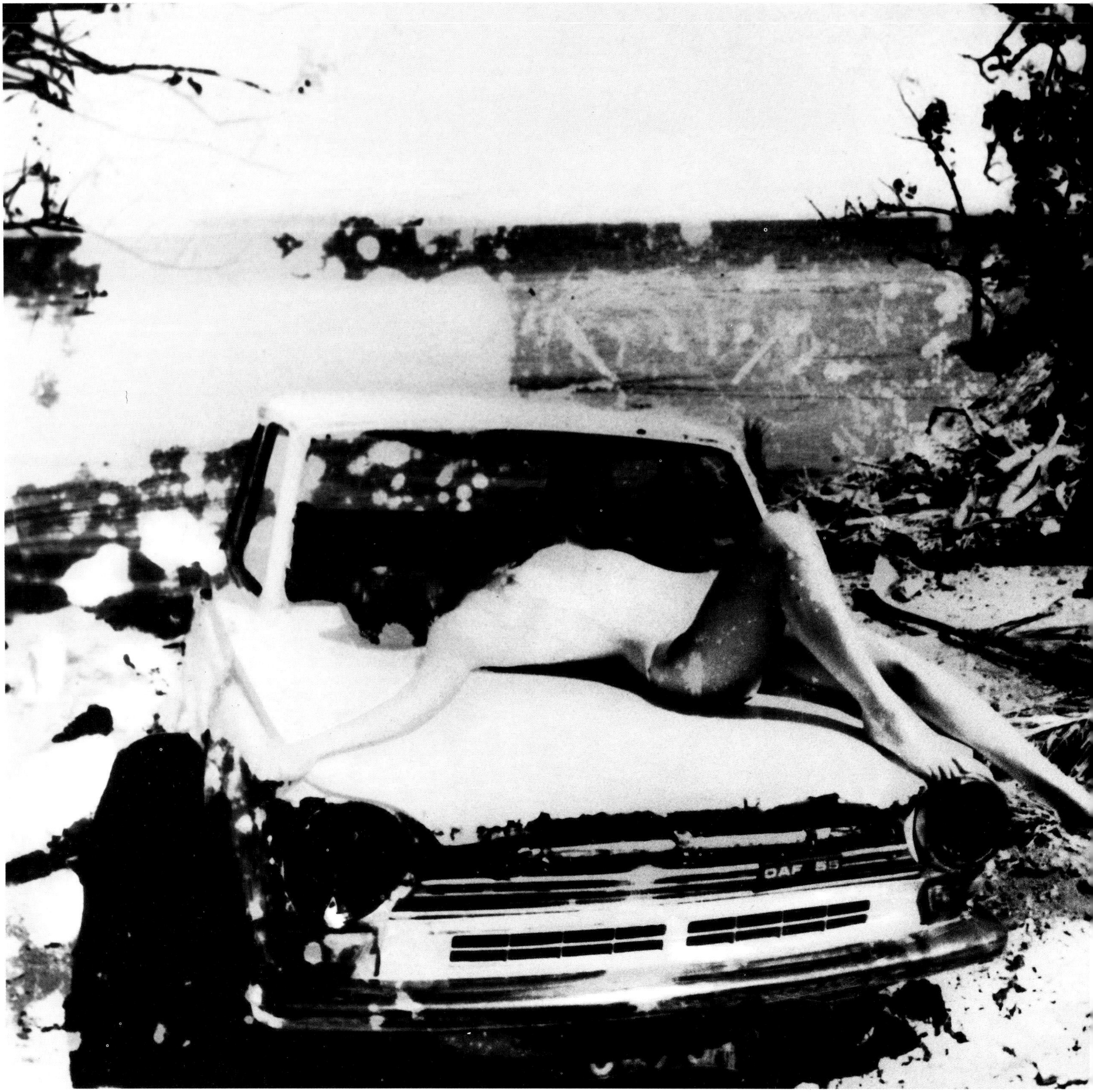
DAF 55

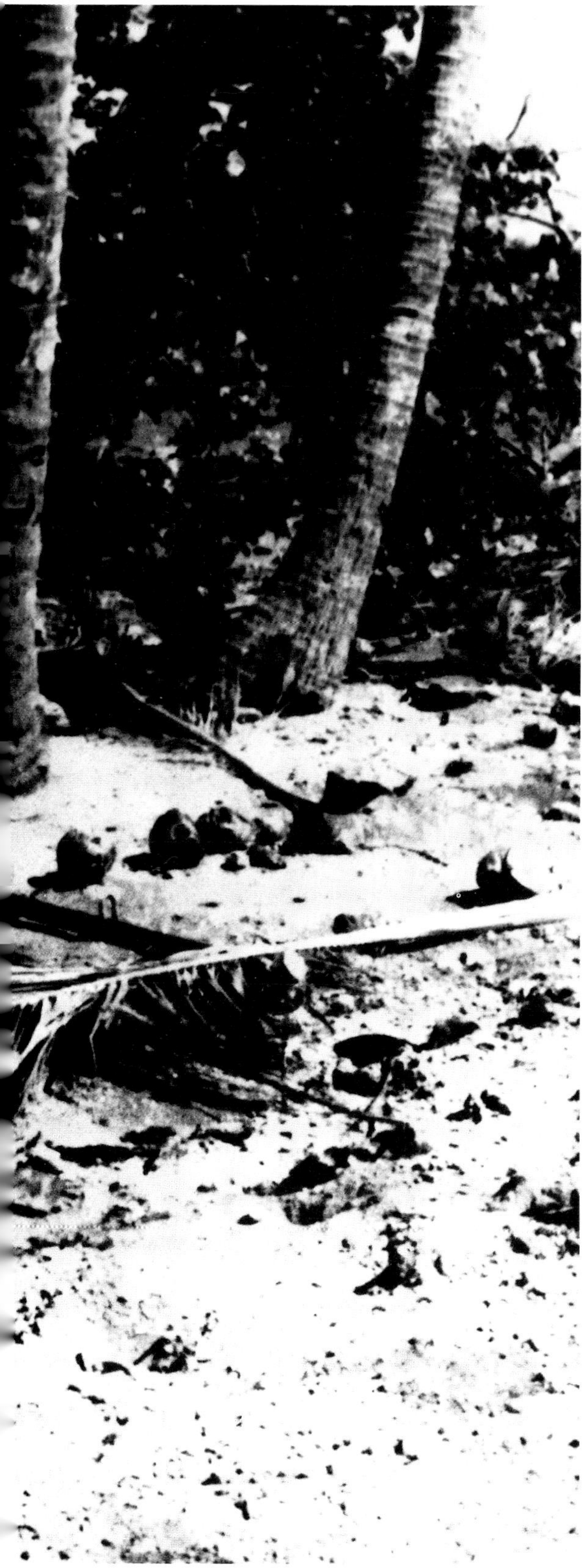

PLATE CVII

DAVID BAILEY

Untitled 1983

Taken from his most recent book, *Nudes 1981-1984*, this shot has the appearance of a film still. This "filmic quality" and the atmosphere of foreboding recall the 1960's paintings of British pop artist Richard Hamilton.

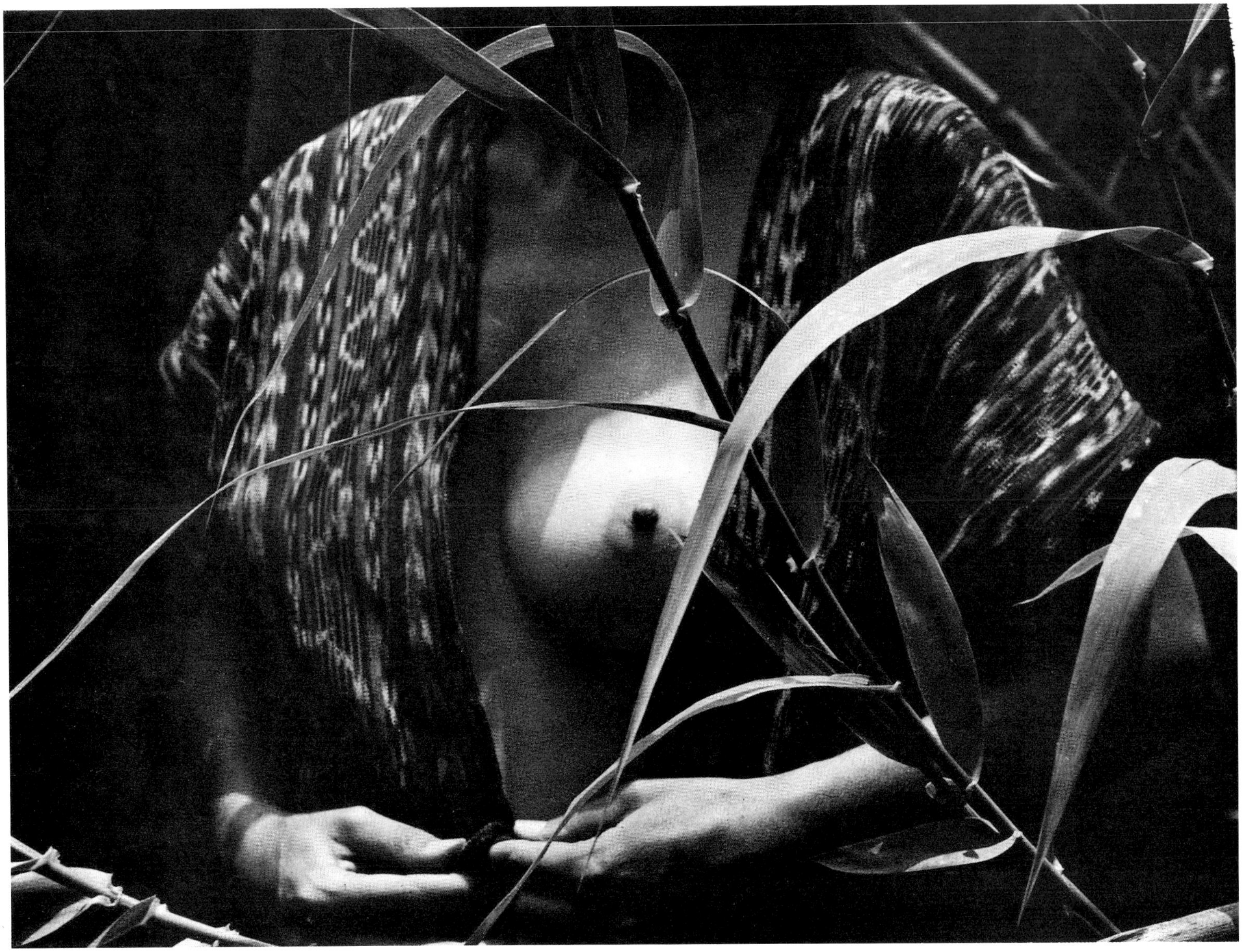

PLATE CVIII
MANUEL ALVAREZ BRAVO
Fruta Prohibida 1977
Photographers Gallery, London

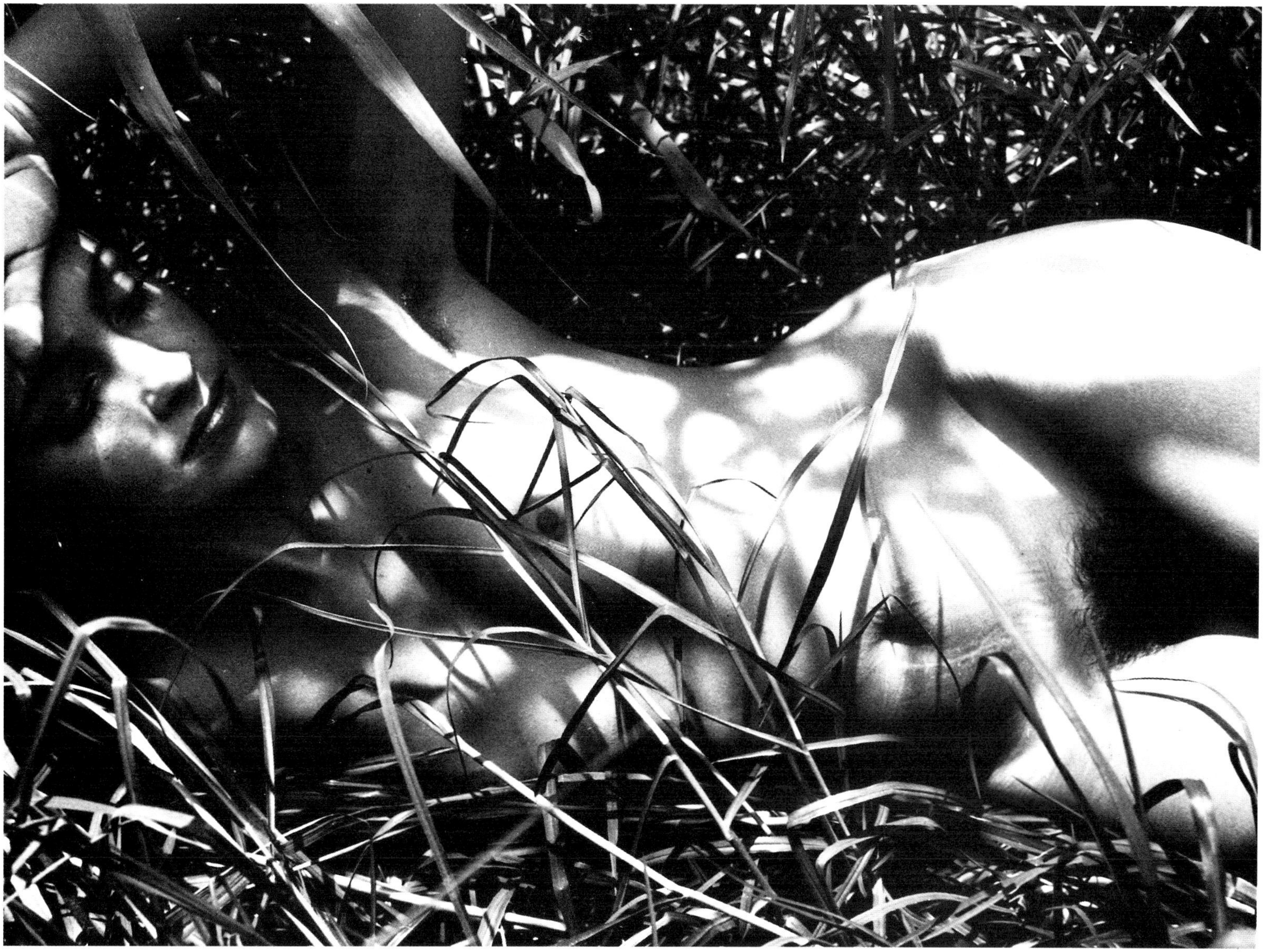

PLATE CIX
MANUEL ALVAREZ BRAVO
Catalina 1978
Photographers Gallery, London

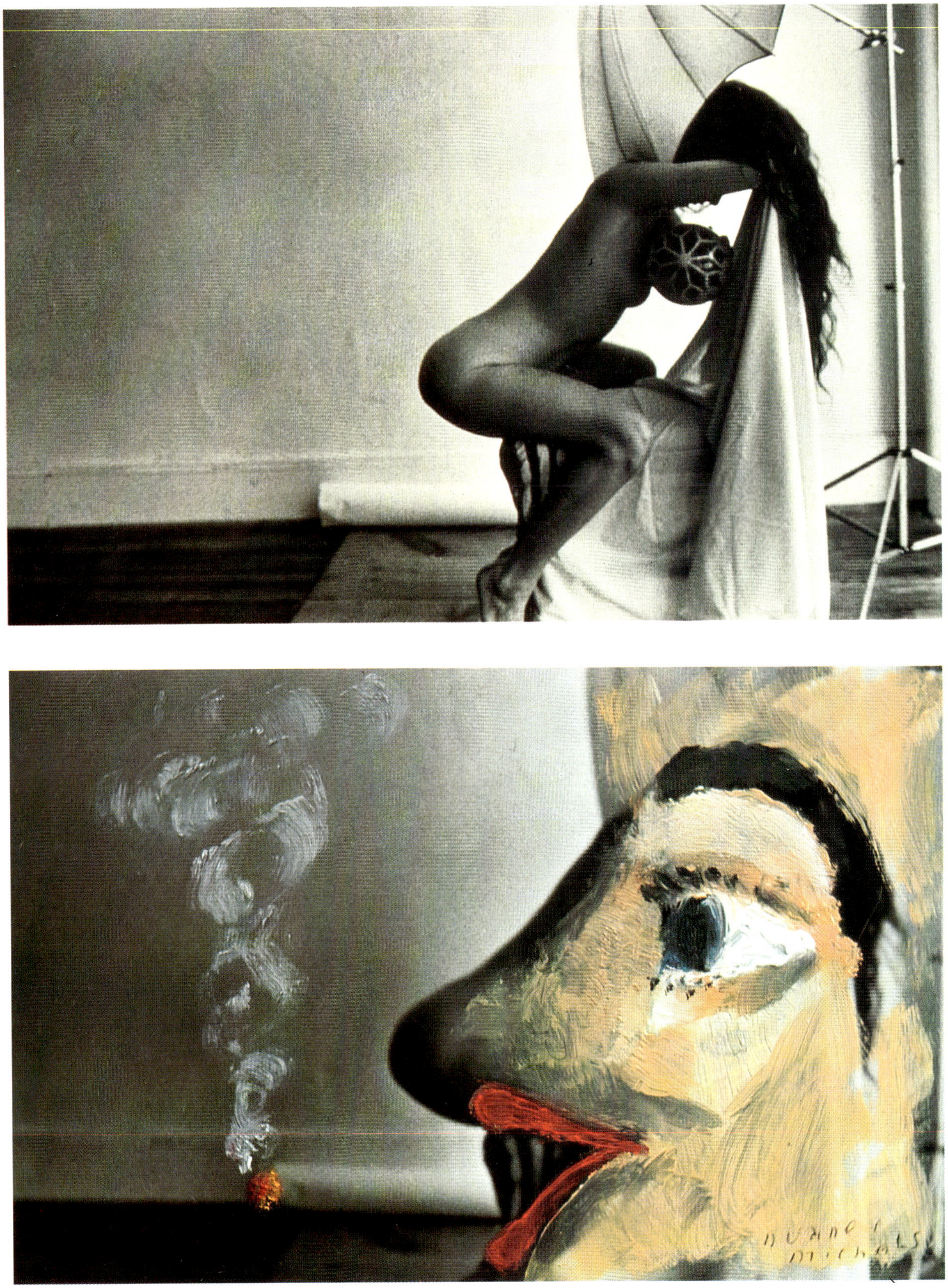

PLATE CX
DUANE MICHALS
Portrait of Esta Greenfield Smoking a Cigarette (Diptych) 1978
Sidney Janis Gallery, New York

Of painting on top of photographs, Michals says: "The gesture alone meant that I had 'disrespected' the traditional photograph. This was upsetting, yet terribly exciting."

NUDE NARRATIVES

Until the 1970s, historians and critics of photography had gone unchallenged in deciding that great photographs were exclusively those which objectively recorded the subject matter as presented to the photographer. Photographs in which the photographer had intervened to manipulate what was in front of his lens were written off as aberrations, unworthy of serious study, or completely ignored. Many great names are omitted, even from recent surveys of the history of photography, because they upset these narrow definitions, in a manner which recalls Russia's official denial of the existence of abstract Constructivist art in the pre-Stalin period of the Revolution.

Once such prejudices are carefully examined, they are soon exposed for what they are, since in fact every photograph involves some degree of manipulation of reality on the part of the practitioner. Certain photographers have always embraced the notion of seeking responsibility for as much as possible of the content of their pictures, but there is as yet no universally accepted generic term for this branch of the medium. The critic A.D. Coleman coined the term "the directorial mode." Tom Hopkinson, former editor of *Picture Post*, drew a useful distinction between what he calls "hunters" and "fixers": "Hunters go out looking for their pictures; fixers largely make theirs in the studio and darkroom." As someone who, professionally, had been more likely to use the work of hunters, Hopkinson recognized, without standing in judgment, that fixers were those for whom ". . . photography is a technique for realizing and making actual their inner fantasies, or for revealing some aspect of the physical world which they feel has been unappreciated or overlooked."

A backlash in favour of the fixers or directorial photographers began around 1970. LES KRIMS (PLATES CXXV, CXXVI and CXXVII) threw down the gauntlet to the Cartier-Bresson school by referring to his humorous fictions as "anti-decisive moments." Krims was one of the first of the new generation of directorial photographers whose work was widely published. Not surprisingly, Bailey was immediately attracted to his work. This was partly due to Krims' bizarre and often controversial subject matter: the quirky dramas he creates tell us as much in their own way about America as do straight documentary photographs. But Bailey was also pleased by the growing acceptance of arranged tableaux in photography: he was, after all, working in the directorial mode himself in his fashion and advertising photography.

Krims underlined the successful retrieval of his kind of photography when he wrote "I call these images fictions because that is what they truly are. These images are products of my imagination that would not have happened, could not have been found. They are before you because I physically caused them to occur in a specifically planned and directed way . . . It is possible to create any image one thinks of: this possibility, of course, is contingent on being able to think and create. The greatest source of photographic imagery is the mind." Krims was freed to make startlingly autobiographical pictures such as "Mom's Snaps, Pasted," for which he somehow persuaded his mother to pose naked with her snapshots of Les stuck to her body and the wall behind. Another early Krims, "The Static Electric Effect of Minnie Mouse on Mickey Mouse Balloons" (PLATE CXXVII) was a must for Bailey, since Krims treated with such wit the Disney characters who had been among Bailey's first childhood heroes (and who have cropped up often in Bailey's own work).

Many of Krims' early works were made in black and white on high contrast Kodalith paper, but more recently he has turned with great success to colour, in which he has created increasingly complex, densely packed, almost chaotic interior environments (PLATES CXXV and CXXVI).

Les Krims' fondness for illogical and absurd subjects and his conscious parodying of documentary photography inevitably recall the anti-rational aims of the Surrealists. "Photography is credible:" says Bailey, "we believe it is telling the truth, even when we should know better. This is why I find photographs which depict what is obviously unreal so fascinating. We are no longer conditioned to expect painting to deal with reality, but photographs that enter the forbidden territory have a kind of subversive edge." PIERRE BOUCHER, an underrated French Surrealist painter and photographer, produced marvellous, if contrived, nudes in the 1930s, which raise some of the problems inherent in Surrealist photography (PLATES CXX and CXXI).

The headless woman amid the ruins of a Moroccan temple (PLATE CXXI) is a photomontage, a scissors and paste job. Although expertly executed, the use of collage has broken the even surface we expect to see in a photographic print, thus forsaking the photograph's inherent veracity. It was perhaps for this reason that few of the leading Surrealist photographers employed this technique, preferring ploys which left the surface intact, such as double exposure. Marcel Natkin, writing in 1937, was clearly an admirer of Boucher's picture, which he felt was "hallucinating in its petrified somberness, and takes the onlooker far away into a world of phantasmagoria." Natkin also offered a clue to Boucher's use of photography: "What his pencil has sketched is completed by photography, which he looks upon as a second string to his bow." Boucher was equally adept at superimposing two negatives, as the dramatic spatial dislocation evident in Bailey's other choice amply demonstrates (PLATE CXVI).

Boucher's predilection for ruinous buildings and double exposures uncannily foreshadowed certain aspects of the work of the great American photographer, CLARENCE JOHN LAUGHLIN. To describe Laughlin as a Surrealist or a narrative photographer is misleading: he prided himself on "the wide range of subject matter with which I have dealt. The implication is that the creative photographer should be able to put the stamp of *his* way of seeing on whatever material he touches." Laughlin felt that his work went beyond "documentation" or "purism" into what he liked to call "the third world of photography." The poet Jonathan Williams depicted him as "the Master of Ignored Ghastliness, the Eldritch, the Psychopompous, the Metamorphic, the Mephitic, the Fearsome, and now and then of Trumpery and the Fulsome."

Laughlin was born in Louisiana in 1905. Initially a poet and writer, he did not take up photography until 1935. His early efforts were in the mould of purist photographers he admired, such as Paul Strand and Edward Weston. But "By 1939 (because of my pre-sensitizing by literature etc), I had embarked on creating pictures in which specific people were intuitively arranged against specifically chosen backgrounds – often with various subjects added – all in terms of internal compulsions. Study of the resulting pictures would sometimes reveal their hidden meanings at a later date." For Laughlin, the camera became the tool which might "reveal the mystery that is behind all things." Instead of the purists' concentration on the "thing-in-itself" Laughlin was concerned with the "thing-beyond-itself."

His unfashionable theories ensured that Laughlin was kept out of the mainstream of American photography. Possibly feeling misunderstood, Laughlin frequently added an explanatory text to his photographs. Some of his most famous pictures, such as "The Repulsive Bed" and "The Auto-Eroticists," treat sexual themes in a disturbing and dramatic way, but his nudes are comparatively scarce. Of "Figure with Iron Flames" (PLATE CXIII) he wrote: "A double exposure dealing with those who are obsessed. The head of the figure has become hard and round and rigid (suggesting fixity); the chain of compulsion is attached to her head; while from her skull break the iron flames of the repression that has her in bondage. The hard tomb forms indicate the rigid world in which the obsessed live." The "Memento of the Mae West Period" (PLATE CXXVIII) has never been published before and attracted Bailey's attention because "it's not quite what I had expected of Laughlin." It stands as a literal example of Laughlin's attempt to "create a mythology from our contemporary world," a complex still-life construction prescient of recent photographic tableaux.

"Prime Cut" (PLATE CXXIII) is a compelling example of the sinister wit which often pervades the work of another American master of staged fantasies, ARTHUR TRESS. Born in Brooklyn in 1940, Tress is one of the younger exponents of narrative photography; his most obvious stylistic forerunners are Clarence John Laughlin and Ralph Eugene Meatyard. Tress' method seems to be to analyse his subjects' personalities and then to persuade them to act out a metaphorical story of his own imagining. The photographer Duane Michals wrote of being photographed by Tress: ". . . you will become an actor. You will perform in his theater and that drama one soon realizes is one's own. Don't be surprised if Arthur suddenly asks you to put your mother in a wheelbarrow, and don't be amazed to find yourself doing it."

"Prime Cut" dates from 1979 and is part of a series Tress was making at that time of voyeuristic homosexual fantasies. It has also carried the title "Butchers' Fantasy" and was made in the butcher's shop belonging to a friend of his. In common with much of Tress' work, this image can be read as macabre and aggressive on the one hand, or equally as having a detached, if somewhat ghoulish, humour.

Like his contemporary Paul Outerbridge, GEORGE PLATT LYNES found that the prevailing moral climate prevented the publication or exhibition of all but a few of his nudes during his lifetime. Their eroticism was of a detached kind, always underpinned by his formal concerns with line and volume, qualities which remained in evidence even in his most fantastic project, a series illustrating Greek mythological subjects made between 1936 and 1940. Lynes died prematurely in 1955, and it is only in the last decade that his nudes have become widely known.

Born in New Jersey in 1907, Lynes made his first visit to Paris in 1925, where he was introduced into an artistic circle which included Gertrude Stein, Jean Cocteau and Pavel Tchelitchew. Returning to the United States, he opened a bookshop in 1927 and published a series of booklets written by Stein, Ernest Hemingway and René Crevel, with illustrations by Cocteau and Tchelitchew. At the same time, he took up photography, exhibiting his first portraits in the bookstore. When we consider that Lynes, in common with Clarence John Laughlin and others, pursued allegorical, theatrical and narrative themes in his photography, it is significant that they shared direct literary origins and interests.

Back in Europe in 1930, Lynes met Julian Levy and collaborated with him on a group of surrealistic still lifes. In 1932, Levy included Lynes' photographs in the pioneering exhibition *Surrealisme* at his New York gallery. The following year Lynes was able to open a studio in New York City, where he became highly successful, initially for his portraits of personalities and later as a fashion photographer. He quickly grew disenchanted with the limitations imposed by fashion magazines and advertising clients, and his unpublished nudes became the major outlet for his imagination. Before his death he destroyed many of his prints and negatives, including most of his fashion work.

"Actaeon" (PLATE CXII), in its almost camp theatricality, can be seen as an offshoot of another important branch of Lynes' activities, that of official photographer to the American Ballet. Choreographer George Balanchine wrote in tribute to Lynes' photographs of the New York City Ballet: "Lynes' secret was his sense of plasticity: his genius for lighting figures in space so that his bodies seemed to exist in actual aery ambience, akin to three-dimensional vitality in sculpture." In 1945, Lynes moved to Hollywood, where he was head of Condé Nast's studio, mainly photographing fashion for *Vogue*'s sister magazine, *Glamour*. The three-year period he spent there is generally written off as a failure and his friend and admirer Cecil Beaton thought that he was "killed" by Hollywood, explaining that Lynes refused to "indulge in grotesque flattery or the fashionable retouching" of his portraits. A problem in assessing his work for *Glamour* exists since he subsequently destroyed so much of it, but a thorough examination of the magazine reveals that he frequently produced innovative and exciting work, often, unusually for him, outside the studio.

Beaton's opinion was certainly accurate in that Lynes' career, despite attempts to re-establish himself as a fashion photographer, took a downturn after his return to New York in 1948. In 1951 he was declared bankrupt; cancer forced him to give up his studio in 1955 and six months later he died. Throughout this period he continued to photograph nudes privately, concentrating on exploring the sexual psyche via photography. In this context it is interesting that, among the more obvious photographic collections, there is a repository of his work at the Kinsey Institute for Research in Sex, Gender and Reproduction in Bloomington, Indiana.

What might be termed the Post-Modernist reaction of younger photographers against established photographic canons has largely been located in the United States. A notable exception to this is the work of BERNARD FAUCON, a young French photographer who is still in his thirties. For the opening exhibition of the Victoria & Albert Museum's new photography galleries, *Personal Choice*, Bailey was asked to select two photographs: he chose one by JOEL-PETER WITKIN (PLATES CXXIII-CXXV) and one by Bernard Faucon (PLATES CXVIII and CXIX). "They start at opposite poles," wrote Bailey, "Witkin bizarre and Faucon ordinary; both leave you visually paranoid." He referred to Faucon's photograph giving us a "sense of security, by introducing so much nostalgia." The same might be said for "The Crucifixion" (PLATE CXVIII), though again any feeling of familiarity evaporates when we register that this strange tableau is played out by plastic dummy children with blank stares. Recently he has forsaken the dummy children, using a live couple who edge into his picture frame in the series "The Rooms of Love" (PLATE CXIX).

Joel-Peter Witkin's photographs "have a Victorian presence;" comments Bailey, "on the one hand they seem rather cozy and domestic, a feeling which is soon shattered by these unfriendly images." He says they recall for him "those sepia Victorian engravings of the devil you used to see in books as a child. Every day I want to read something new, an opinion, a point of view. My greatest pleasure in life is to see a new image, or one I never thought of . . . In the new I'm looking for things forgotten. For we know everything: it's up to the poet to jog our memories, to help us remember."

In the last five or six years, Witkin's photographs have achieved great celebrity and are included in the collections of some of the world's major museums. They have frequently been published in photographic magazines but, in Britain at least, have not yet reached a wider public. Those encountering these images for the first time may perhaps understand the artist's intentions more clearly, or at least trust his sincerity, by knowing something of his life, which has been explained in some detail in the specialist press.

Witkin was born in Brooklyn in 1939 to a Jewish father and a Catholic mother. He has told of the mark left by his first conscious visual experience, which occurred when he was six years old: "Out of it I see many roots extending to my visual work in my use of severed heads, masks, and my concerns with violence, pain and death. We were going to church. While walking down the hallway to the entrance of the building, we heard an incredible crash mixed with screaming and cries for help. The accident had involved three cars, all with families in them. Somehow, in the confusion, I was no longer holding my mother's hand. At the place where I stood at the curb I could see something rolling from one of the overturned cars. It stopped at the curb where I stood. It was the head of a little girl. I bent down to touch the face, to ask it – but before I could touch it I was carried away."

His first serious photographs were made in the mid-1950s. His brother was a painter who had chosen Coney Island freaks as his subject. Joel-Peter took pictures for his brother, including some of a hermaphrodite with whom Joel-Peter had his first sexual experience. Shortly after this the freak show moved south and, having lost his ready-made subject matter, Witkin resolved to create his own settings in which he could enact and direct his strange rituals. Much of his inspiration came from paintings, from artists as diverse as Rembrandt, Goya, Bosch, Klimt, Kubin, Balthus and Beckmann. In 1961, he began work as a printer of colour photographs, attending evening classes in sculpture. Since he was not a full-time student he knew he would be drafted into the U.S. Army so, in order to continue photography, he enlisted for three years and trained to be a combat photographer. One of his duties was to record forms of death from accidents on manoeuvres and suicides. After being discharged from the army – where he had attempted suicide himself – Witkin resolved to make photographs which would lead to a better understanding of his own troubled psyche. He has stated: "In order to know if I were truly alive, I'd make the invisible visible! Photography would be the means to bring God down to earth – to exist for me in the photographic images I would create."

Witkin left New York in 1975 to become a graduate student of photography at the University of New Mexico. It was here that the body of work by which he is known began to develop. He undertook the serious study of the history of art and photography, one outcome of which was that he now seeks to give his prints a physical quality of being aged. This he achieves by making scratch marks on his negatives, printing through tissue and by selective colour toning. Faces will often be erased by scratching, or obscured by masks, so that the meaning of the image is not diluted by reference to a specific personality.

Witkin has written about one such photograph, selected by Bailey, "I.D. Photograph from Purgatory: Two Women with Stomach Irritations," dating from 1982 (PLATE CXV): "One of these two women is obviously pregnant and the other had had an operation because her spleen had burst when she ran into a parking pole, which is why her stomach was buttoned up. The masks I used came from some drawings I was making at the time that I felt would change the shape of the human figure if used with the addition of the photographically made eyes I glued to them. There's a connection here with Miro, African masks and shields, for a face basically is what we project to the world or a shield is used as a kind of weapon of love or hate. I lit my models very much like a mug shot, or like an I.D. photograph is usually lit. The curious thing about this photograph, and many of the photographs I make, is that I can believe in something so crazy and preposterous as this image that exists only as a photograph."

Witkin's preoccupation with death and sexual deviations has led his supporters' arguments, understandably enough, to take on a certain defensiveness. His work does not need defending, but it might require explanation, as it clearly raises many important issues. That any photographs still have the power to shock is in itself perhaps surprising. The Romantic and Symbolist art to which Witkin's photographs most closely relate no longer challenges taboos with such a jolt, not even the more extreme works of Goya, Fuseli, Félicien Rops or Egon Schiele. Equally, the supposedly numbing effect of present-day war reportage photographs, such as those taken in Vietnam and Beirut, seems not to have brutalized our senses to the point where Witkin's images leave us unmoved. Van Deren Coke has perhaps summed it up best: "Witkin's admirably inventive when it comes to giving us an intimate view of the dark side of our make-up. Most photographers have dealt with what is known. Witkin gives us glimpses of the unknown as he has seen it."[10]

In 1966, when the American photographer DUANE MICHALS began to present his photographs as multiple-print sequences rather than single images, he was in a sense taking the photo-narrative to its logical conclusion. Of course he did not invent the method, which can be traced back to Muybridge in the nineteenth century or even earlier, yet he was undoubtedly one of the most prominent and influential of the recent revivers of this practice. Bailey's admiration for Michals' work, in which he finds the "mix of innocence and sophistication" particularly appealing, is in some ways surprising. In general, Bailey prefers photographs which get their message across in a single image and usually steers clear of the texts or captions which accompany many of Michals' sequences. It is in the nature of these sequences that they have a cumulative effect which is greater than the power of any individual images; nevertheless, Bailey has chosen one photograph from a dream sequence which he feels does stand up in isolation (PLATE CXI). His other choice is more accurately described as a diptych: the "Portrait of Esta Greenfield Smoking a Cigarette" (PLATE CX) struck a chord with Bailey because of the way Michals transformed the reading of the second image by his amusing painted additions. Bailey, too, has on occasion let his enthusiasm for painting spill over into his photographs (PLATE XCVI).

Since 1960, Duane Michals has made a successful living as a portrait and fashion photographer. He is relatively unusual in that he has continued this work in parallel with his "art" photography intended for books or galleries. The work he publishes in sequences and his other "private" pictures are of a highly personal, often autobiographical nature, which is rare in photography. He has spoken of the "enormous amount of vulnerability in poets, because they're still speaking in the first person singular," and in many ways he is a first person singular photographer, using his camera to question reality and relationships. Some of his sequences he has characterized as cinematic rather than narrative, which is an important distinction, and others, those with lengthier texts, as more literary. He acknowledges the influence of photographers such as Atget, Bill Brandt and George Platt Lynes, and the Surrealist painters De Chirico, Balthus and Magritte. Michals' techniques also bear comparison with Surrealist photographers. As he says, "It's very funny that here I am, probably with no official photographic training, yet I'm the one who does all the photographic tricks: I do double exposures, I do the blurs, I do the sandwiching, I do all those things that I always thought that people much more technically suited than me to doing these things should be doing . . . I love doing it. I love anything the camera can do. So a painter takes advantage of the drips and the dribbles and the splashes and the accidents. Well, I like to take advantage of the machine, and these are the things that the camera can do."

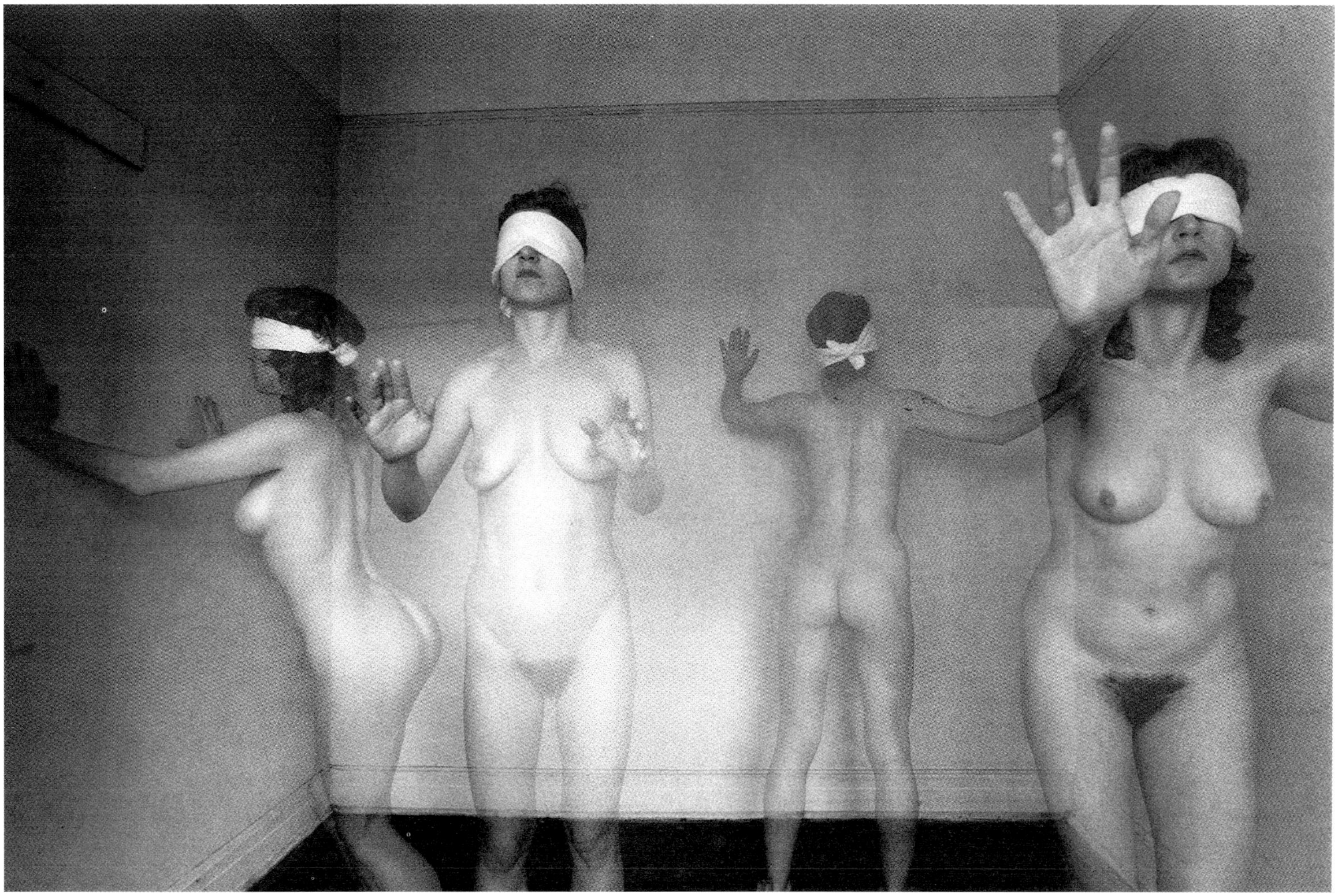

PLATE CXI
DUANE MICHALS
Violent Women 1983
Courtesy the photographer

"The nude has always been part of my work," explains Duane Michals. "There's something about the nude body that makes the person 'nonspecific', universal. The moment the person puts on clothing, a point of view is defined, a social class established."

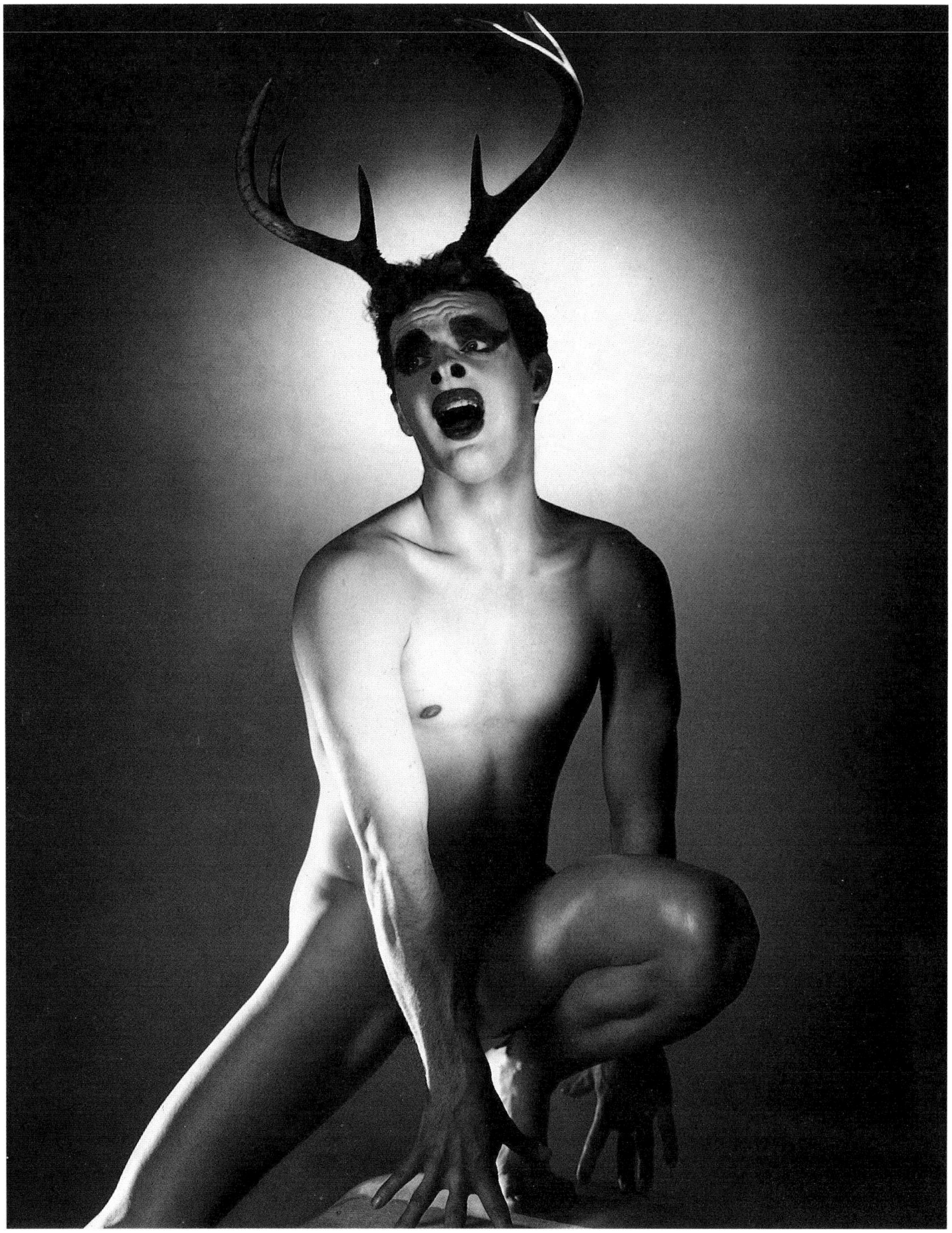

PLATE CXII

GEORGE PLATT LYNES

Actaeon c.1937-39

Robert Miller Gallery, New York

Lynes' depictions of Greek myths sometimes teeter on the edge of bathos or camp, but are usually rescued by his acknowledgement of the element of theater and by his sensitive lighting.

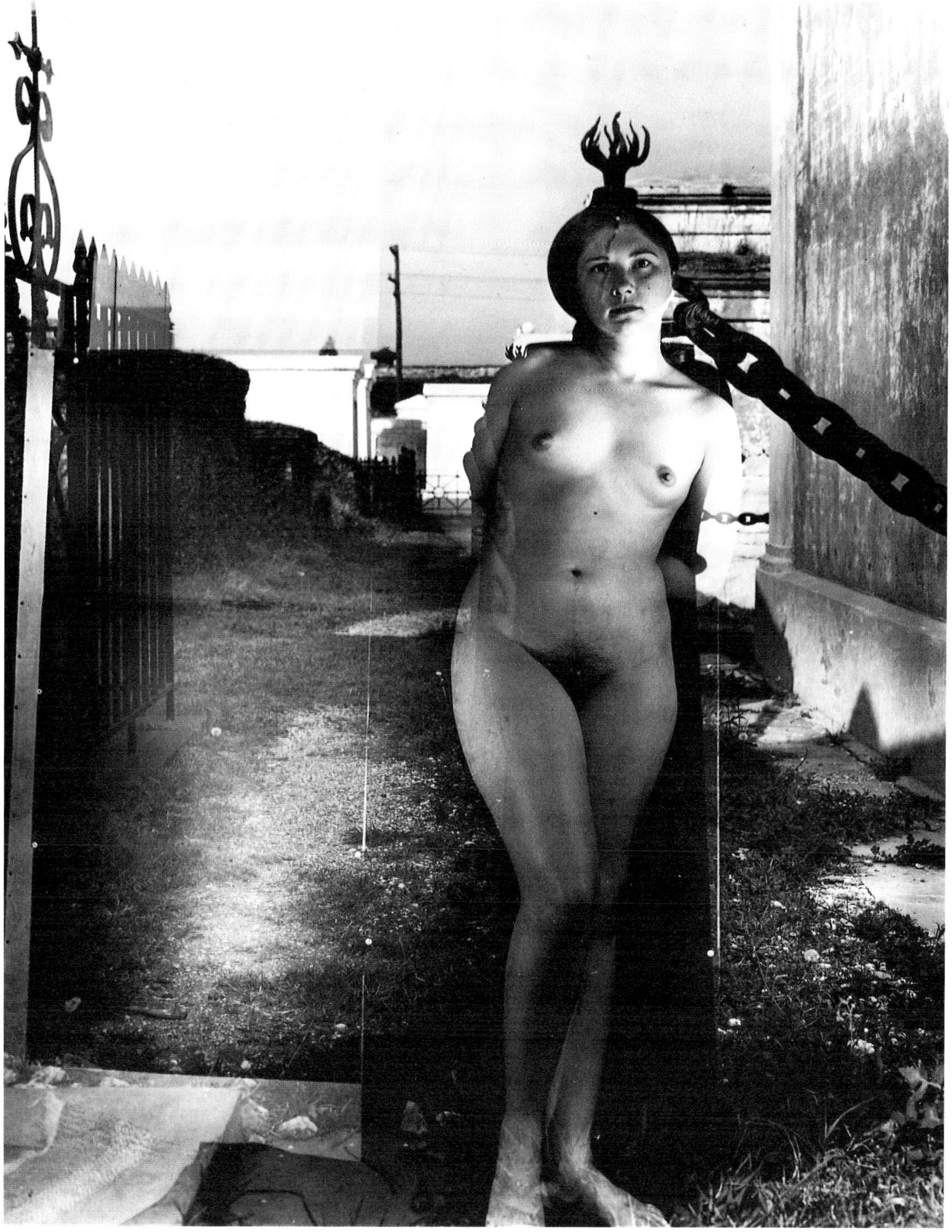

PLATE CXIII
CLARENCE JOHN LAUGHLIN
Figure with Iron Flames 1940
Historic New Orleans Collection/Robert Miller Gallery, New York

Laughlin classified his work in twenty-three different categories, and "Figure with Iron Flames" he placed in the group *Poems of the Inner World*, which contained many of his most original and disquieting images.

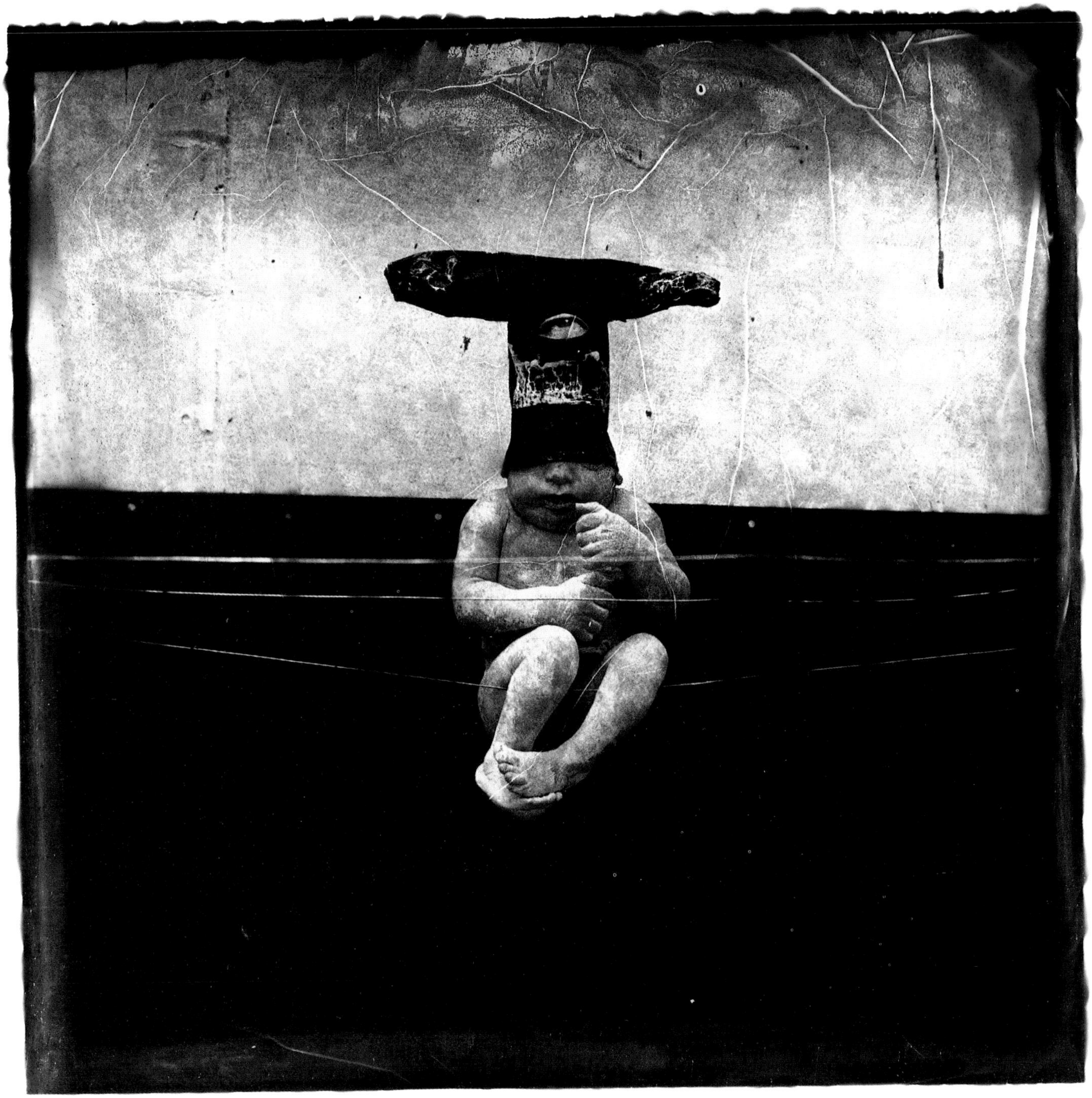

PLATE CXIV
JOEL-PETER WITKIN
Counting Lesson in Purgatory 1982
Courtesy the photographer, Pace/McGill, New York and Fraenkel Gallery, San Francisco

Witkin explains: "Most of my work comes about through my association with aesthetics and art history, rather than things which have happened to me personally."

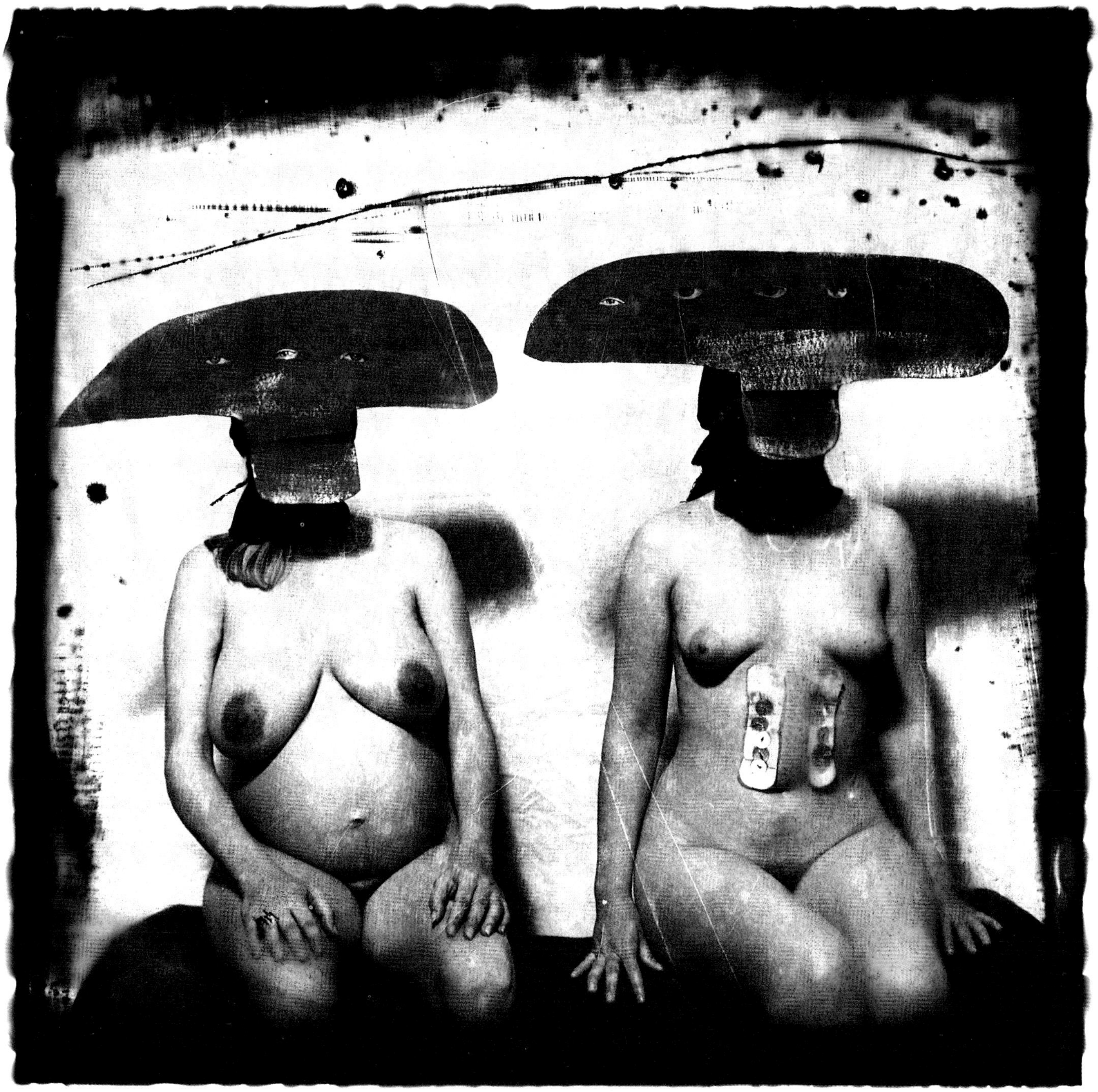

PLATE CXV
JOEL-PETER WITKIN
I.D. Photograph from Purgatory.
Two Women with Stomach Irritations 1982
Courtesy the photographer, Pace/McGill, New York and Fraenkel Gallery, San Francisco

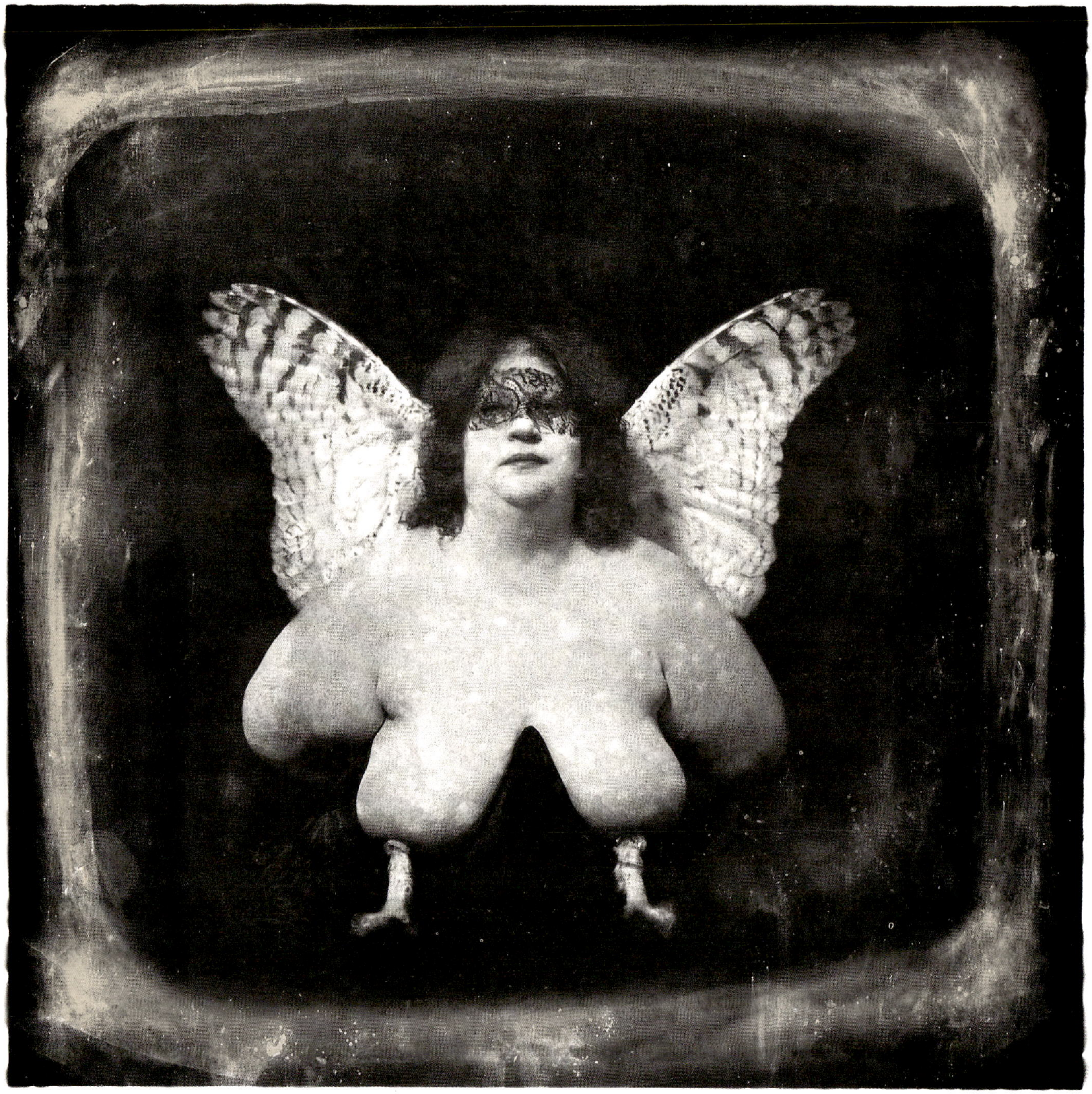

PLATE CXVI
JOEL-PETER WITKIN
Bird of Quevada 1982
Courtesy the photographer, Pace/McGill, New York and Fraenkel Gallery, San Francisco

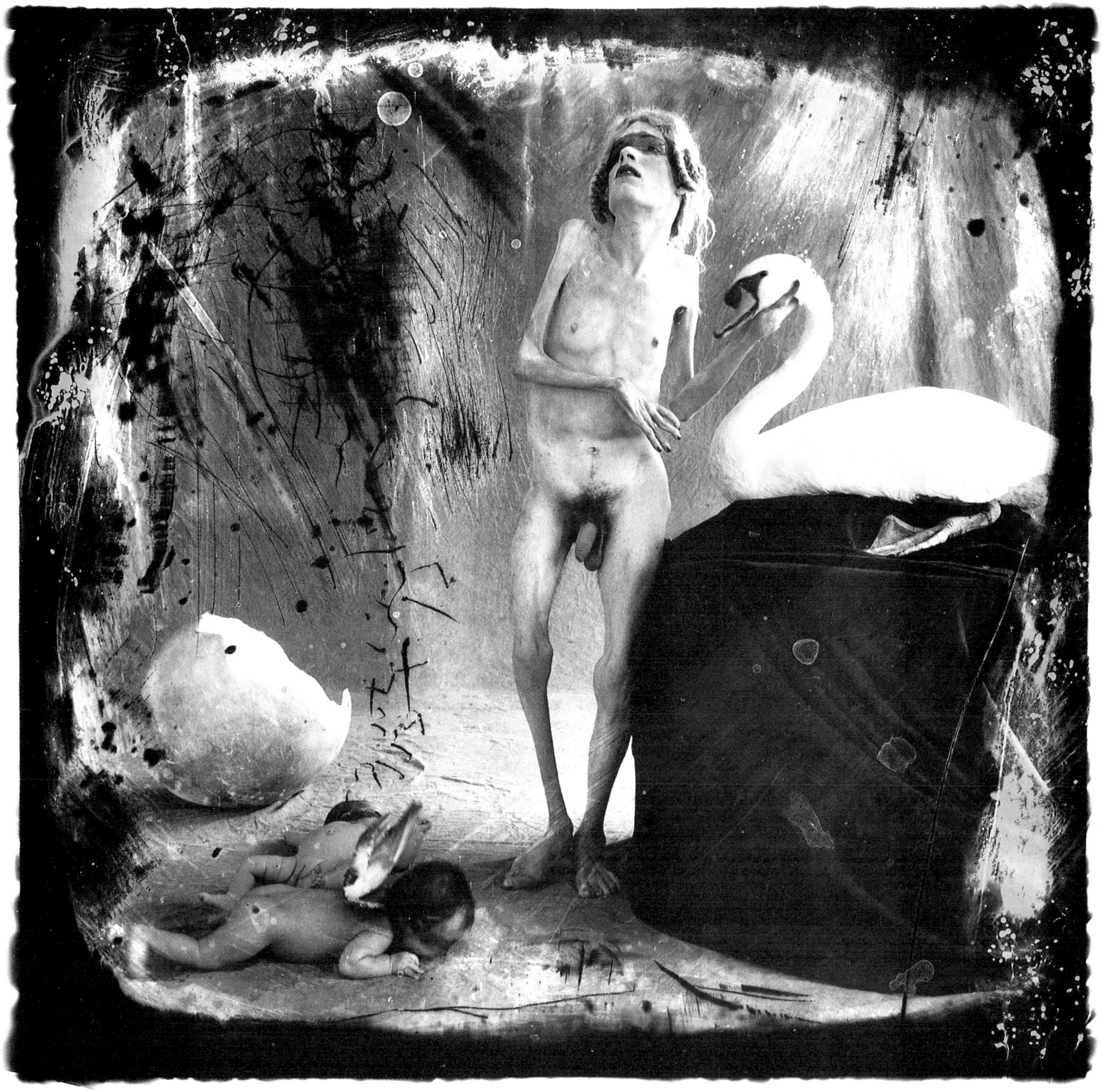

PLATE CXXVII
JOEL-PETER WITKIN
Leda 1986
Courtesy the photographer, Pace/MacGill, New York and Fraenkel Gallery, San Francisco

Witkins' treatment of the Greek myth of Leda and the swan is far removed from that of Leonardo.

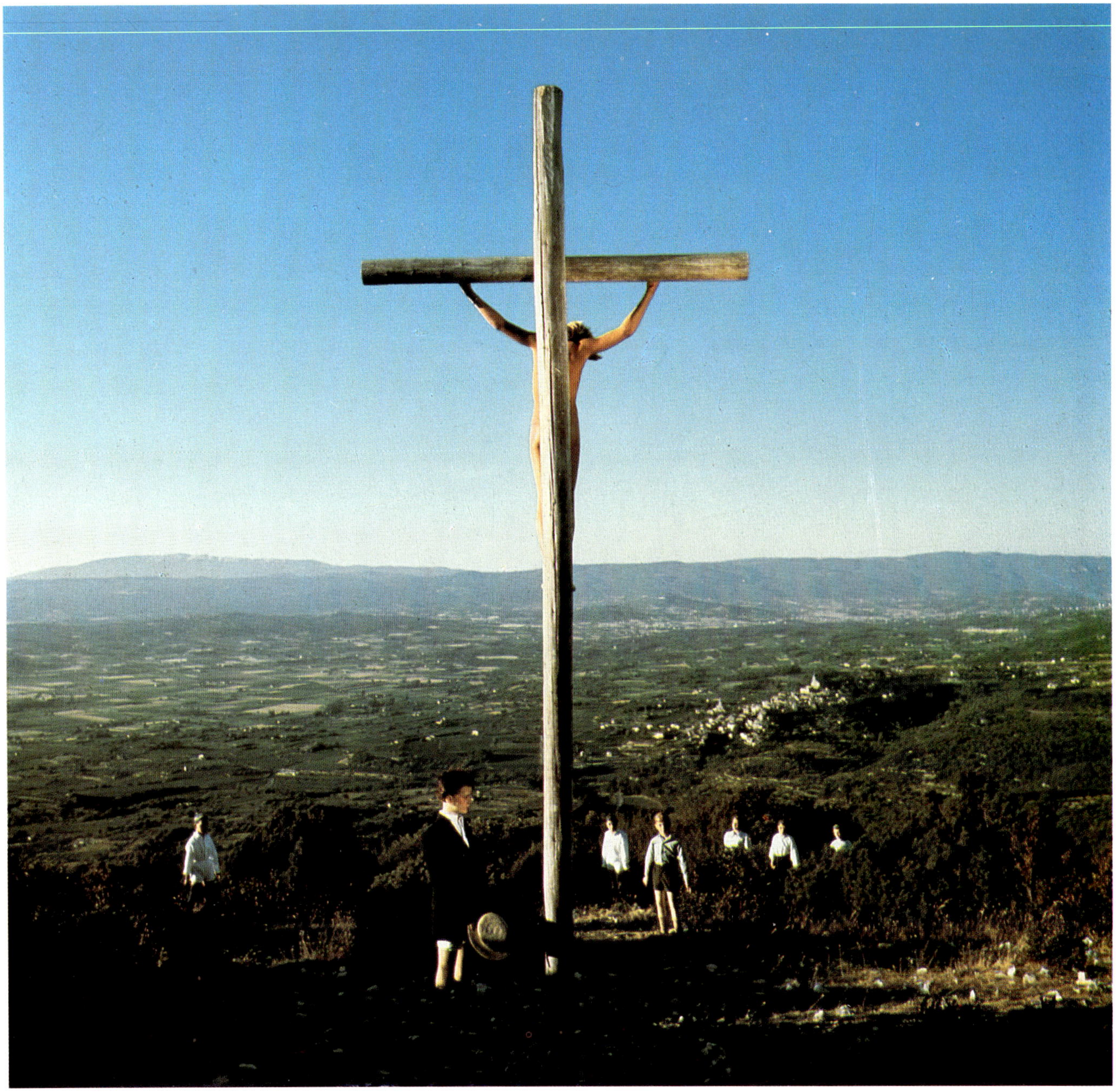

PLATE CXVIII
BERNARD FAUCON
Crucifixion 1980
Galerie Agatha Gaillard, Paris/Bernard Faucon

Faucon's tableaux are exercises in ambiguity and dislocation. He is fascinated by childhood, but the seemingly innocent scenes (mostly acted out by mannequins) are disrupted by violence or chaos, reminiscent of the breakdown of order depicted in Golding's *Lord of the Flies*.

In the *Chambres d'Amour* series Faucon shows us conspicuously empty rooms, with changing clues to a human presence.

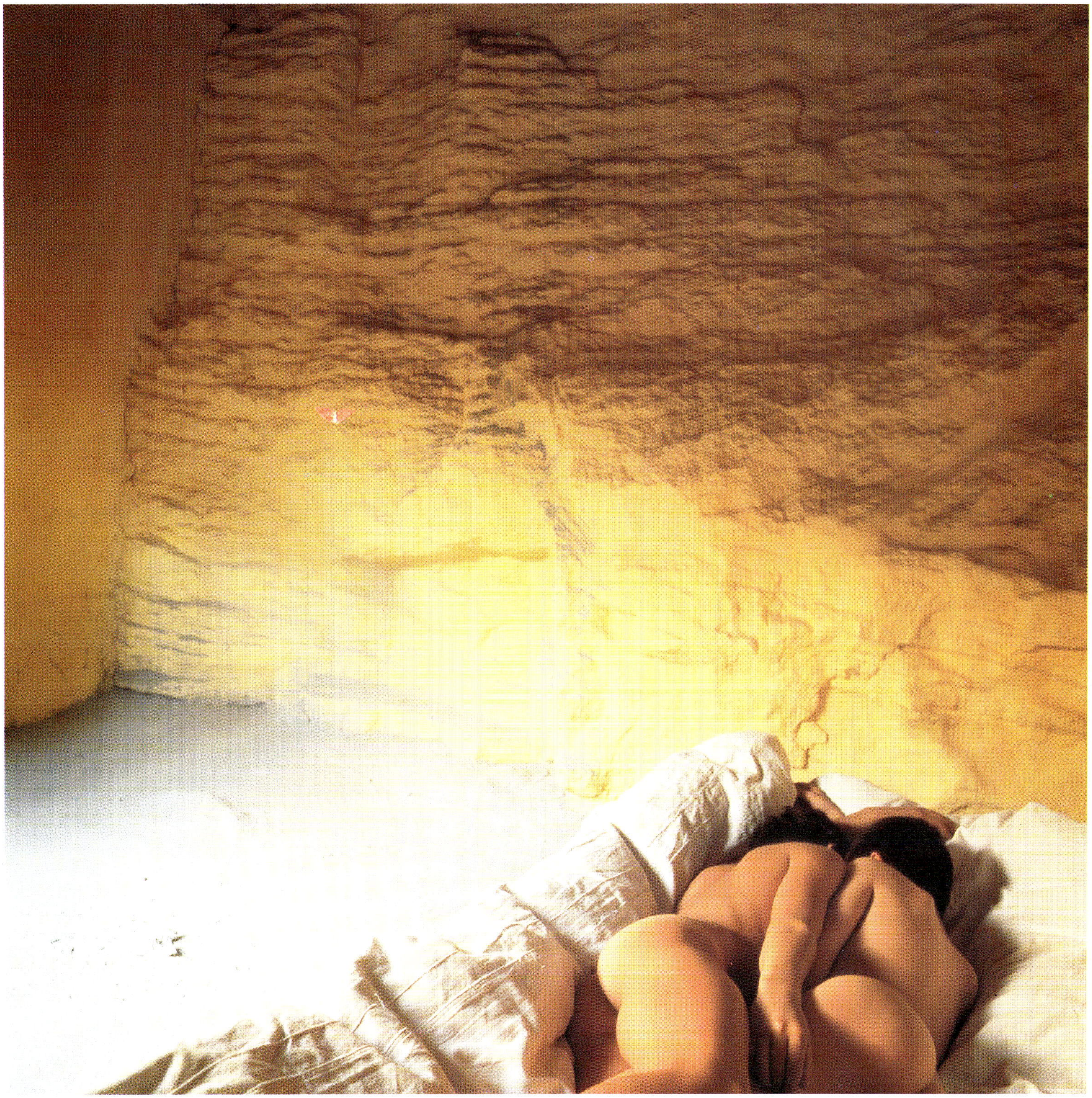

PLATE CXIX
BERNARD FAUCON
The Sixteenth Room of Love 1985
Galerie Agathe Gaillard, Paris/Bernard Faucon

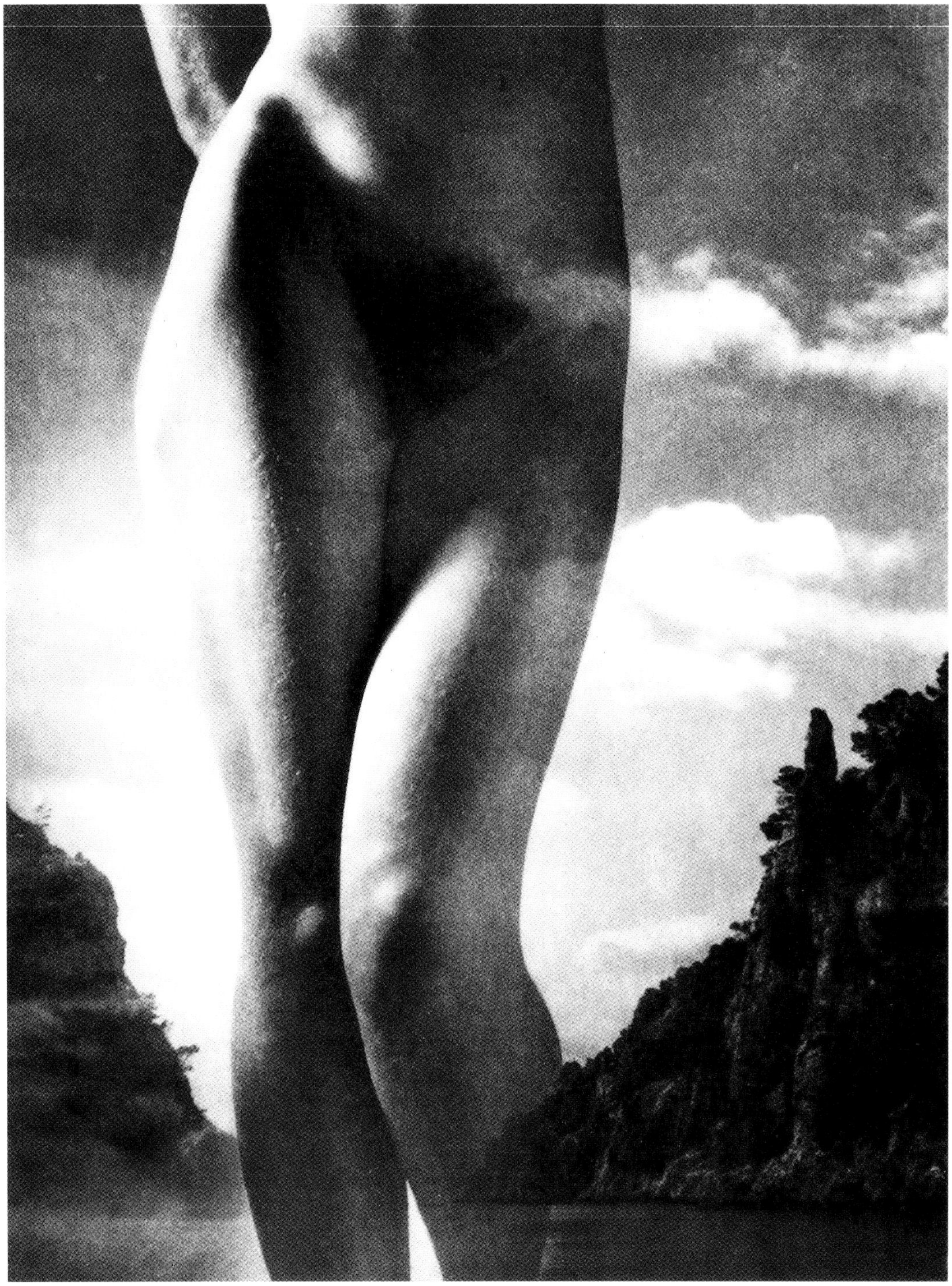

PLATE CXX
PIERRE BOUCHER
Untitled c.1935
PHOTOGRAVURE
Private Collection, London

Boucher's photographs, using a wide range of techniques inspired by Surrealism, were used to illustrate the book *Truquages en photographie* (Tricks in Photography), which was published in 1938.

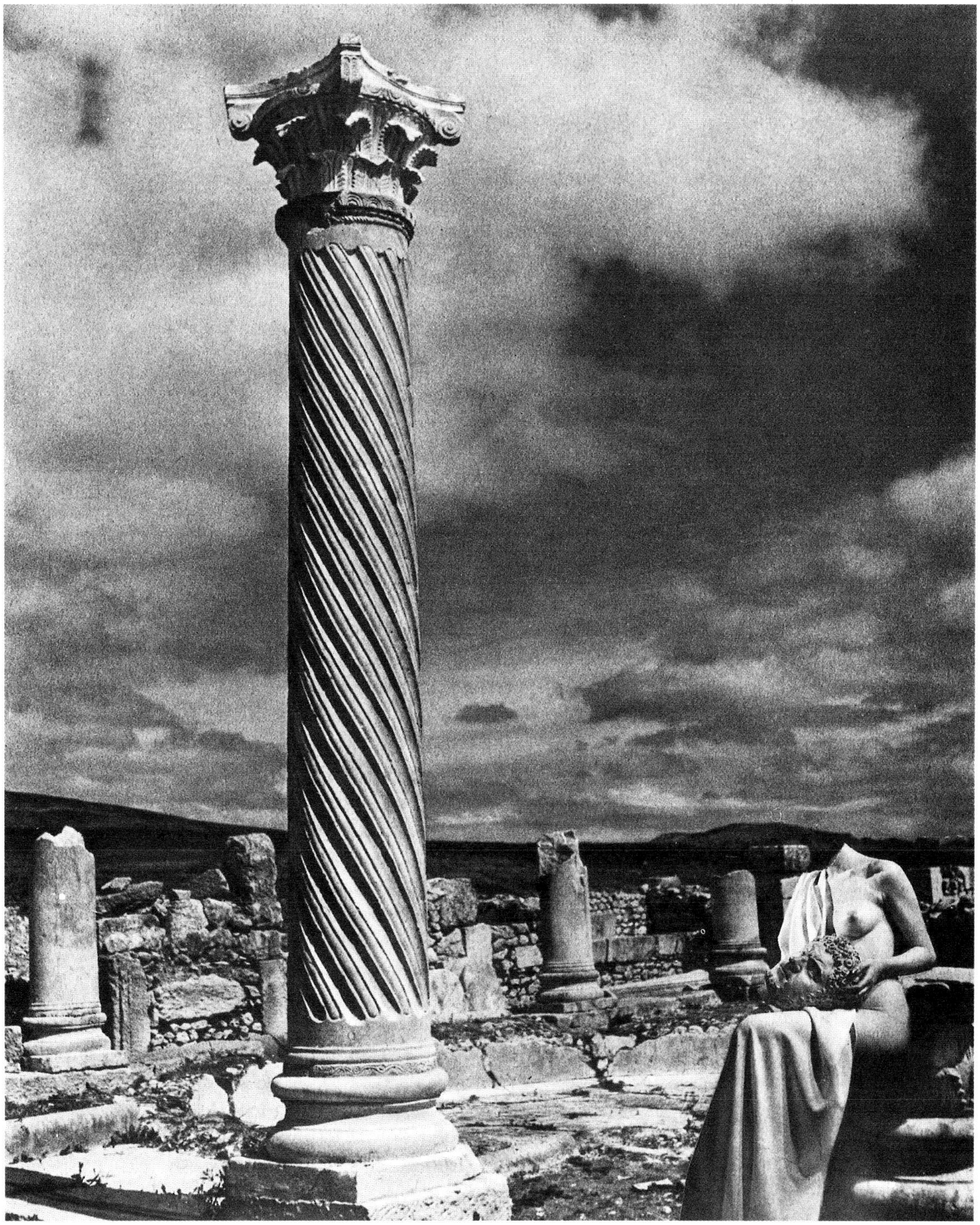

PLATE CXXI
PIERRE BOUCHER
Untitled c.1935
PHOTOGRAVURE
Private Collection

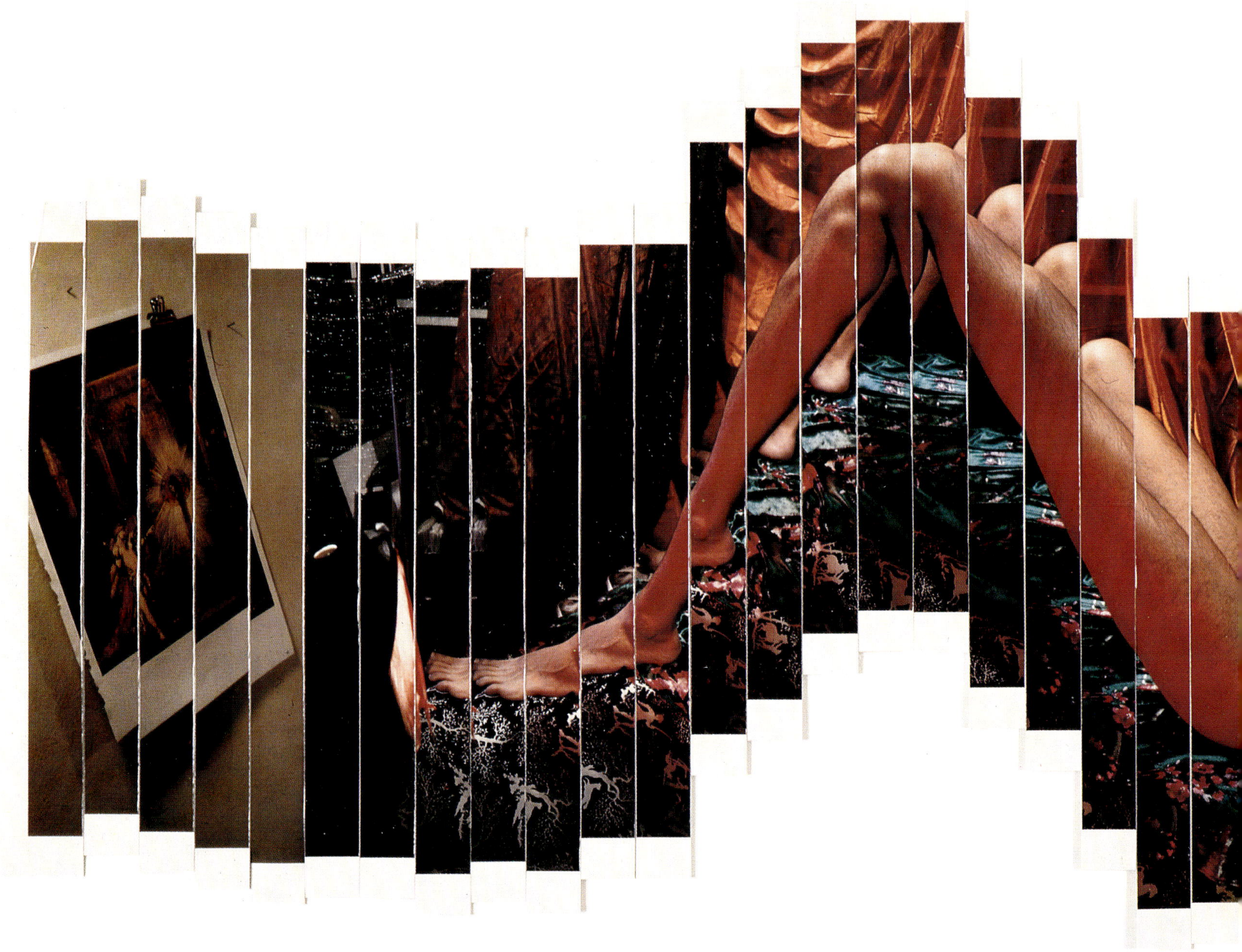

PLATE CXXII
LUCAS SAMARAS
Panorama – Blau 1983
MULTIPLE POLAROIDS
Roger M. Dalsheimer Collection

An artist in various media, Samaras first used Polaroids in 1969. Since then he has greatly expanded his applications of several Polaroid formats. Originally incorporating Polaroids into his works in other media, such as his boxes, films and sculptures, more recently Samaras has concentrated on purely photographic imagery, still exploring his self-directed slices of autobiography.

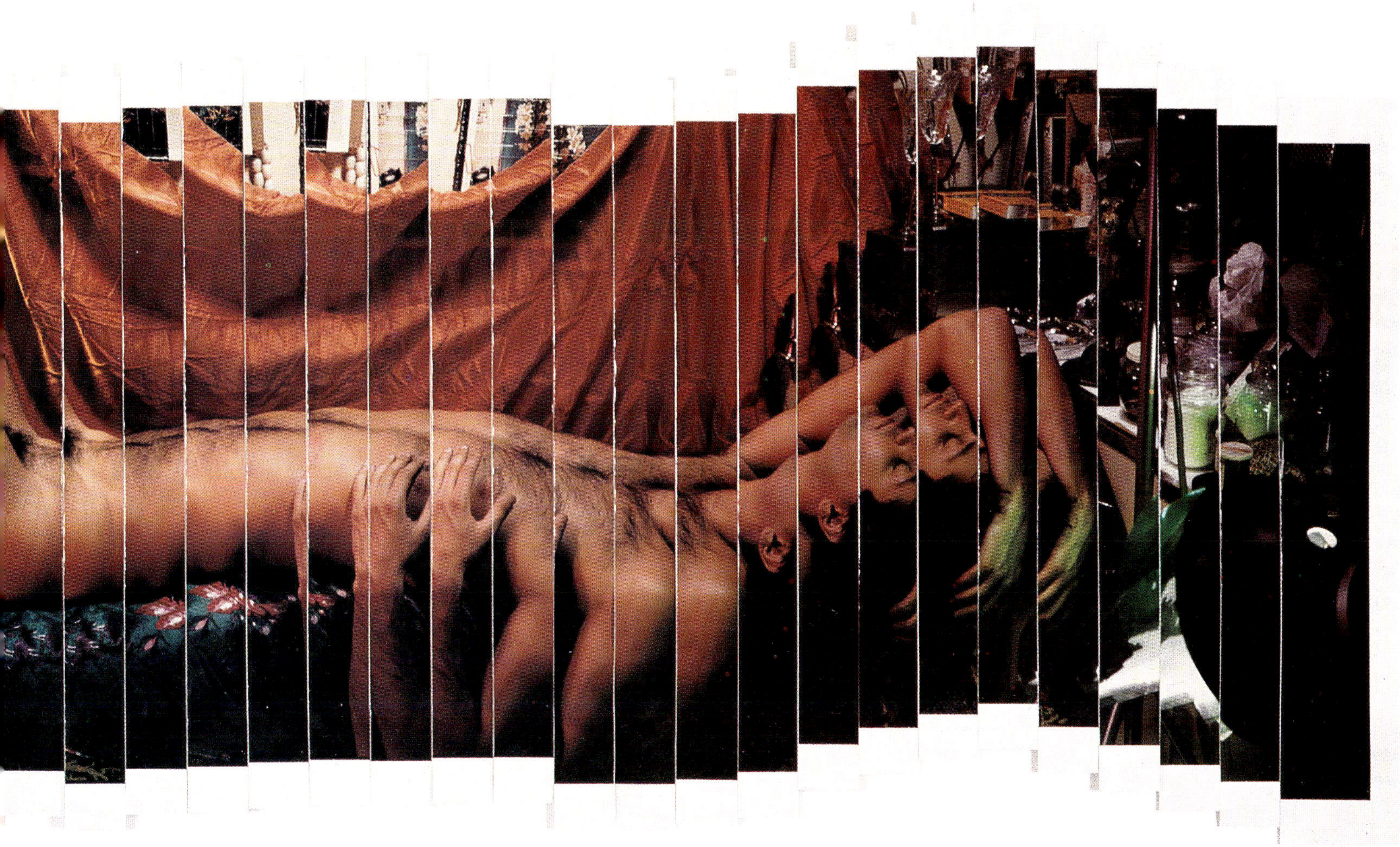

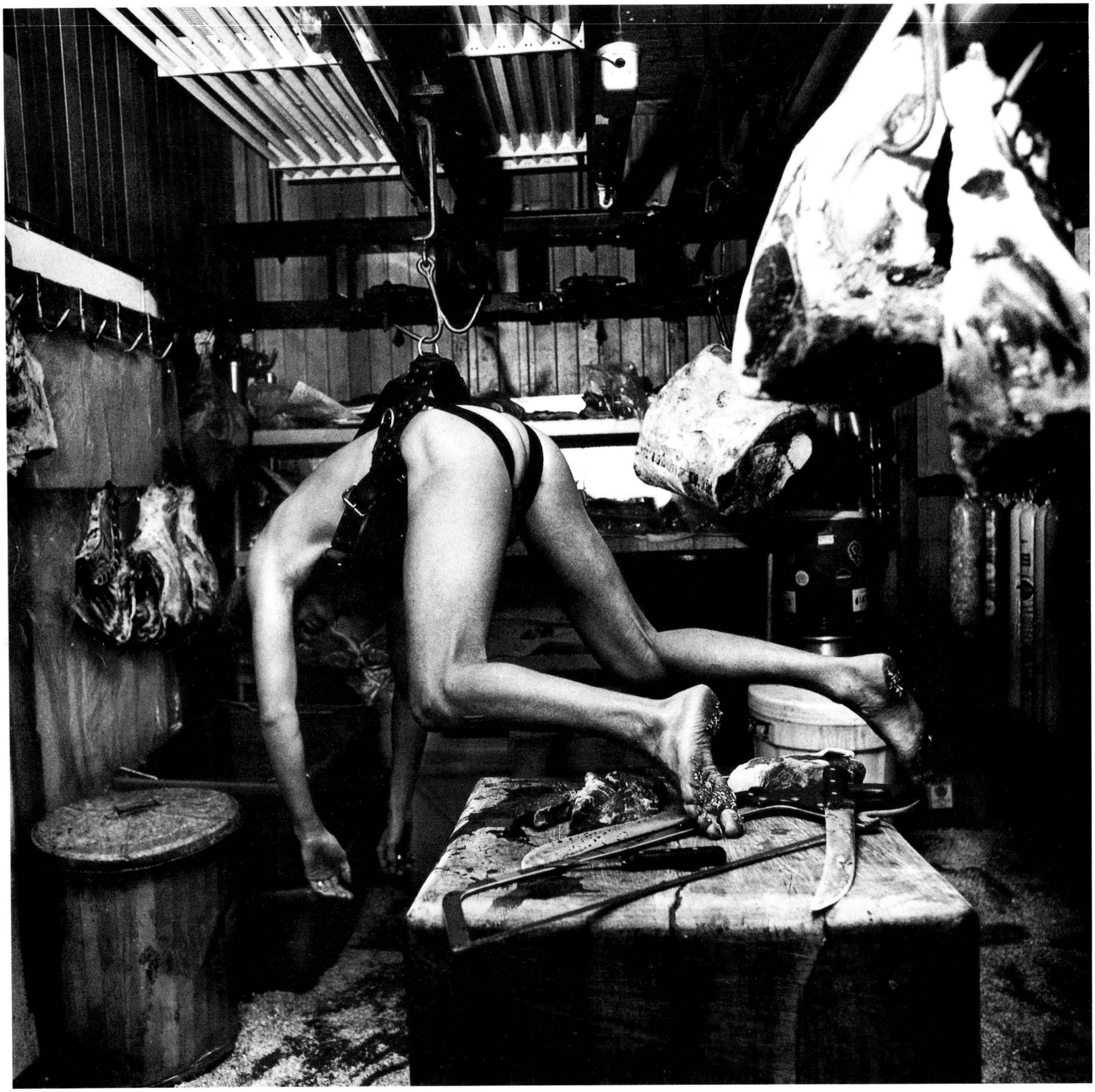

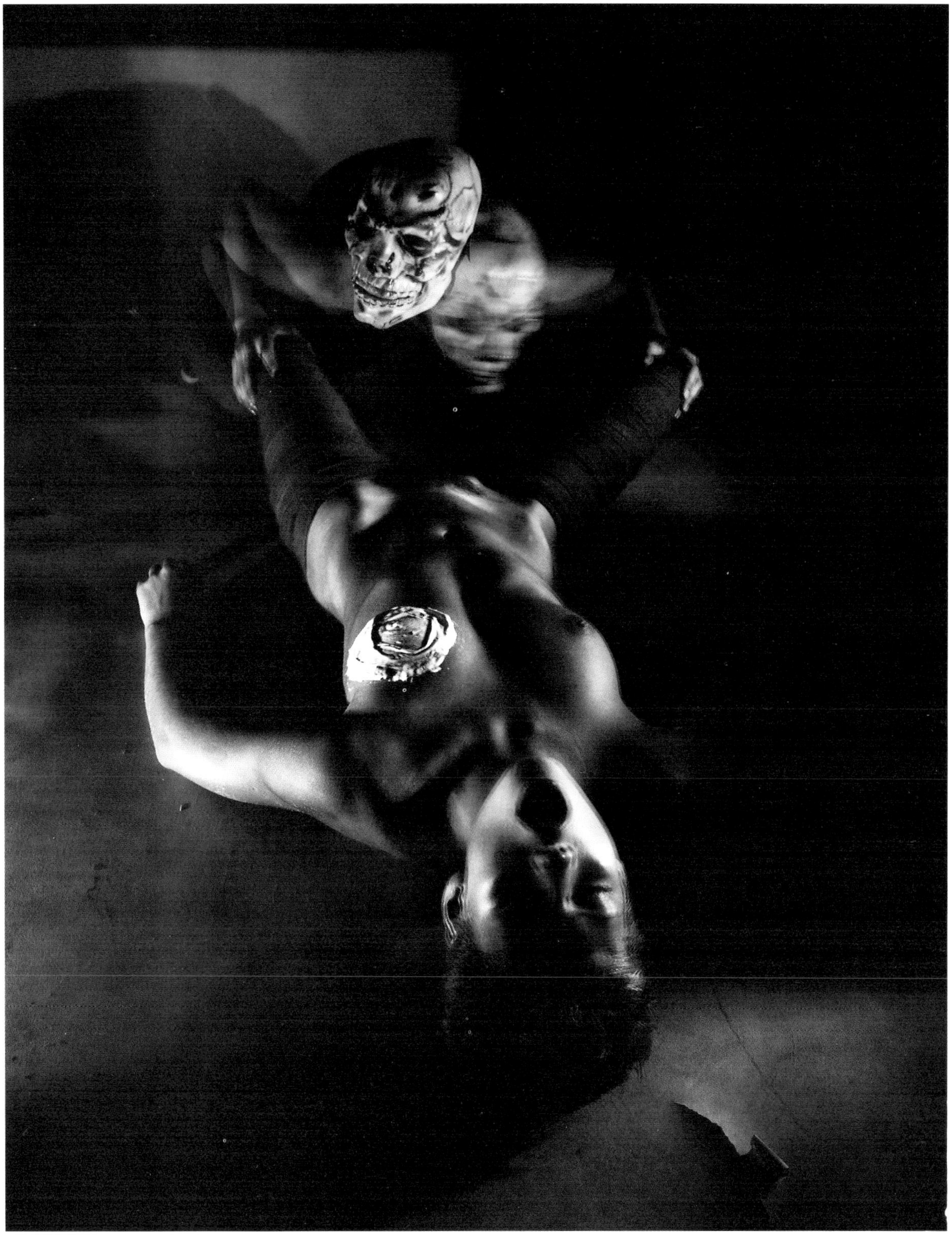

PLATE CXXIII (Far left)
ARTHUR TRESS
Prime Cut 1979
Photographers Gallery, London

Tress' photographs cleverly exploit the medium's documentary credibility, while clearly being the product of his imagination. They do record a reality, but a reality which is conceived and directed by the photographer to act as a metaphor for something outside the immediate event being recorded. The actors play out parts in Tress' continuing autobiography.

PLATE CXXIV (Left)
DAVID BAILEY
Untitled 1983

Bailey's most recent series of nudes, from which this photograph was taken, was published in 1984 as a sixty-three image sequence. The story began with the birth of Venus, enshrouded, from the sea and developed by way of highly personal and sometimes arcane symbolism to a female crucifixion at the end.

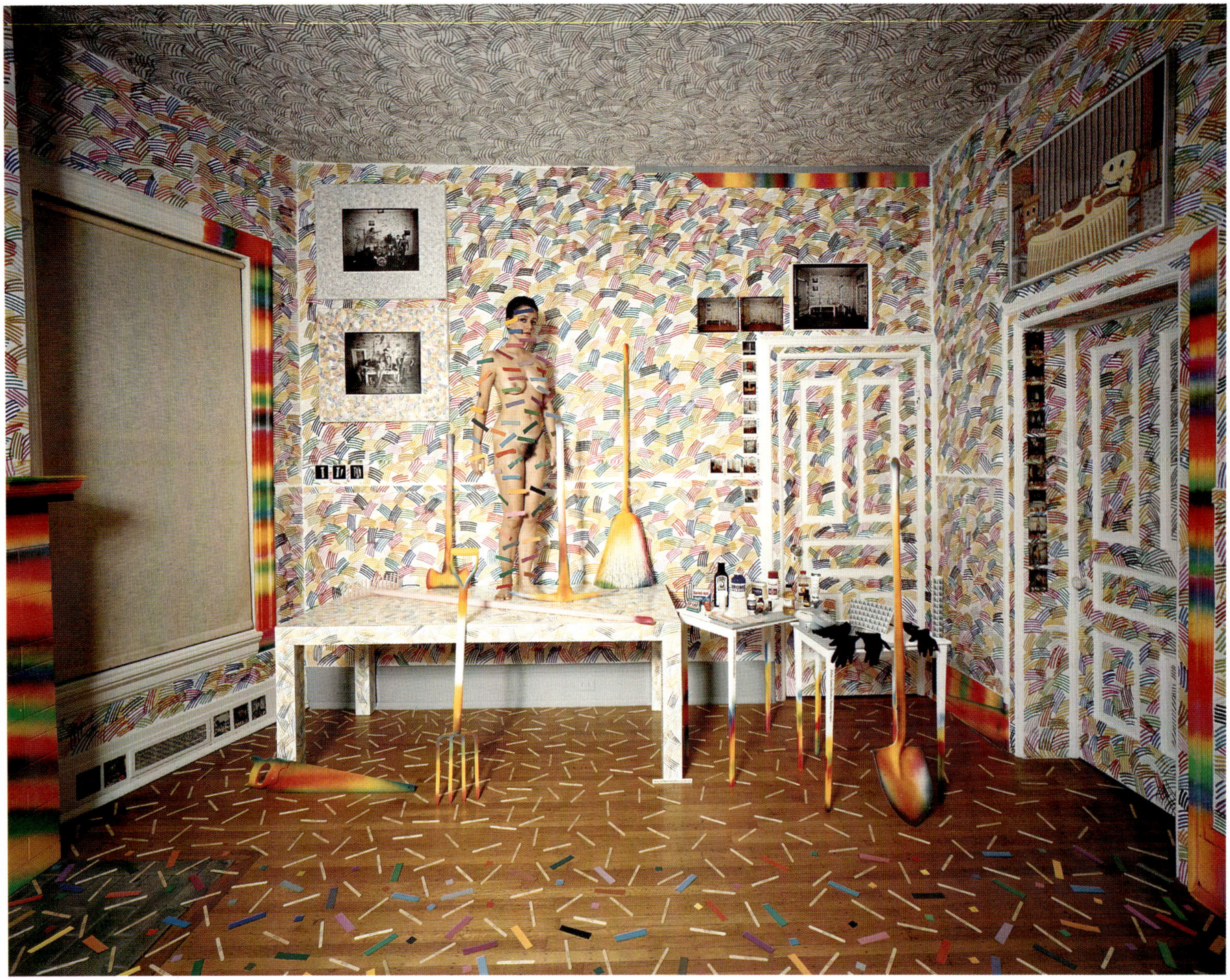

PLATE CXXV

LES KRIMS

A Rake's Revisionist Regress: . . . Buffalo Fashion: Christmas Presents for Nuns: an Assortment of Effective Remedies: Nancy N. Memorial Sticks Scattered: She Had Any Number of Lines: and a Coloured Picture 1980. (Image with bands of vibrant colour)

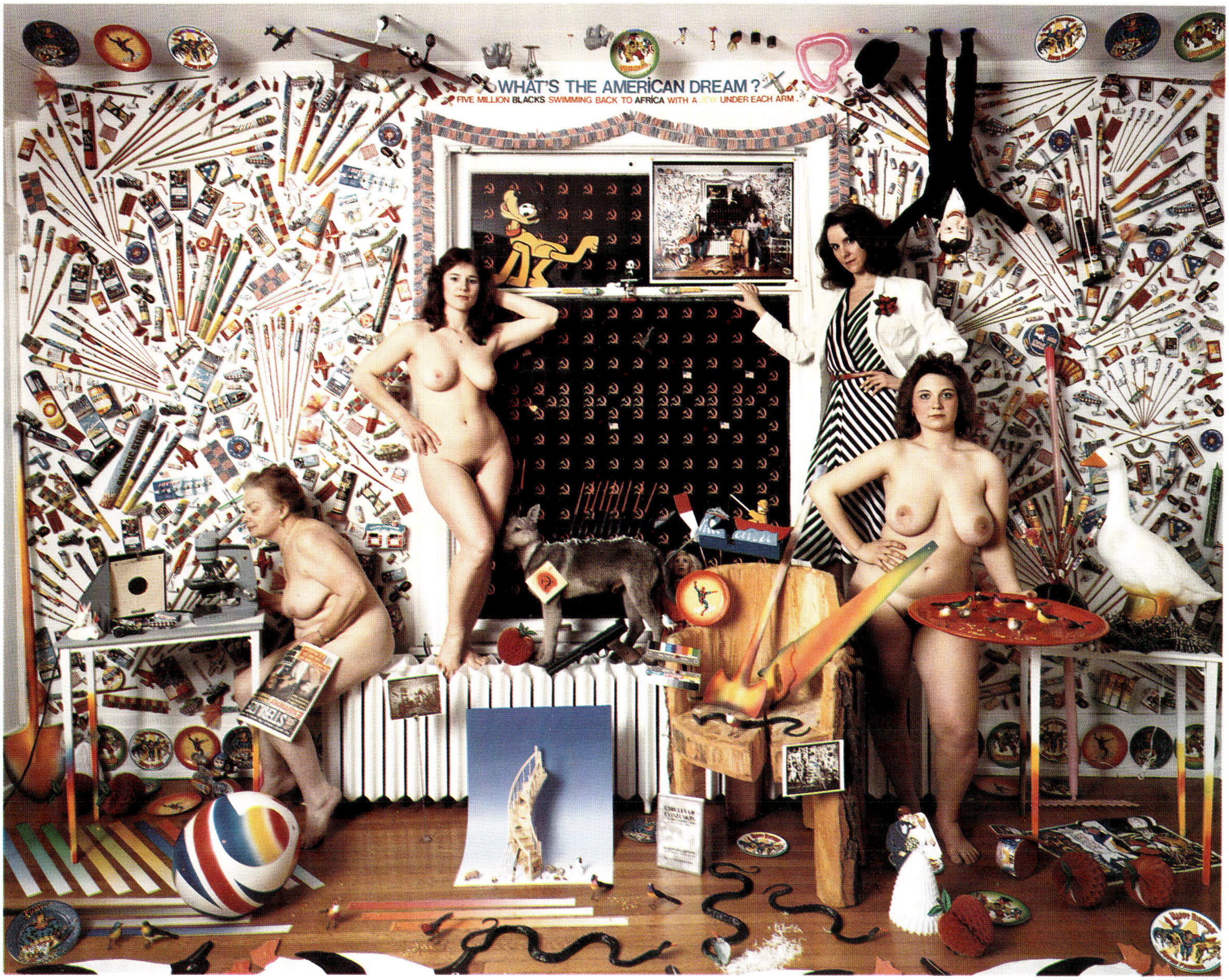

PLATE CXXVI
LES KRIMS
A Marxist View: Madam Curious: Bark Art: Art Bark (for ART PARK): a Chinese Entertainment: Irving's Pens: Something to Look at Spotting Upside Down: Hollis's Hersheys: and Four Lovely Women Posing . . . 1983/84. (Image with four women)
Courtesy the photographer

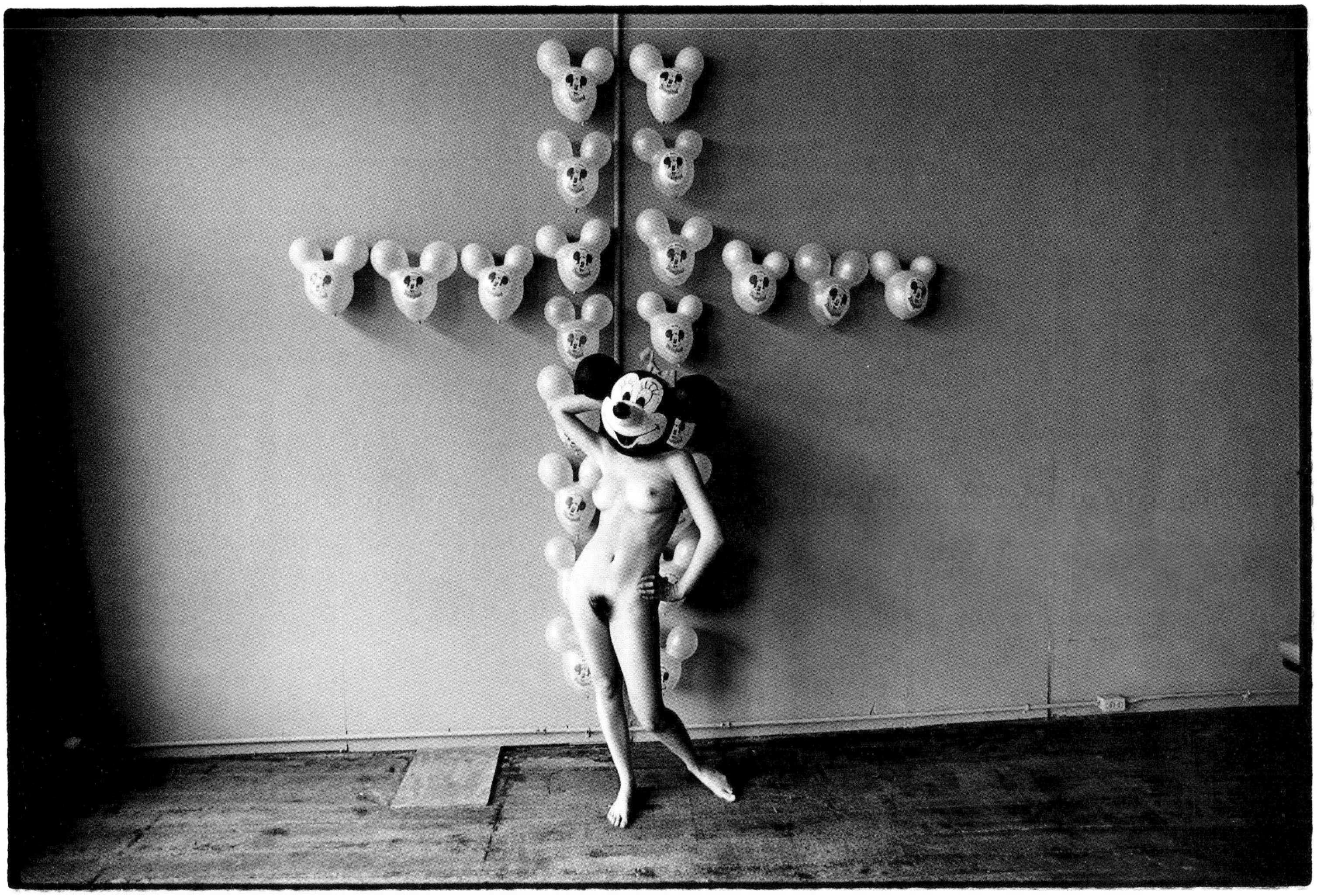

PLATE CXXVII
LES KRIMS
The Static Electric Effect of Minnie Mouse on Mickey Mouse
Balloons 1968
Courtesy the photographer

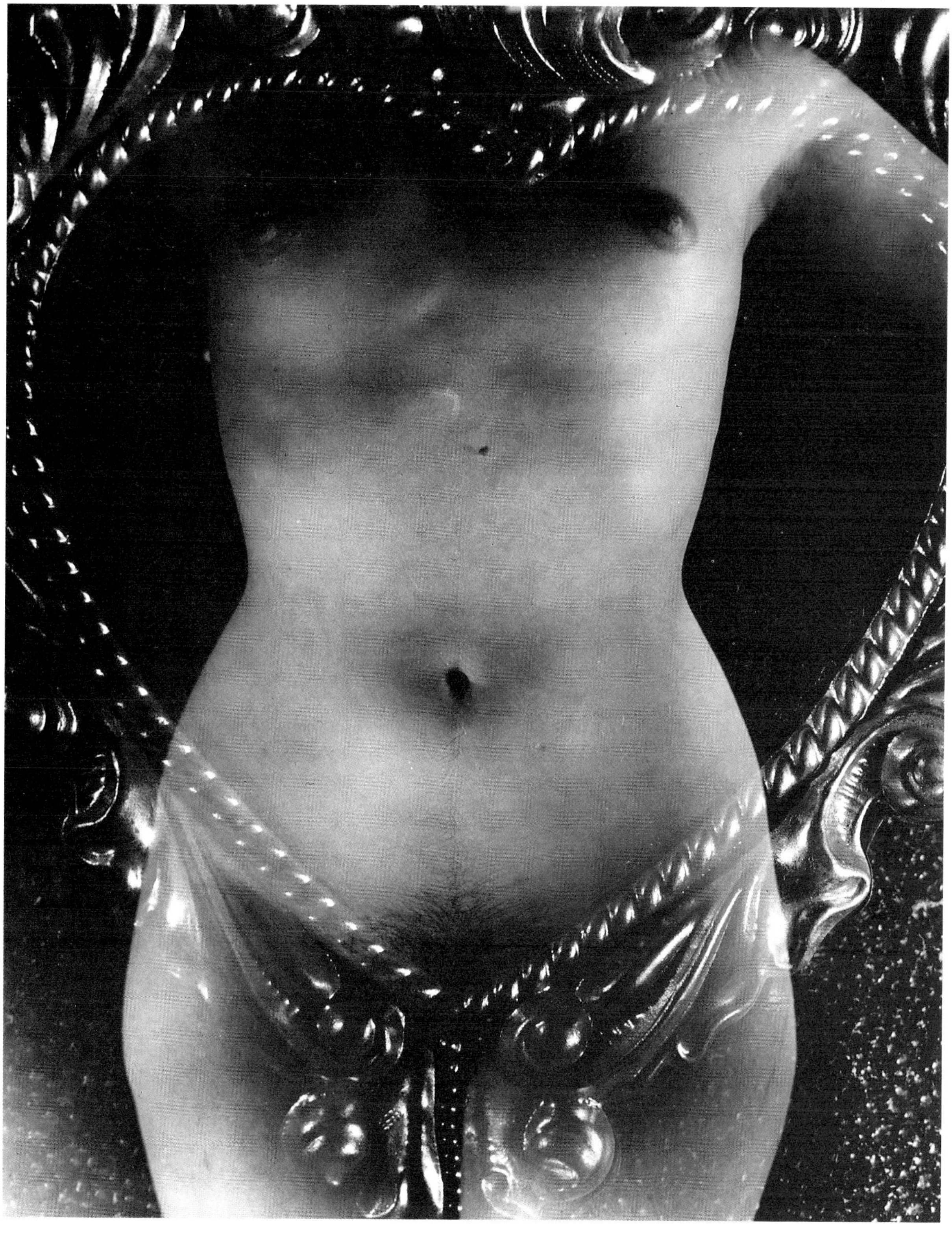

PLATE CXXVIII
CLARENCE JOHN LAUGHLIN
Memento of the Mae West Period 1940
Historic New Orleans Collection/Robert Miller Gallery, New York

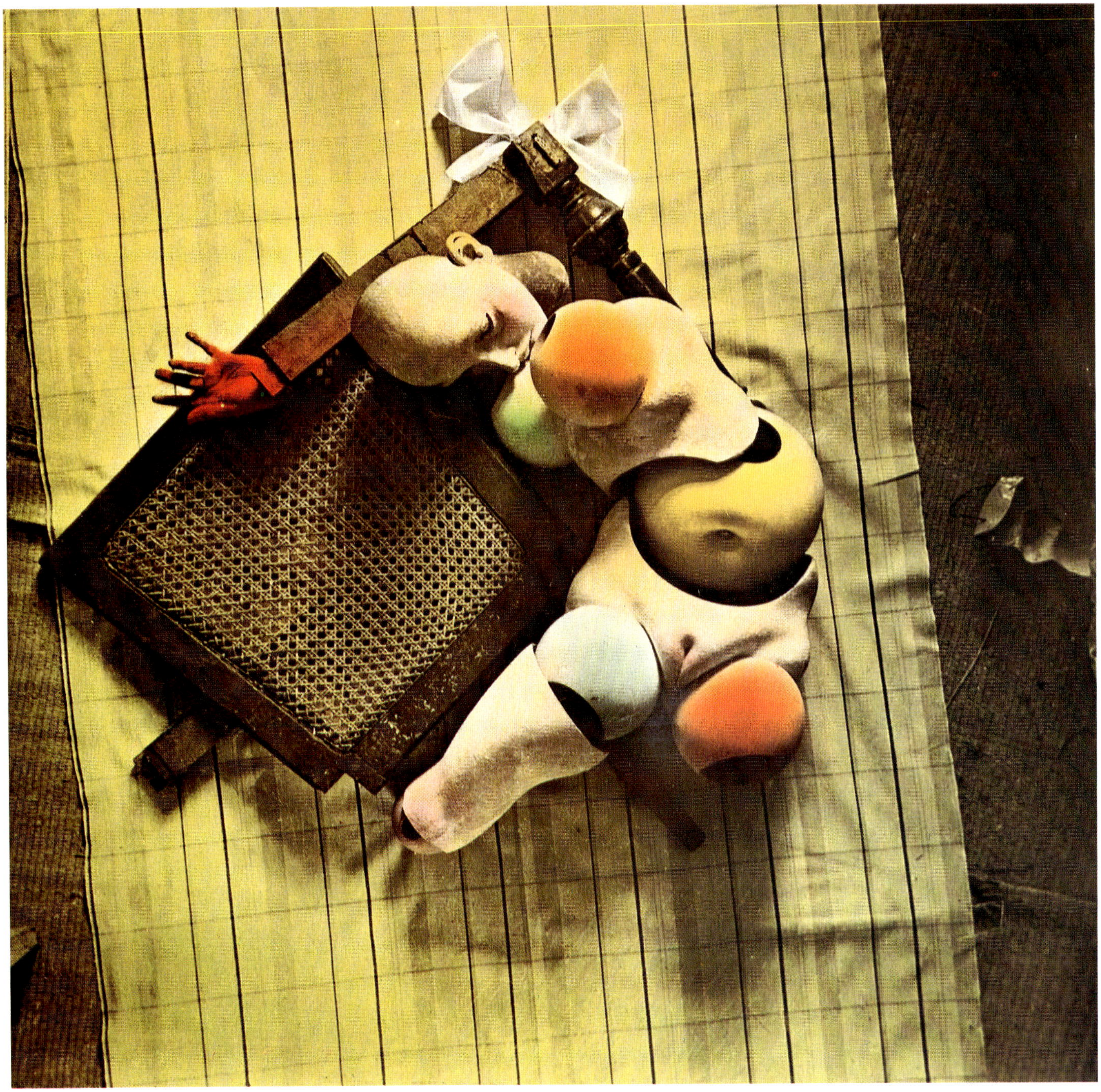

PLATE CXXIX
HANS BELLMER
Unnumbered plate from *Les Jeux de la Poupée* 1949
David Dawson, London

Bellmer's obsessive interest in dismembered dolls began in 1932, when he attended a performance of Offenbach's opera *The Tales of Hoffman*. He used the camera to record his own sculptures, though the photographic images were often modified subsequently, for example with the addition of coloured tints to the print.